# MY AUTOBIOGRAPHY
## "Chapters" from the
## North American Review

## Mark Twain

With an Introduction by
Thomas Wortham
*University of California at Los Angeles*

DOVER PUBLICATIONS, INC.

*Bibliographical Note*

This Dover edition, first published in 1999, is an unabridged reprint of *Chapters from My Autobiography,* by Mark Twain, first published in twenty-five installments in the *North American Review,* from September 1906 through December 1907. A new introduction was written for this edition by Professor Thomas Wortham, and the pages have been renumbered consecutively for easy reference.

*Library of Congress Cataloging-in-Publication Data*

Twain, Mark, 1835–1910.
  [Autobiography]
  My autobiography : "chapters" from the North American review / Mark Twain.
    p. cm.
  ". . . unabridged reprint of Chapters from My Autobiography . . . first published in twenty-five installments in The North American Review, from September 1906 through December 1907"—T.p. verso.
  Includes new introd. by Thomas Wortham.
  ISBN 0-486-40898-1 (pbk.)
    1. Twain, Mark, 1835–1910. 2. Authors, American—19th century—Biography. 3. Humorists, American—19th century—Biography. I. Title.
PS1331 .A2 1999
818'.409—dc21
[B]

99-050284

Manufactured in the United States of America
Dover Publications, Inc., 31 East 2nd Street, Mineola, N.Y. 11501

# INTRODUCTION TO THE DOVER EDITION

*"I do like to hear myself talk."*—Mark Twain

Samuel Clemens found the dictation of his autobiography a pleasure. A lifetime of lecturing and after-dinner speaking had made oral performance second nature to him, and the presence of an audience, even if only an admiring stenographer, worked like a charm. The idea for his telling his life story came from Olivia Clemens, who during the months of her final illness in Florence, Italy, in 1904 must have sensed that these reminiscences would provide her forlorn husband with some sort of distraction from the crisis at hand. And she was right. On January 16 Clemens wrote to his old literary friend and collaborator William Dean Howells:

> Dear 'Owells—
> I've struck it! And I will give it away—to you. You will never know how much enjoyment you have lost until you get to dictating your autobiography; then you will realize, with a pang, that you might have been doing it all your life if you had only had the luck to think of it. And you will be astonished (& charmed) to see how like *talk* it is, & how real it sounds, & how well & compactly & sequentially it constructs itself, & what a dewy & breezy & woodsy freshness it has, & what a darling & worshipful absence of the signs of starch, & flatiron, & labor & fuss & the other artificialities!

This series of dictations lasted until Olivia's death the following June, and it wasn't until Clemens was back in New York in 1906 that he began the project again in earnest.

His enthusiasm knew no bounds. The autobiographical project would, he soon predicted, replace to the world the loss of the great library at Alexandria, that matchless repository of classical literature and learning that was burned on the orders of the caliph Omar, A.D. 642. As he talked over the matter with Howells, "the scheme enlarged itself in our riotous fancy. We said it should be not only a book, it should be a library, not only a library, but a literature." Why this high estimation? Simply because it would be the first time in literature that a man told the truth about himself and about the men and women he had known.

There had been earlier attempts at writing his life, as far back as 1870, exercises in memory related most generally to works of fiction he was at the time either writing or planning to write. But these earlier attempts, put down by pen on paper and following a fairly chronological line, were not to his liking. Life for Clemens was always uppermost in his imagination a performance. In 1904 his secretary Isabel Lyon noted in her diary: "His idea of *writing* an autobiography had never proved successful, for to his mind autobiography is like narrative and should be spoken." The author of *The Adventures of Huckleberry Finn, A Connecticut Yankee in King Arthur's Court,* and *Personal Recollections of Joan of Arc* was a master at first-person narration, a mode of storytelling in which he could draw richly upon the oral traditions of Southwestern humor and the frontier tall tale that he had learned so well during his literary apprenticeship. "Dictated things are talk," he wrote to a correspondent in February 1907, "and talk is all the better and all the more natural when it stumbles a little here and there."

And a great deal of talking he did. During 1906 he dictated his reminiscences on 134 different days, and while the pace slowed down the next year, the project continued until very shortly before his death in 1910, altogether some half-million words. Propped up in bed with his amanuensis by his side— and on occasion a newspaper photographer present to record for the nation's readers the soon-familiar "deathbed" images, thereby reinforcing the idea that he was indeed talking "as from the grave"—Clemens was as happy as the remnants of his life in these final months could allow. He enjoyed in particular the spontaneity and free association of these dictations: "Start it at no particular time of your life; wander at your free will all over your life; talk only about the thing which interests you for the moment; drop it the moment its interest threatens to pale, and turn your talk upon the new and more interesting thing that has intruded itself into your mind meantime." He did not desire to provide anything resembling a chronological narrative—an arrangement, he complained, "that starts you at the cradle & drives you straight for the grave, with no side-excursions permitted on the way." After all, "the side-excursions are the life of our life-voyage, & should be, also, of its history." Or as he said on another occasion: "the truth is, a person's memory has no more sense than his conscience, and no appreciation whatever of values and proportions." This is the freedom from order that only fools and the very wise can appreciate.

Just as Olivia Clemens first imagined, autobiography provided her husband with a sort of bittersweet, even sentimental, entertainment. At other times it meant a settling of old scores. That too was fun. Unlike his friend Howells, for whom memory was hell, Clemens found freedom in the act of remembering, a temporary escape from the hell that his world seemed at times to have become in these final years. He had experienced this even before he took to dictating his life. In 1897–98, the family having retreated to Vienna in its attempt to recover from the tragic death of Susy and the shame and the hardship of bankruptcy, Clemens clearly found great solace in composing his reminiscences of Quarles Farm (the thirteenth installment published in the *North American Review* for 1 March 1907), certainly among the most moving pages later included in the *Chapters:* "I remember . . . I know . . . I see . . . I can call it all back and make it as real as it ever was, and as blessed . . . For I have been there." Even in the madness of night, there might be found clarity and serenity in sweet memory.

But it is not all sunshine and happiness in these pages. Melancholy gloom intrudes. The account of the family's young ducks being maimed by the snapping turtles in the pond of the Clemens household in Hartford, and thereby made fit only for the dinner table, reverberates with an unsettling admission of culpability and guilt on the part of a parent who, if he should insist upon taking credit for life's joys, must also assume responsibility for its terrors and heartbreaks. Without that omniscient and all-controlling God that Clemens had been taught to believe in in youth, but later rejected, man was left utterly alone in a world he had so imperfectly created, and at enormous expense.

Though initially Clemens had not planned to publish any of

these dictations during his lifetime, two natural impulses caused him to change his mind in the summer of 1906: the desire for money and the desire to control his public image. The $30,000 paid him by the *North American Review* for the twenty-five "chapters" (a princely sum in those days, equal to over $500,000 today) enabled him to build his new house at Redding, Connecticut. More important (and far more complicated) was his need to control how his admiring public would regard him after his death, to create a life in words that might be judged less harshly by others than the life of deeds was judged by himself. His involvement in the preparation of copy as well as the care he took in proofreading individual installments give these "chapters" an authority that the other autobiographical compilations made from the dictated material in later years clearly lack. Though they generated considerable interest at the time, including complaints from family members of several of those whom Clemens had not treated kindly in his recollections, these "chapters" have been for too many years neglected, overshadowed by those other arrangements of the autobiographical materials that were more fortunate in being published in book form: Albert Bigelow Paine's *Mark Twain's Autobiography* (1924), Bernard De Voto's *Mark Twain in Eruption* (1940), and Charles Neider's *The Autobiography of Mark Twain* (1959). Even with the eventual publication, in the near future, of the entire autobiographical record that Clemens left, these "chapters" will still be important to any understanding of his life and imagination, because it was the portrait—and the book—that he imagined.

The question always implicit in any reader's encounter with autobiography is, How truthful are these reminiscences? Clemens's earliest biographer, Albert Bigelow Paine, a man he had picked for the job and for whose sake the dictations were in part undertaken, later found that they "bore only an atmospheric relation to history":

> They [are] aspects of biography rather than its veritable narrative; and built largely—sometimes wholly—from an imagination that, with age, had dominated memory, creating details, even reversing them, yet with a perfect sincerity of purpose on the part of the narrator to set down the literal and unvarnished truth.

Certainly those looking for details relating to the public moments of Clemens's life, including his ordeals and successes as a writer, will be disappointed in these pages. As he announces at the very beginning, "this autobiography of mine does not select from my life its showy episodes, but deals mainly in the common experiences which go to make up the life of the average human being, because these episodes are of a sort which he is familiar with in his own life." Rarely does he dwell upon the celebrated persons he has come in contact with, but rather the uncelebrated, who "were just as interesting to him." In particular it is Samuel Clemens "family man," spirited son and brother, loving father and husband, faithful friend and faithfuller enemy, who emerges from these pages, a man defined by human associations and circumstances. And if, in order to tell the truth about this life, his imagination has to massage facts a little, so be it: this is the province of art, the saving power of the imagination. It is not enough to remember only what has happened; one must remember with even greater clarity what may appear to many others not to have happened.

Samuel Clemens spent his life studying human nature, and among the things about mankind that he learned was that our "lies" also tell profound truths about ourselves, revealing as they do those innermost fears and doubts, the complicated character we try to hide behind the public mask. In the end it all balances out. Though Clemens gives credit for these observations regarding the autobiographer's art to John Hay, the great statesman who was his friend for forty years, the words are entirely his own:

> He *will* tell the truth in spite of himself, for his facts and his fictions will work loyally together for the protection of the reader; each fact and each fiction will be a dab of paint, each will fall in its right place, and together they will paint his portrait; not the portrait *he* thinks they are painting, but his real portrait, the inside of him, the soul of him, his character.

He explained the matter as simply as truth could be told to a correspondent many years before: "A man's private thoughts can never be a lie; what he thinks, is to him the truth, always."

Or as he now wrote to old friend Howells about these remarkable "chapters," the truth hides "between the lines" for the courageous reader to find.

Thomas Wortham
*University of California at Los Angeles*

*Note:* All dates and page numbers on the chapter openings in this edition refer to the *North American Review,* where the chapters originally appeared.

# CONTENTS

# Chapter I

## September 7, 1906. Pages 321–30.

PREFATORY NOTE.—Mr. Clemens began to write his autobiography many years ago, and he continues to add to it day by day. It was his original intention to permit no publication of his memoirs until after his death; but, after leaving "Pier No. 70," he concluded that a considerable portion might now suitably be given to the public. It is that portion, garnered from the quarter-million of words already written, which will appear in this REVIEW during the coming year. No part of the autobiography will be published in book form during the lifetime of the author.—EDITOR N. A. R.

## INTRODUCTION.

I INTEND that this autobiography shall become a model for all future autobiographies when it is published, after my death, and I also intend that it shall be read and admired a good many centuries because of its form and method—a form and method whereby the past and the present are constantly brought face to face, resulting in contrasts which newly fire up the interest all along, like contact of flint with steel. Moreover, this autobiography of mine does not select from my life its showy episodes, but deals mainly in the common experiences which go to make up the life of the average human being, because these episodes are of

a sort which he is familiar with in his own life, and in which he
sees his own life reflected and set down in print. The usual,
conventional autobiographer seems to particularly hunt out those
occasions in his career when he came into contact with celebrated
persons, whereas his contacts with the uncelebrated were just as
interesting to him, and would be to his reader, and were vastly
more numerous than his collisions with the famous.

Howells was here yesterday afternoon, and I told him the whole
scheme of this autobiography and its apparently systemless system—only apparently systemless, for it is not really that. It is a
deliberate system, and the law of the system is that I shall talk
about the matter which for the moment interests me, and cast
it aside and talk about something else the moment its interest
for me is exhausted. It is a system which follows no charted
course and is not going to follow any such course. It is a
system which is a complete and purposed jumble—a course which
begins nowhere, follows no specified route, and can never reach an
end while I am alive, for the reason that, if I should talk to the
stenographer two hours a day for a hundred years, I should still
never be able to set down a tenth part of the things which have
interested me in my lifetime. I told Howells that this autobiography of mine would live a couple of thousand years, without
any effort, and would then take a fresh start and live the rest of
the time.

He said he believed it would, and asked me if I meant to make
a library of it.

I said that that was my design; but that, if I should live long
enough, the set of volumes could not be contained merely in a
city, it would require a State, and that there would not be any
multi-billionaire alive, perhaps, at any time during its existence
who would be able to buy a full set, except on the instalment plan.

Howells applauded, and was full of praises and endorsement,
which was wise in him and judicious. If he had manifested a
different spirit, I would have thrown him out of the window. I
like criticism, but it must be my way.

---

## I.

Back of the Virginia Clemenses is a dim procession of ancestors stretching back to Noah's time. According to tradition, some
of them were pirates and slavers in Elizabeth's time. But this

is no discredit to them, for so were Drake and Hawkins and the others. It was a respectable trade, then, and monarchs were partners in it. In my time I have had desires to be a pirate myself. The reader—if he will look deep down in his secret heart, will find—but never mind what he will find there; I am not writing his Autobiography, but mine. Later, according to tradition, one of the procession was Ambassador to Spain in the time of James 1, or of Charles I, and married there and sent down a strain of Spanish blood to warm us up. Also, according to tradition, this one or another—Geoffrey Clement, by name—helped to sentence Charles to death.

I have not examined into these traditions myself, partly because I was indolent, and partly because I was so busy polishing up this end of the line and trying to make it showy; but the other Clemenses claim that they have made the examination and that it stood the test. Therefore I have always taken for granted that I did help Charles out of his troubles, by ancestral proxy. My instincts have persuaded me, too. Whenever we have a strong and persistent and ineradicable instinct, we may be sure that it is not original with us, but inherited—inherited from away back, and hardened and perfected by the petrifying influence of time. Now I have been always and unchangingly bitter against Charles, and I am quite certain that this feeling trickled down to me through the veins of my forebears from the heart of that judge; for it is not my disposition to be bitter against people on my own personal account. I am not bitter against Jeffreys. I ought to be, but I am not. It indicates that my ancestors of James II's time were indifferent to him; I do not know why; I never could make it out; but that is what it indicates. And I have always felt friendly toward Satan. Of course that is ancestral; it must be in the blood, for I could not have originated it.

. . . . And so, by the testimony of instinct, backed by the assertions of Clemenses who said they had examined the records, I have always been obliged to believe that Geoffrey Clement the martyr-maker was an ancestor of mine, and to regard him with favor, and in fact pride. This has not had a good effect upon me, for it has made me vain, and that is a fault. It has made me set myself above people who were less fortunate in their ancestry than I, and has moved me to take them down a peg, upon occasion, and say things to them which hurt them before company.

A case of the kind happened in Berlin several years ago. William Walter Phelps was our Minister at the Emperor's Court, then, and one evening he had me to dinner to meet Count S., a cabinet minister. This nobleman was of long and illustrious descent. Of course I wanted to let out the fact that I had some ancestors, too; but I did not want to pull them out of their graves by the ears, and I never could seem to get the chance to work them in in a way that would look sufficiently casual. I suppose Phelps was in the same difficulty. In fact he looked distraught, now and then—just as a person looks who wants to uncover an ancestor purely by accident, and cannot think of a way that will seem accidental enough. But at last, after dinner, he made a try. He took us about his drawing-room, showing us the pictures, and finally stopped before a rude and ancient engraving. It was a picture of the court that tried Charles I. There was a pyramid of judges in Puritan slouch hats, and below them three bareheaded secretaries seated at a table. Mr. Phelps put his finger upon one of the three, and said with exulting indifference—

" An ancestor of mine."

I put my finger on a judge, and retorted with scathing languidness—

" Ancestor of mine. But it is a small matter. I have others."

It was not noble in me to do it. I have always regretted it since. But it landed him. I wonder how he felt? However, it made no difference in our friendship, which shows that he was fine and high, notwithstanding the humbleness of his origin. And it was also creditable in me, too, that I could overlook it. I made no change in my bearing toward him, but always treated him as an equal.

But it was a hard night for me in one way. Mr. Phelps thought I was the guest of honor, and so did Count S.; but I didn't, for there was nothing in my invitation to indicate it. It was just a friendly offhand note, on a card. By the time dinner was announced Phelps was himself in a state of doubt. Something had to be done; and it was not a handy time for explanations. He tried to get me to go out with him, but I held back; then he tried S., and he also declined. There was another guest, but there was no trouble about him. We finally went out in a pile. There was a decorous plunge for seats, and I got the one at Mr. Phelps's left, the Count captured the one facing

Phelps, and the other guest had to take the place of honor, since he could not help himself. We returned to the drawing-room in the original disorder. I had new shoes on, and they were tight. At eleven I was privately crying; I couldn't help it, the pain was so cruel. Conversation had been dead for an hour. S. had been due at the bedside of a dying official ever since half past nine. At last we all rose by one blessed impulse and went down to the street door without explanations—in a pile, and no precedence; and so, parted.

The evening had its defects; still, I got my ancestor in, and was satisfied.

Among the Virginian Clemenses were Jere. (already mentioned), and Sherrard. Jere. Clemens had a wide reputation as a good pistol-shot, and once it enabled him to get on the friendly side of some drummers when they wouldn't have paid any attention to mere smooth words and arguments. He was out stumping the State at the time. The drummers were grouped in front of the stand, and had been hired by the opposition to drum while he made his speech. When he was ready to begin, he got out his revolver and laid it before him, and said in his soft, silky way—

" I do not wish to hurt anybody, and shall try not to; but I have got just a bullet apiece for those six drums, and if you should want to play on them, don't stand behind them."

Sherrard Clemens was a Republican Congressman from West Virginia in the war days, and then went out to St. Louis, where the James Clemens branch lived, and still lives, and there he became a warm rebel. This was after the war. At the time that he was a Republican I was a rebel; but by the time he had become a rebel I was become (temporarily) a Republican. The Clemenses have always done the best they could to keep the political balances level, no matter how much it might inconvenience them. I did not know what had become of Sherrard Clemens; but once I introduced Senator Hawley to a Republican mass meeting in New England, and then I got a bitter letter from Sherrard from St. Louis. He said that the Republicans of the North—no, the " mudsills of the North "—had swept away the old aristocracy of the South with fire and sword, and it ill became me, an aristocrat by blood, to train with that kind of swine. Did I forget that I was a Lambton?

That was a reference to my mother's side of the house. As I have already said, she was a Lambton—Lambton with a p, for some of the American Lamptons could not spell very well in early times, and so the name suffered at their hands. She was a native of Kentucky, and married my father in Lexington in 1823, when she was twenty years old and he twenty-four. Neither of them had an overplus of property. She brought him two or three negroes, but nothing else, I think. They removed to the remote and secluded village of Jamestown, in the mountain solitudes of east Tennessee. There their first crop of children was born, but as I was of a later vintage I do not remember anything about it. I was postponed—postponed to Missouri. Missouri was an unknown new State and needed attractions.

I think that my eldest brother, Orion, my sisters Pamela and Margaret, and my brother Benjamin were born in Jamestown. There may have been others, but as to that I am not sure. It was a great lift for that little village to have my parents come there. It was hoped that they would stay, so that it would become a city. It was supposed that they would stay. And so there was a boom; but by and by they went away, and prices went down, and it was many years before Jamestown got another start. I have written about Jamestown in the " Gilded Age," a book of mine, but it was from hearsay, not from personal knowledge. My father left a fine estate behind him in the region round about Jamestown— 75,000 acres.* When he died in 1847 he had owned it about twenty years. The taxes were almost nothing (five dollars a year for the whole), and he had always paid them regularly and kept his title perfect. He had always said that the land would not become valuable in his time, but that it would be a commodious provision for his children some day. It contained coal, copper, iron and timber, and he said that in the course of time railways would pierce to that region, and then the property would be property in fact as well as in name. It also produced a wild grape of a promising sort. He had sent some samples to Nicholas Longworth, of Cincinnati, to get his judgment upon them, and Mr. Longworth had said that they would make as good wine as his Catawbas. The land contained all these riches; and also oil, but my father did not know that, and of course in those early days he would have cared nothing about it if he had known it. The oil

* Correction. 1906: it was above 100,000, it appears.

was not discovered until about 1895. I wish I owned a couple of acres of the land now. In which case I would not be writing Autobiographies for a living. My father's dying charge was, " Cling to the land and wait; let nothing beguile it away from you." My mother's favorite cousin, James Lampton, who figures in the " Gilded Age " as " Colonel Sellers," always said of that land—and said it with blazing enthusiasm, too,—" There's millions in it—millions!" It is true that he always said that about everything—and was always mistaken, too; but this time he was right; which shows that a man who goes around with a prophecy-gun ought never to get discouraged; if he will keep up his heart and fire at everything he sees, he is bound to hit something by and by.

Many persons regarded " Colonel Sellers " as a fiction, an invention, an extravagant impossibility, and did me the honor to call him a " creation "; but they were mistaken. I merely put him on paper as he was; he was not a person who could be exaggerated. The incidents which looked most extravagant, both in the book and on the stage, were not inventions of mine but were facts of his life; and I was present when they were developed. John T. Raymond's audiences used to come near to dying with laughter over the turnip-eating scene; but, extravagant as the scene was, it was faithful to the facts, in all its absurd details. The thing happened in Lampton's own house, and I was present. In fact I was myself the guest who ate the turnips. In the hands of a great actor that piteous scene would have dimmed any manly spectator's eyes with tears, and racked his ribs apart with laughter at the same time. But Raymond was great in humorous portrayal only. In that he was superb, he was wonderful—in a word, great; in all things else he was a pigmy of the pigmies.

The real Colonel Sellers, as I knew him in James Lampton, was a pathetic and beautiful spirit, a manly man, a straight and honorable man, a man with a big, foolish, unselfish heart in his bosom, a man born to be loved; and he was loved by all his friends, and by his family worshipped. It is the right word. To them he was but little less than a god. The real Colonel Sellers was never on the stage. Only half of him was there. Raymond could not play the other half of him; it was above his level. That half was made up of qualities of which Raymond was wholly destitute.

For Raymond was not a manly man, he was not an honorable man nor an honest one, he was empty and selfish and vulgar and ignorant and silly, and there was a vacancy in him where his heart should have been. There was only one man who could have played the whole of Colonel Sellers, and that was Frank Mayo.*

It is a world of surprises. They fall, too, where one is least expecting them. When I introduced Sellers into the book, Charles Dudley Warner, who was writing the story with me, proposed a change of Sellers's Christian name. Ten years before, in a remote corner of the West, he had come across a man named Eschol Sellers, and he thought that Eschol was just the right and fitting name for our Sellers, since it was odd and quaint and all that. I liked the idea, but I said that that man might turn up and object. But Warner said it couldn't happen; that he was doubtless dead by this time, a man with a name like that couldn't live long; and be he dead or alive we must have the name, it was exactly the right one and we couldn't do without it. So the change was made. Warner's man was a farmer in a cheap and humble way. When the book had been out a week, a college-bred gentleman of courtly manners and ducal upholstery arrived in Hartford in a sultry state of mind and with a libel suit in his eye, and *his* name was Eschol Sellers! He had never heard of the other one, and had never been within a thousand miles of him. This damaged aristocrat's programme was quite definite and businesslike: the American Publishing Company must suppress the edition as far as printed, and change the name in the plates, or stand a suit for $10,000. He carried away the Company's promise and many apologies, and we changed the name back to Colonel Mulberry Sellers, in the plates. Apparently there is nothing that cannot happen. Even the existence of two unrelated men wearing the impossible name of Eschol Sellers is a possible thing.

James Lampton floated, all his days, in a tinted mist of magnificent dreams, and died at last without seeing one of them realized. I saw him last in 1884, when it had been twenty-six years since I ate the basin of raw turnips and washed them down with a bucket of water in his house. He was become old and white-headed, but he entered to me in the same old breezy

---

* Raymond was playing "Colonel Sellers" in 1876 and along there. About twenty years later Mayo dramatized "Pudd'nhead Wilson" and played the title rôle delightfully.

way of his earlier life, and he was all there, yet—not a detail
wanting: the happy light in his eye, the abounding hope in his
heart, the persuasive tongue, the miracle-breeding imagination
—they were all there: and before I could turn around he was polishing up his Aladdin's lamp and flashing the secret riches of the
world before me. I said to myself, " I did not overdraw him by
a shade, I set him down as he was; and he is the same man to-
day. Cable will recognize him." I asked him to excuse me
a moment, and ran into the next room, which was Cable's; Cable
and I were stumping the Union on a reading tour. I said—

" I am going to leave your door open, so that you can listen.
There is a man in there who is interesting."

I went back and asked Lampton what he was doing now. He
began to tell me of a " small venture " he had begun in New
Mexico through his son; " only a little thing—a mere trifle—
partly to amuse my leisure, partly to keep my capital from lying idle, but mainly to develop the boy—develop the boy; fortune's wheel is ever revolving, he may have to work for his living
some day—as strange things have happened in this world. But
it's only a little thing—a mere trifle, as I said."

And so it was—as he began it. But under his deft hands it
grew, and blossomed, and spread—oh, beyond imagination. At
the end of half an hour he finished; finished with the remark,
uttered in an adorably languid manner:

" Yes, it is but a trifle, as things go nowadays—a bagatelle—
but amusing. It passes the time. The boy thinks great things of
it, but he is young, you know, and imaginative; lacks the experience which comes of handling large affairs, and which tem-
pers the fancy and perfects the judgment. I suppose there's
a couple of millions in it, possibly three, but not more, I think;
still, for a boy, you know, just starting in life, it is not bad. I
should not want him to make a fortune—let that come later.
It could turn his head, at his time of life, and in many ways
be a damage to him."

Then he said something about his having left his pocketbook
lying on the table in the main drawing-room at home, and about
its being after banking hours, now, and—

I stopped him, there, and begged him to honor Cable and me
by being our guest at the lecture—with as many friends as
might be willing to do us the like honor. He accepted. And he

thanked me as a prince might who had granted us a grace.  The reason I stopped his speech about the tickets was because I saw that he was going to ask me to furnish them to him and let him pay next day; and I knew that if he made the debt he would pay it if he had to pawn his clothes.  After a little further chat he shook hands heartily and affectionately, and took his leave. Cable put his head in at the door, and said—

" That was Colonel Sellers."

MARK TWAIN.

(To be Continued.)

# Chapter II

September 21, 1906. Pages 449–60.

PREFATORY NOTE.—Mr. Clemens began to write his autobiography many years ago, and he continues to add to it day by day. It was his original intention to permit no publication of his memoirs until after his death; but, after leaving "Pier No. 70," he concluded that a considerable portion might now suitably be given to the public. It is that portion, garnered from the quarter-million of words already written, which will appear in this REVIEW during the coming year. No part of the autobiography will be published in book form during the lifetime of the author.—EDITOR N. A. R.

## II.

MY experiences as an author began early in 1867. I came to New York from San Francisco in the first month of that year and presently Charles H. Webb, whom I had known in San Francisco as a reporter on *The Bulletin,* and afterward editor of *The Californian,* suggested that I publish a volume of sketches. I had but a slender reputation to publish it on, but I was charmed and excited by the suggestion and quite willing to venture it if some industrious person would save me the trouble of gathering the sketches together. I was loath to do it myself, for from the beginning of my sojourn in this world there was a persistent vacancy in me where the industry ought to be. ("Ought to was"

11

is better, perhaps, though the most of the authorities differ as to this.)

Webb said I had some reputation in the Atlantic States, but I knew quite well that it must be of a very attenuated sort. What there was of it rested upon the story of " The Jumping Frog." When Artemus Ward passed through California on a lecturing tour, in 1865 or '66, I told him the " Jumping Frog " story, in San Francisco, and he asked me to write it out and send it to his publisher, Carleton, in New York, to be used in padding out a small book which Artemus had prepared for the press and which needed some more stuffing to make it big enough for the price which was to be charged for it.

It reached Carleton in time, but he didn't think much of it, and was not willing to go to the typesetting expense of adding it to the book. He did not put it in the waste-basket, but made Henry Clapp a present of it, and Clapp used it to help out the funeral of his dying literary journal, *The Saturday Press.* " The Jumping Frog " appeared in the last number of that paper, was the most joyous feature of the obsequies, and was at once copied in the newspapers of America and England. It certainly had a wide celebrity, and it still had it at the time that I am speaking of—but I was aware that it was only the frog that was celebrated. It wasn't I. I was still an obscurity.

Webb undertook to collate the sketches. He performed this office, then handed the result to me, and I went to Carleton's establishment with it. I approached a clerk and he bent eagerly over the counter to inquire into my needs; but when he found that I had come to sell a book and not to buy one, his temperature fell sixty degrees, and the old-gold intrenchments in the roof of my mouth contracted three-quarters of an inch and my teeth fell out. I meekly asked the privilege of a word with Mr. Carleton, and was coldly informed that he was in his private office. Discouragements and difficulties followed, but after a while I got by the frontier and entered the holy of holies. Ah, now I remember how I managed it! Webb had made an appointment for me with Carleton; otherwise I never should have gotten over that frontier. Carleton rose and said brusquely and aggressively,

" Well, what can I do for you?"

I reminded him that I was there by appointment to offer him my book for publication. He began to swell, and went on swelling and swelling and swelling until he had reached the dimensions of a god of about the second or third degree. Then the fountains of his great deep were broken up, and for two or three minutes I couldn't see him for the rain. It was words, only words, but they fell so densely that they darkened the atmosphere. Finally he made an imposing sweep with his right hand, which comprehended the whole room and said,

" Books—look at those shelves! Every one of them is loaded with books that are waiting for publication. Do I want any more? Excuse me, I don't. Good morning."

Twenty-one years elapsed before I saw Carleton again. I was then sojourning with my family at the Schweitzerhof, in Luzerne. He called on me, shook hands cordially, and said at once, without any preliminaries,

" I am substantially an obscure person, but I have at least one distinction to my credit of such colossal dimensions that it entitles me to immortality—to wit: I refused a book of yours, and for this I stand without competitor as the prize ass of the nineteenth century."

It was a most handsome apology, and I told him so, and said it was a long-delayed revenge but was sweeter to me than any other that could be devised; that during the lapsed twenty-one years I had in fancy taken his life several times every year, and always in new and increasingly cruel and inhuman ways, but that now I was pacified, appeased, happy, even jubilant; and that thenceforth I should hold him my true and valued friend and never kill him again.

I reported my adventure to Webb, and he bravely said that not all the Carletons in the universe should defeat that book; he would publish it himself on a ten per cent. royalty. And so he did. He brought it out in blue and gold, and made a very pretty little book of it. I think he named it " The Celebrated Jumping Frog of Calaveras County, and Other Sketches," price $1.25. He made the plates and printed and bound the book through a job-printing house, and published it through the American News Company.

In June I sailed in the *Quaker City* Excursion. I returned in November, and in Washington found a letter from Elisha Bliss, of the American Publishing Company of Hartford, offering me five per cent. royalty on a book which should recount the adventures of the Excursion. In lieu of the royalty, I was offered the al-

ternative of ten thousand dollars cash upon delivery of the manuscript. I consulted A. D. Richardson and he said "take the
royalty." I followed his advice and closed with Bliss. By my
contract I was to deliver the manuscript in July of 1868. I wrote
the book in San Francisco and delivered the manuscript within
contract time. Bliss provided a multitude of illustrations for
the book, and then stopped work on it. The contract date for the
issue went by, and there was no explanation of this. Time drifted along and still there was no explanation. I was lecturing all
over the country; and about thirty times a day, on an average, I
was trying to answer this conundrum:

" When is your book coming out?"

I got tired of inventing new answers to that question, and by
and by I got horribly tired of the question itself. Whoever asked
it became my enemy at once, and I was usually almost eager to
make that appear.

As soon as I was free of the lecture-field I hastened to Hartford to make inquiries. Bliss said that the fault was not his;
that he wanted to publish the book but the directors of his Company were staid old fossils and were afraid of it. They had examined the book, and the majority of them were of the opinion
that there were places in it of a humorous character. Bliss said
the house had never published a book that had a suspicion like
that attaching to it, and that the directors were afraid that a departure of this kind would seriously injure the house's reputation; that he was tied hand and foot, and was not permitted to
carry out his contract. One of the directors, a Mr. Drake—at
least he was the remains of what had once been a Mr. Drake—
invited me to take a ride with him in his buggy, and I went along.
He was a pathetic old relic, and his ways and his talk were also
pathetic. He had a delicate purpose in view and it took him some
time to hearten himself sufficiently to carry it out, but at last he
accomplished it. He explained the house's difficulty and distress,
as Bliss had already explained it. Then he frankly threw himself and the house upon my mercy and begged me to take away
" The Innocents Abroad " and release the concern from the contract. I said I wouldn't—and so ended the interview and the
buggy excursion. Then I warned Bliss that he must get to work
or I should make trouble. He acted upon the warning, and set
up the book and I read the proofs. Then there was another long

wait and no explanation. At last toward the end of July (1896, I think), I lost patience and telegraphed Bliss that if the book was not on sale in twenty-four hours I should bring suit for damages.

That ended the trouble. Half a dozen copies were bound and placed on sale within the required time. Then the canvassing began, and went briskly forward. In nine months the book took the publishing house out of debt, advanced its stock from twenty-five to two hundred, and left seventy thousand dollars profit to the good. It was Bliss that told me this—but if it was true, it was the first time that he had told the truth in sixty-five years. He was born in 1804.

---

### III.

. . . This was in 1849. I was fourteen years old, then. We were still living in Hannibal, Missouri, on the banks of the Mississippi, in the new " frame " house built by my father five years before. That is, some of us lived in the new part, the rest in the old part back of it—the " L." In the autumn my sister gave a party, and invited all the marriageable young people of the village. I was too young for this society, and was too bashful to mingle with young ladies, anyway, therefore I was not invited— at least not for the whole evening. Ten minutes of it was to be my whole share. I was to do the part of a bear in a small fairy play. I was to be disguised all over in a close-fitting brown hairy stuff proper for a bear. About half past ten I was told to go to my room and put on this disguise, and be ready in half an hour. I started, but changed my mind; for I wanted to practise a little, and that room was very small. I crossed over to the large unoccupied house on the corner of Main and Hill streets,* unaware that a dozen of the young people were also going there to dress for their parts. I took the little black slave boy, Sandy, with me, and we selected a roomy and empty chamber on the second floor. We entered it talking, and this gave a couple of half-dressed young ladies an opportunity to take refuge behind a screen undiscovered. Their gowns and things were hanging on hooks behind the door, but I did not see them; it was Sandy that shut the door, but all his heart was in the theatricals, and he was as unlikely to notice them as I was myself.

That was a rickety screen, with many holes in it, but as I did

* That house still stands.

not know there were girls behind it, I was not disturbed by that detail. If I had known, I could not have undressed in the flood of cruel moonlight that was pouring in at the curtainless windows; I should have died of shame. Untroubled by apprehensions, I stripped to the skin and began my practice. I was full of ambition; I was determined to make a hit; I was burning to establish a reputation as a bear and get further engagements; so I threw myself into my work with an abandon that promised great things. I capered back and forth from one end of the room to the other on all fours, Sandy applauding with enthusiasm; I walked upright and growled and snapped and snarled; I stood on my head, I flung handsprings, I danced a lubberly dance with my paws bent and my imaginary snout sniffing from side to side; I did everything a bear could do, and many things which no bear could ever do and no bear with any dignity would want to do, anyway; and of course I never suspected that I was making a spectacle of myself to any one but Sandy. At last, standing on my head, I paused in that attitude to take a minute's rest. There was a moment's silence, then Sandy spoke up with excited interest and said—

"Marse Sam, has you ever seen a smoked herring?"

"No. What is that?"

"It's a fish."

"Well, what of it? Anything peculiar about it?"

"Yes, suh, you bet you dey is. *Dey eats 'em guts and all!*"

There was a smothered burst of feminine snickers from behind the screen! All the strength went out of me and I toppled forward like an undermined tower and brought the screen down with my weight, burying the young ladies under it. In their fright they discharged a couple of piercing screams—and possibly others, but I did not wait to count. I snatched my clothes and fled to the dark hall below, Sandy following. I was dressed in half a minute, and out the back way. I swore Sandy to eternal silence, then we went away and hid until the party was over. The ambition was all out of me. I could not have faced that giddy company after my adventure, for there would be two performers there who knew my secret, and would be privately laughing at me all the time. I was searched for but not found, and the bear had to be played by a young gentleman in his civilized clothes. The house was still and everybody asleep when I finally ventured home. I was very heavy-hearted, and full of a sense of disgrace. Pinned to my pillow I found a slip of paper which bore a line that did not lighten my heart, but only made my face burn. It was written in a laboriously disguised hand, and these were its mocking terms:

"You probably couldn't have played *bear,* but you played *bare* very well—oh, very very well!"

We think boys are rude, unsensitive animals, but it is not so in all cases. Each boy has one or two sensitive spots, and if you can find out where they are located you have only to touch them and you can scorch him as with fire. I suffered miserably over that episode. I expected that the facts would be all over the village in the morning, but it was not so. The secret remained confined to the two girls and Sandy and me. That was some appeasement of my pain, but it was far from sufficient—the main trouble remained: I was under four mocking eyes, and it might as well have been a thousand, for I suspected all girls' eyes of being the ones I so dreaded. During several weeks I could not look any young lady in the face; I dropped my eyes in confusion when any one of them smiled upon me and gave me greeting; and I said to myself, "*That is one of them,*" and got quickly away. Of course I was meeting the right girls everywhere, but if they ever let slip any betraying sign I was not bright enough to catch it. When I left Hannibal four years later, the secret was still a secret; I had never guessed those girls out, and was no longer expecting to do it. Nor wanting to, either.

One of the dearest and prettiest girls in the village at the time of my mishap was one whom I will call Mary Wilson, because that was not her name. She was twenty years old; she was dainty and sweet, peach-bloomy and exquisite, gracious and lovely in character, and I stood in awe of her, for she seemed to me to be made out of angel-clay and rightfully unapproachable by an unholy ordinary kind of a boy like me. I probably never suspected her. But—

The scene changes. To Calcutta — forty - seven years later. It was in 1896. I arrived there on my lecturing trip. As I entered the hotel a divine vision passed out of it, clothed in the glory of the Indian sunshine—the Mary Wilson of my long-vanished boyhood! It was a startling thing. Before I could recover from the bewildering shock and speak to her she was gone. I thought maybe I had seen an apparition, but it was not so, she

was flesh. She was the granddaughter of the other Mary, the
original Mary. That Mary, now a widow, was up-stairs, and
presently sent for me. She was old and gray-haired, but she looked
young and was very handsome. We sat down and talked. We
steeped our thirsty souls in the reviving wine of the past, the beautiful past, the dear and lamented past; we uttered the names that
had been silent upon our lips for fifty years, and it was as if they
were made of music; with reverent hands we unburied our dead,
the mates of our youth, and caressed them with our speech; we
searched the dusty chambers of our memories and dragged forth
incident after incident, episode after episode, folly after folly,
and laughed such good laughs over them, with the tears running
down; and finally Mary said suddenly, and without any leading
up—

"Tell me! What is the special peculiarity of smoked herrings?"

It seemed a strange question at such a hallowed time as this.
And so inconsequential, too. I was a little shocked. And yet I
was aware of a stir of some kind away back in the deeps of my
memory somewhere. It set me to musing—thinking—searching.
Smoked herrings. Smoked herrings. The peculiarity of smo. . . .
I glanced up. Her face was grave, but there was a dim and
shadowy twinkle in her eye which— All of a sudden I knew!
and far away down in the hoary past I heard a remembered voice
murmur, "Dey eats 'em guts and all!"

"At—last! I've found one of you, anyway! Who was the
other girl?"

But she drew the line there. She wouldn't tell me.

## IV.

. . . But it was on a bench in Washington Square that I saw
the most of Louis Stevenson. It was an outing that lasted an
hour or more, and was very pleasant and sociable. I had come
with him from his house, where I had been paying my respects
to his family. His business in the Square was to absorb the sunshine. He was most scantily furnished with flesh, his clothes
seemed to fall into hollows as if there might be nothing inside
but the frame for a sculptor's statue. His long face and lank hair
and dark complexion and musing and melancholy expression
seemed to fit these details justly and harmoniously, and the alto-

gether of it seemed especially planned to gather the rays of your observation and focalize them upon Stevenson's special distinction and commanding feature, his splendid eyes. They burned with a smouldering rich fire under the penthouse of his brows, and they made him beautiful.

. . . . . . . .

I said I thought he was right about the others, but mistaken as to Bret Harte; in substance I said that Harte was good company and a thin but pleasant talker; that he was always bright, but never brilliant; that in this matter he must not be classed with Thomas Bailey Aldrich, nor must any other man, ancient or modern; that Aldrich was always witty, always brilliant, if there was anybody present capable of striking his flint at the right angle; that Aldrich was as sure and prompt and unfailing as the red-hot iron on the blacksmith's anvil—you had only to hit it competently to make it deliver an explosion of sparks. I added—

" Aldrich has never had his peer for prompt and pithy and witty and humorous sayings. None has equalled him, certainly none has surpassed him, in the felicity of phrasing with which he clothed these children of his fancy. Aldrich was always brilliant, he couldn't help it, he is a fire-opal set round with rose diamonds; when he is not speaking, you know that his dainty fancies are twinkling and glimmering around in him; when he speaks the diamonds flash. Yes, he was always brilliant, he will always be brilliant; he will be brilliant in hell—you will see."

Stevenson, smiling a chuckly smile, " I hope not."

" Well, you will, and he will dim even those ruddy fires and look like a transfigured Adonis backed against a pink sunset."

. . . . . . . .

There on that bench we struck out a new phrase—one or the other of us, I don't remember which — " submerged renown." Variations were discussed: " submerged fame," " submerged reputation," and so on, and a choice was made; " submerged renown " was elected, I believe. This important matter rose out of an incident which had been happening to Stevenson in Albany. While in a book-shop or book-stall there he had noticed a long rank of small books, cheaply but neatly gotten up, and bearing such titles as " Davis's Selected Speeches," " Davis's Selected Poetry," Davis's this and Davis's that and Davis's the other thing; compilations, every one of them, each with a brief, compact, intelligent and useful introductory chapter by this same Davis, whose first name I have forgotten. Stevenson had begun the matter with this question:

"Can you name the American author whose fame and acceptance stretch widest in the States?"

I thought I could, but it did not seem to me that it would be modest to speak out, in the circumstances. So I diffidently said nothing. Stevenson noticed, and said—

"Save your delicacy for another time—you are not the one. For a shilling you can't name the American author of widest note and popularity in the States. But I can."

Then he went on and told about that Albany incident. He had inquired of the shopman—

"Who is this Davis?"

The answer was—

"An author whose books have to have freight-trains to carry them, not baskets. Apparently you have not heard of him?"

Stevenson said no, this was the first time. The man said—

"Nobody has heard of Davis: you may ask all around and you will see. You never see his name mentioned in print, not even in advertisement; these things are of no use to Davis, not any more than they are to the wind and the sea. You never see one of Davis's books floating on top of the United States, but put on your diving armor and get yourself lowered away down and down and down till you strike the dense region, the sunless region of eternal drudgery and starvation wages—there you'll find them by the million. The man that gets that market, his fortune is made, his bread and butter are safe, for those people will never go back on him. An author may have a reputation which is confined to the surface, and lose it and become pitied, then despised, then forgotten, entirely forgotten— the frequent steps in a surface reputation. A surface reputation, however great, is always mortal, and always killable if you go at it right—with pins and needles, and quiet slow poison, not with the club and tomahawk. But it is a different matter with the submerged reputation—down in the deep water; once a favorite there, always a favorite; once beloved, always beloved; once respected, always respected, honored, and believed in. For, what the reviewer says never finds its way down into those placid deeps; nor the newspaper sneers, nor any breath of the winds of slander blowing above. Down there they never hear of these things. Their idol may be painted clay, up there at the surface, and fade and waste and crumble and blow away, there being much weather there; but down below he is gold and adamant and indestructible."

---

## V.

This is from this morning's paper:

### MARK TWAIN LETTER SOLD.

*Written to Thomas Nast, it Proposed a Joint Tour.*

A Mark Twain autograph letter brought $43 yesterday at the auction by the Merwin-Clayton Company of the library and correspondence of the late Thomas Nast, cartoonist. The letter is nine pages note-paper, is dated Hartford, Nov. 12, 1877, and is addressed to Nast. It reads in part as follows:

HARTFORD, *Nov. 12.*

MY DEAR NAST: I did not think I should ever stand on a platform again until the time was come for me to say I die innocent. But the same old offers keep arriving that have arriven every year, and been every year declined—$500 for Louisville, $500 for St. Louis, $1,000 gold for two nights in Toronto, half gross proceeds for New York, Boston, Brooklyn, &c. I have declined them all just as usual, though sorely tempted as usual.

Now, I do not decline because I mind talking to an audience, but because (1) travelling alone is so heart-breakingly dreary, and (2) shouldering the whole show is such cheer-killing responsibility.

Therefore I now propose to you what you proposed to me in November, 1867—ten years ago, (when I was unknown,) viz.; That you should stand on the platform and make pictures, and I stand by you and blackguard the audience. I should enormously enjoy meandering around (to big towns—don't want to go to little ones) with you for company.

The letter includes a schedule of cities and the number of appearances planned for each.

This is as it should be. This is worthy of all praise. I say it myself lest other competent persons should forget to do it. It appears that four of my ancient letters were sold at auction, three of them at twenty-seven dollars, twenty-eight dollars, and twenty-nine dollars respectively, and the one above mentioned at forty-three dollars. There is one very gratifying circumstance about this, to wit: that my literature has more than held its own as regards money value through this stretch of thirty-six years. I judge that the forty-three-dollar letter must have gone at about ten cents a word, whereas if I had written it to-day its market

rate would be thirty cents—so I have increased in value two or
three hundred per cent. I note another gratifying circumstance
—that a letter of General Grant's sold at something short of
eighteen dollars. I can't rise to General Grant's lofty place in the
estimation of this nation, but it is a deep happiness to me to know
that when it comes to epistolary literature he can't sit in the
front seat along with me.

This reminds me—nine years ago, when we were living in Tedworth Square, London, a report was cabled to the American journals that I was dying. I was not the one. It was another
Clemens, a cousin of mine,—Dr. J. Ross Clemens, now of St.
Louis—who was due to die but presently escaped, by some chi-
canery or other characteristic of the tribe of Clemens. The London representatives of the American papers began to flock in,
with American cables in their hands, to inquire into my condition.
There was nothing the matter with me, and each in his turn was
astonished, and disappointed, to find me reading and smoking in
my study and worth next to nothing as a text for transatlantic
news. One of these men was a gentle and kindly and grave and
sympathetic Irishman, who hid his sorrow the best he could, and
tried to look glad, and told me that his paper, the *Evening Sun,*
had cabled him that it was reported in New York that I was dead.
What should he cable in reply? I said—

" Say the report is greatly exaggerated."

He never smiled, but went solemnly away and sent the cable
in those words. The remark hit the world pleasantly, and to this
day it keeps turning up, now and then, in the newspapers when
people have occasion to discount exaggerations.

The next man was also an Irishman. He had his New York
cablegram in his hand—from the New York *World*—and he was
so evidently trying to get around that cable with invented soft-
nesses and palliations that my curiosity was aroused and I wanted
to see what it did really say. So when occasion offered I slipped
it out of his hand. It said,

" If Mark Twain dying send five hundred words. If dead send
a thousand."

Now that old letter of mine sold yesterday for forty-three dollars. When I am dead it will be worth eighty-six.

MARK TWAIN,

*(To be continued.)*

# Chapter III

October 5, 1906. Pages 577–89.

PREFATORY NOTE.—Mr. Clemens began to write his autobiography many years ago, and he continues to add to it day by day. It was his original intention to permit no publication of his memoirs until after his death; but, after leaving " Pier No. 70," he concluded that a considerable portion might now suitably be given to the public. It is that portion, garnered from the quarter-million of words already written, which will appear in this REVIEW during the coming year. No part of the autobiography will be published in book form during the lifetime of the author.—EDITOR N. A. R.

## VI.

TO-MORROW will be the thirty-sixth anniversary of our marriage. My wife passed from this life one year and eight months ago, in Florence, Italy, after an unbroken illness of twenty-two months' duration.

I saw her first in the form of an ivory miniature in her brother Charley's stateroom in the steamer " Quaker City," in the Bay of Smyrna, in the summer of 1867, when she was in her twenty-second year. I saw her in the flesh for the first time in New York in the following December. She was slender and beautiful and girlish—and she was both girl and woman. She remained both girl and woman to the last day of her life. Under a grave

23

and gentle exterior burned inextinguishable fires of sympathy, energy, devotion, enthusiasm, and absolutely limitless affection. She was *always* frail in body, and she lived upon her spirit, whose hopefulness and courage were indestructible. Perfect truth, perfect honesty, perfect candor, were qualities of her character which were born with her. Her judgments of people and things were sure and accurate. Her intuitions almost never deceived her. In her judgments of the characters and acts of both friends and strangers, there was always room for charity, and this charity never failed. I have compared and contrasted her with hundreds of persons, and my conviction remains that hers was the most perfect character I have ever met. And I may add that she was the most winningly dignified person I have ever known. Her character and disposition were of the sort that not only invites worship, but commands it. No servant ever left her service who deserved to remain in it. And, as she could choose with a glance of her eye, the servants she selected did in almost all cases deserve to remain, and they *did* remain. She was always cheerful; and she was always able to communicate her cheerfulness to others. During the nine years that we spent in poverty and debt, she was always able to reason me out of my despairs, and find a bright side to the clouds, and make me see it. In all that time, I never knew her to utter a word of regret concerning our altered circumstances, nor did I ever know her children to do the like. For she had taught them, and they drew their fortitude from her. The love which she bestowed upon those whom she loved took the form of worship, and in that form it was returned—returned by relatives, friends and the servants of her household. It was a strange combination which wrought into one individual, so to speak, by marriage—her disposition and character and mine. She poured out her prodigal affections in kisses and caresses, and in a vocabulary of endearments whose profusion was always an astonishment to me. I was born *reserved* as to endearments of speech and caresses, and hers broke upon me as the summer waves break upon Gibraltar. I was reared in that atmosphere of reserve. As I have already said, in another chapter, I never knew a member of my father's family to kiss another member of it except once, and that at a death-bed. And our village was not a kissing community. The kissing and caressing ended with courtship—along with the deadly piano-playing of that day.

She had the heart-free laugh of a girl. It came seldom, but when it broke upon the ear it was as inspiring as music. I heard it for the last time when she had been occupying her sick-bed for more than a year, and I made a written note of it at the time—a note not to be repeated.

To-morrow will be the thirty-sixth anniversary. We were married in her father's house in Elmira, New York, and went next day, by special train, to Buffalo, along with the whole Langdon family, and with the Beechers and the Twichells, who had solemnized the marriage. We were to live in Buffalo, where I was to be one of the editors of the Buffalo "Express," and a part owner of the paper. I knew nothing about Buffalo, but I had made my household arrangements there through a friend, by letter. I had instructed him to find a boarding-house of as respectable a character as my light salary as editor would command. We were received at about nine o'clock at the station in Buffalo, and were put into several sleighs and driven all over America, as it seemed to me—for, apparently, we turned all the corners in the town and followed all the streets there were—I scolding freely, and characterizing that friend of mine in very uncomplimentary words for securing a boarding-house that apparently had no definite locality. But there was a conspiracy—and my bride knew of it, but I was in ignorance. Her father, Jervis Langdon, had bought and furnished a new house for us in the fashionable street, Delaware Avenue, and had laid in a cook and housemaids, and a brisk and electric young coachman, an Irishman, Patrick McAleer—and we were being driven all over that city in order that one sleighful of those people could have time to go to the house, and see that the gas was lighted all over it, and a hot supper prepared for the crowd. We arrived at last, and when I entered that fairy place my indignation reached high-water mark, and without any reserve I delivered my opinion to that friend of mine for being so stupid as to put us into a boarding-house whose terms would be far out of my reach. Then Mr. Langdon brought forward a very pretty box and opened it, and took from it a deed of the house. So the comedy ended very pleasantly, and we sat down to supper.

The company departed about midnight, and left us alone in our new quarters. Then Ellen, the cook, came in to get orders for the morning's marketing—and neither of us knew whether beefsteak was sold by the barrel or by the yard. We exposed our ignorance, and Ellen was full of Irish delight over it. Patrick McAleer, that brisk young Irishman, came in to get his orders for next day—and that was our first glimpse of him. . . .

Our first child, Langdon Clemens, was born the 7th of November, 1870, and lived twenty-two months. Susy was born the 19th of March, 1872, and passed from life in the Hartford home, the 18th of August, 1896. With her, when the end came, were Jean and Katy Leary, and John and Ellen (the gardener and his wife). Clara and her mother and I arrived in England from around the world on the 31st of July, and took a house in Guildford. A week later, when Susy, Katy and Jean should have been arriving from America, we got a letter instead.

It explained that Susy was slightly ill—nothing of consequence. But we were disquieted, and began to cable for later news. This was Friday. All day no answer—and the ship to leave Southampton next day, at noon. Clara and her mother began packing, to be ready in case the news should be bad. Finally came a cablegram saying, " Wait for cablegram in the morning." This was not satisfactory—not reassuring. I cabled again, asking that the answer be sent to Southampton, for the day was now closing. I waited in the post-office that night till the doors were closed, toward midnight, in the hope that good news might still come, but there was no message. We sat silent at home till one in the morning, waiting—waiting for we knew not what. Then we took the earliest morning train, and when we reached Southampton the message was there. It said the recovery would be long, but certain. This was a great relief to me, but not to my wife. She was frightened. She and Clara went aboard the steamer at once and sailed for America, to nurse Susy. I remained behind to search for a larger house in Guildford.

That was the 15th of August, 1896. Three days later, when my wife and Clara were about half-way across the ocean, I was standing in our dining-room thinking of nothing in particular, when a cablegram was put into my hand. It said, " Susy was peacefully released to-day."

It is one of the mysteries of our nature that a man, all unprepared, can receive a thunder-stroke like that and live. There is but one reasonable explanation of it. The intellect is stunned by the shock, and but gropingly gathers the meaning of the words.

The power to realize their full import is mercifully wanting. The mind has a dumb sense of vast loss—that is all. It will take mind and memory months, and possibly years, to gather together the details, and thus learn and know the whole extent of the loss. A man's house burns down. The smoking wreckage represents only a ruined home that was dear through years of use and pleasant associations. By and by, as the days and weeks go on, first he misses this, then that, then the other thing. And, when he casts about for it, he finds that it was in that house. Always it is an *essential*—there was but one of its kind. It cannot be replaced. It was in that house. It is irrevocably lost. He did not realize that it was an essential when he had it; he only discovers it now when he finds himself balked, hampered, by its absence. It will be years before the tale of lost essentials is complete, and not till then can he truly know the magnitude of his disaster.

The 18th of August brought me the awful tidings. The mother and the sister were out there in mid-Atlantic, ignorant of what was happening; flying to meet this incredible calamity. All that could be done to protect them from the full force of the shock was done by relatives and good friends. They went down the Bay and met the ship at night, but did not show themselves until morning, and then only to Clara. When she returned to the stateroom she did not speak, and did not need to. Her mother looked at her and said:

" Susy is dead."

At half past ten o'clock that night, Clara and her mother completed their circuit of the globe, and drew up at Elmira by the same train and in the same car which had borne them and me Westward from it one year, one month, and one week before. And again Susy was there—not waving her welcome in the glare of the lights, as she had waved her farewell to us thirteen months before, but lying white and fair in her coffin, in the house where she was born.

The last thirteen days of Susy's life were spent in our own house in Hartford, the home of her childhood, and always th. dearest place in the earth to her. About her she had faithful old friends—her pastor, Mr. Twichell, who had known her from the cradle, and who had come a long journey to be with her; her uncle and aunt, Mr. and Mrs. Theodore Crane; Patrick, the coachman; Katy, who had begun to serve us when Susy was a child of eight years; John and Ellen, who had been with us many years. Also Jean was there.

At the hour when my wife and Clara set sail for America, Susy was in no danger. Three hours later there came a sudden change for the worse. Meningitis set in, and it was immediately apparent that she was death-struck. That was Saturday, the 15th of August.

"That evening she took food for the last time," (Jean's letter to me). The next morning the brain-fever was raging. She walked the floor a little in her pain and delirium, then succumbed to weakness and returned to her bed. Previously she had found hanging in a closet a gown which she had seen her mother wear. She thought it was her mother, dead, and she kissed it, and cried. About noon she became blind (an effect of the disease) and bewailed it to her uncle.

From Jean's letter I take this sentence, which needs no comment:

"About one in the afternoon Susy spoke for the last time."

It was only one word that she said when she spoke that last time, and it told of her longing. She groped with her hands and found Katy, and caressed her face, and said "Mamma."

How gracious it was that, in that forlorn hour of wreck and ruin, with the night of death closing around her, she should have been granted that beautiful illusion—that the latest vision which rested upon the clouded mirror of her mind should have been the vision of her mother, and the latest emotion she should know in life the joy and peace of that dear imagined presence.

About two o'clock she composed herself as if for sleep, and never moved again. She fell into unconsciousness and so remained two days and five hours, until Tuesday evening at seven minutes past seven, when the release came. She was twenty-four years and five months old.

On the 23d, her mother and her sisters saw her laid to rest—she that had been our wonder and our worship.

In one of her own books I find some verses which I will copy here. Apparently, she always put borrowed matter in quotation marks. These verses lack those marks, and therefore I take them to be her own:

Love came at dawn, when all the world was fair,
  When crimson glories' bloom and sun were rife;
Love came at dawn, when hope's wings fanned the air,
  And murmured, " I am life."

Love came at eve, and when the day was done,
  When heart and brain were tired, and slumber pressed;
Love came at eve, shut out the sinking sun,
  And whispered, " I am rest."

The summer seasons of Susy's childhood were spent at Quarry Farm, on the hills east of Elmira, New York; the other seasons of the year at the home in Hartford. Like other children, she was blithe and happy, fond of play; *un*like the average of children, she was at times much given to retiring within herself, and trying to search out the hidden meanings of the deep things that make the puzzle and pathos of human existence, and in all the ages have baffled the inquirer and mocked him. As a little child aged seven, she was oppressed and perplexed by the maddening repetition of the stock incidents of our race's fleeting sojourn here, just as the same thing has oppressed and perplexed maturer minds from the beginning of time. A myriad of men are born; they labor and sweat and struggle for bread; they squabble and scold and fight; they scramble for little mean advantages over each other; age creeps upon them; infirmities follow; shames and humiliations bring down their prides and their vanities; those they love are taken from them, and the joy of life is turned to aching grief. The burden of pain, care, misery, grows heavier year by year; at length, ambition is dead, pride is dead; vanity is dead; longing for release is in their place. It comes at last— the only unpoisoned gift earth ever had for them—and they vanish from a world where they were of no consequence; where they achieved nothing; where they were a mistake and a failure and a foolishness; there they have left no sign that they have existed—a world which will lament them a day and forget them forever. Then another myriad takes their place, and copies all they did, and goes along the same profitless road, and vanishes as they vanished—to make room for another, and another, and a million other myriads, to follow the same arid path through the same desert, and accomplish what the first myriad, and all the myriads that came after it, accomplished—nothing!

" Mamma, what is it all for?" asked Susy, preliminarily stating the above details in her own halting language, after long brooding over them alone in the privacy of the nursery.

A year later, she was groping her way alone through another sunless bog, but this time she reached a rest for her feet. For a week, her mother had not been able to go to the nursery, evenings, at the child's prayer hour. She spoke of it—was sorry for it, and said she would come to-night, and hoped she could continue to come every night and hear Susy pray, as before. Noticing that the child wished to respond, but was evidently troubled as to how to word her answer, she asked what the difficulty was. Susy explained that Miss Foote (the governess) had been teaching her about the Indians and their religious beliefs, whereby it appeared that they had not only a God, but several. This had set Susy to thinking. As a result of this thinking, she had stopped praying. She qualified this statement—that is, she modified it—saying she did not now pray "in the same way" as she had formerly done. Her mother said:

"Tell me about it, dear."

"Well, mamma, the Indians believed they knew, but now we know they were wrong. By and by, it can turn out that we are wrong. So now I only pray that there may be a God and a Heaven —or something better."

I wrote down this pathetic prayer in its precise wording, at the time, in a record which we kept of the children's sayings, and my reverence for it has grown with the years that have passed over my head since then. Its untaught grace and simplicity are a child's, but the wisdom and the pathos of it are of all the ages that have come and gone since the race of man has lived, and longed, and hoped, and feared, and doubted.

To go back a year—Susy aged seven. Several times her mother said to her:

"There, there, Susy, you mustn't cry over little things."

This furnished Susy a text for thought. She had been breaking her heart over what had seemed vast disasters—a broken toy; a picnic cancelled by thunder and lightning and rain; the mouse that was growing tame and friendly in the nursery caught and killed by the cat—and now came this strange revelation. For some unaccountable reason, these were not vast calamities. Why? How is the size of calamities measured? What is the rule? There must be some way to tell the great ones from the small ones; what is the law of these proportions? She examined the problem earnestly and long. She gave it her best thought from time to time, for two or three days—but it baffled her—defeated her. And at last she gave up and went to her mother for help.

"Mamma, what is ' *little* things'?"

It seemed a simple question—at first. And yet, before the answer could be put into words, unsuspected and unforeseen difficulties began to appear. They increased; they multiplied; they brought about another defeat. The effort to explain came to a standstill. Then Susy tried to help her mother out—with an instance, an example, an illustration. The mother was getting ready to go down-town, and one of her errands was to buy a long-promised toy-watch for Susy.

"If you forgot the watch, mamma, would that be a little thing?"

She was not concerned about the watch, for she knew it would not be forgotten. What she was hoping for was that the answer would unriddle the riddle, and bring rest and peace to her perplexed little mind.

The hope was disappointed, of course—for the reason that the size of a misfortune is not determinable by an outsider's measurement of it, but only by the measurements applied to it by the person specially affected by it. The king's lost crown is a vast matter to the king, but of no consequence to the child. The lost toy is a great matter to the child, but in the king's eyes it is not a thing to break the heart about. A verdict was reached, but it was based upon the above model, and Susy was granted leave to measure her disasters thereafter with her own tape-line.

As a child, Susy had a passionate temper; and it cost her much remorse and many tears before she learned to govern it, but after that it was a wholesome salt, and her character was the stronger and healthier for its presence. It enabled her to be good with dignity; it preserved her not only from being good for vanity's sake, but from even the appearance of it. In looking back over the long vanished years, it seems but natural and excusable that I should dwell with longing affection and preference upon incidents of her young life which made it beautiful to us, and that I should let its few small offences go unsummoned and unreproached.

In the summer of 1880, when Susy was just eight years of age, the family were at Quarry Farm, as usual at that season of the year.  Hay-cutting time was approaching, and Susy and Clara were counting the hours, for the time was big with a great event for them; they had been promised that they might mount the wagon and ride home from the fields on the summit of the hay mountain.  This perilous privilege, so dear to their age and species, had never been granted them before.  Their excitement had no bounds.  They could talk of nothing but this epoch-making adventure, now.  But misfortune overtook Susy on the very morning of the important day.  In a sudden outbreak of passion, she corrected Clara—with a shovel, or stick, or something of the sort. At any rate, the offence committed was of a gravity clearly beyond the limit allowed in the nursery.  In accordance with the rule and custom of the house, Susy went to her mother to confess, and to help decide upon the size and character of the punishment due.  It was quite understood that, as a punishment could have but one rational object and function—to act as a reminder, and warn the transgressor against transgressing in the same way again—the children would know about as well as any how to choose a penalty which would be rememberable and effective. Susy and her mother discussed various punishments, but none of them seemed adequate.  This fault was an unusually serious one, and required the setting up of a danger-signal in the memory that would not blow out nor burn out, but remain a fixture there and furnish its saving warning indefinitely.  Among the punishments mentioned was deprivation of the hay-wagon ride.  It was noticeable that this one hit Susy hard.  Finally, in the summing up, the mother named over the list and asked:

" Which one do you think it ought to be, Susy?"

Susy studied, shrank from her duty, and asked:

" Which do you think, mamma?"

" Well, Susy, I would rather leave it to you. *You* make the choice yourself."

It cost Susy a struggle, and much and deep thinking and weighing—but she came out where any one who knew her could have foretold she would.

" Well, mamma, I'll make it the hay-wagon, because you know the other things might not make me remember not to do it again, but if I don't get to ride on the hay-wagon I can remember it easily."

In this world the real penalty, the sharp one, the lasting one, never falls otherwise than on the wrong person. It was not *I* that corrected Clara, but the remembrance of poor Susy's lost hayride still brings *me* a pang—after twenty-six years.

Apparently, Susy was born with humane feelings for the animals, and compassion for their troubles. This enabled her to see a new point in an old story, once, when she was only six years old—a point which had been overlooked by older, and perhaps duller, people for many ages. Her mother told her the moving story of the sale of Joseph by his brethren, the staining of his coat with the blood of the slaughtered kid, and the rest of it. She dwelt upon the inhumanity of the brothers; their cruelty toward their helpless young brother; and the unbrotherly treachery which they practised upon him; for she hoped to teach the child a lesson in gentle pity and mercifulness which she would remember. Apparently, her desire was accomplished, for the tears came into Susy's eyes and she was deeply moved. Then she said:

" Poor little kid !"

A child's frank envy of the privileges and distinctions of its elders is often a delicately flattering attention and the reverse of unwelcome, but sometimes the envy is not placed where the beneficiary is expecting it to be placed. Once, when Susy was seven, she sat breathlessly absorbed in watching a guest of ours adorn herself for a ball. The lady was charmed by this homage; this mute and gentle admiration; and was happy in it. And when her pretty labors were finished, and she stood at last perfect, unimprovable, clothed like Solomon in all his glory, she paused, confident and expectant, to receive from Susy's tongue the tribute that was burning in her eyes. Susy drew an envious little sigh and said:

" I wish *I* could have crooked teeth and spectacles !"

Once, when Susy was six months along in her eighth year, she did something one day in the presence of company, which subjected her to criticism and reproof. Afterward, when she was alone with her mother, as was her custom she reflected a little while over the matter. Then she set up what I think—and what the shade of Burns would think—was a quite good philosophical defence.

" Well, mamma, you know I didn't see myself, and so I couldn't know how it looked."

In homes where the near friends and visitors are mainly literary people—lawyers, judges, professors and clergymen—the children's ears become early familiarized with wide vocabularies. It is natural for them to pick up any words that fall in their way; it is natural for them to pick up big and little ones indiscriminately; it is natural for them to use without fear any word that comes to their net, no matter how formidable it may be as to size. As a result, their talk is a curious and funny musketry clatter of little words, interrupted at intervals by the heavy artillery crash of a word of such imposing sound and size that it seems to shake the ground and rattle the windows. Sometimes the child gets a wrong idea of a word which it has picked up by chance, and attaches to it a meaning which impairs its usefulness—but this does not happen as often as one might expect it would. Indeed, it happens with an infrequency which may be regarded as remarkable. As a child, Susy had good fortune with her large words, and she employed many of them. She made no more than her fair share of mistakes. Once when she thought something very funny was going to happen (but it didn't), she was racked and torn with laughter, by anticipation. But, apparently, she still felt sure of her position, for she said, " If it had happened, I should have been transformed [transported] with glee."

And earlier, when she was a little maid of five years, she informed a visitor that she had been in a church only once, and that was the time when Clara was " crucified " [christened]. . . .

In Heidelberg, when Susy was six, she noticed that the Schloss gardens were populous with snails creeping all about everywhere. One day she found a new dish on her table and inquired concerning it, and learned that it was made of snails. She was awed and impressed, and said:

" Wild ones, mamma?"

She was thoughtful and considerate of others—an acquired quality, no doubt. No one seems to be born with it. One hot day, at home in Hartford, when she was a little child, her mother borrowed her fan several times (a Japanese one, value five cents), refreshed herself with it a moment or two, then handed it back with a word of thanks. Susy knew her mother would use the fan all the time if she could do it without putting a deprivation upon its owner. She also knew that her mother could not be persuaded to do that. A relief must be devised somehow; Susy devised it. She got five cents out of her money-box and carried it to Patrick, and asked him to take it down-town (a mile and a half) and buy a Japanese fan and bring it home. He did it— and thus thoughtfully and delicately was the exigency met and the mother's comfort secured. It is to the child's credit that she did not save herself expense by bringing down another and more costly kind of fan from up-stairs, but was content to act upon the impression that her mother desired the Japanese kind—content to accomplish the desire and stop with that, without troubling about the wisdom or unwisdom of it.

Sometimes, while she was still a child, her speech fell into quaint and strikingly expressive forms. Once—aged nine or ten—she came to her mother's room, when her sister Jean was a baby, and said Jean was crying in the nursery, and asked if she might ring for the nurse. Her mother asked:

" Is she crying hard?"—meaning cross, ugly.

" Well, no, mamma. It is a weary, lonesome cry."

It is a pleasure to me to recall various incidents which reveal the delicacies of feeling that were so considerable a part of her budding character. Such a revelation came once in a way which, while creditable to her heart, was defective in another direction. She was in her eleventh year then. Her mother had been making the Christmas purchases, and she allowed Susy to see the presents which were for Patrick's children. Among these was a handsome sled for Jimmy, on which a stag was painted; also, in gilt capitals, the word " Deer." Susy was excited and joyous over everything, until she came to this sled. Then she became sober and silent— yet the sled was the choicest of all the gifts. Her mother was surprised, and also disappointed, and said:

" Why, Susy, doesn't it please you? Isn't it fine?"

Susy hesitated, and it was plain that she did not want to say the thing that was in her mind. However, being urged, she brought it haltingly out:

" Well, mamma, it *is* fine, and of course it *did* cost a good deal —but—but—why should that be mentioned?"

Seeing that she was not understood, she reluctantly pointed to that word " Deer." It was her orthography that was at fault, not her heart. She had inherited both from her mother.

MARK TWAIN.

# Chapter IV

### October 19, 1906. Pages 705–16.

PREFATORY NOTE.—Mr. Clemens began to write his autobiography many years ago, and he continues to add to it day by day. It was his original intention to permit no publication of his memoirs until after his death; but, after leaving "Pier No. 70," he concluded that a considerable portion might now suitably be given to the public. It is that portion, garnered from the quarter-million of words already written, which will appear in this REVIEW during the coming year. No part of the autobiography will be published in book form during the lifetime of the author.—EDITOR N. A. R.

WHEN Susy was thirteen, and was a slender little maid with plaited tails of copper-tinged brown hair down her back, and was perhaps the busiest bee in the household hive, by reason of the manifold studies, health exercises and recreations she had to attend to, she secretly, and of her own motion, and out of love, added another task to her labors—the writing of a biography of me. She did this work in her bedroom at night, and kept her record hidden. After a little, the mother discovered it and filched it, and let me see it; then told Susy what she had done, and how pleased I was, and how proud. I remember that time with a deep pleasure. I had had compliments before, but none that touched me like this; none that could approach it for value in my eyes. It has kept that place always since. I have had no compliment, no praise, no tribute from any source, that was so precious to me as this one was and still is. As I read it *now,* after all these many years, it is still a king's message to me, and brings me the same dear surprise it brought me then—with the pathos added, of the thought that the eager and hasty hand that sketched it and scrawled it will not touch mine again—and I feel as the humble and unexpectant must feel when their eyes fall upon the edict that raises them to the ranks of the noble.

Yesterday while I was rummaging in a pile of ancient note-books of mine which I had not seen for years, I came across a reference to that biography. It is quite evident that several times, at breakfast and dinner, in those long-past days, I was posing for the biography. In fact, I clearly remember that I *was* doing that—and I also remember that Susy detected it. I remember saying a very smart thing, with a good deal of an air, at the breakfast - table one morning, and that Susy observed to her mother privately, a little later, that papa was doing that for the biography.

I cannot bring myself to change any line or word in Susy's sketch of me, but will introduce passages from it now and then just as they came in their quaint simplicity out of her honest heart, which was the beautiful heart of a child. What comes from that source has a charm and grace of its own which may transgress all the recognized laws of literature, if it choose, and yet be literature still, and worthy of hospitality. I shall print the whole of this little biography, before I have done with it—every word, every sentence.

The spelling is frequently desperate, but it was Susy's, and it shall stand. I love it, and cannot profane it. To me, it is gold. To correct it would alloy it, not refine it. It would spoil it. It would take from it its freedom and flexibility and make it stiff and formal. Even when it is most extravagant I am not shocked. It is Susy's spelling, and she was doing the best she could—and nothing could better it for me. . . .

Susy began the biography in 1885, when I was in the fiftieth year of my age, and she just entering the fourteenth of hers. She begins in this way:

We are a very happy family. We consist of Papa, Mamma, Jean, Clara and me. It is papa I am writing about, and I shall have no trouble in not knowing what to say about him, as he is a *very* striking character.

But wait a minute—I will return to Susy presently.

In the matter of slavish imitation, man is the monkey's superior all the time. The average man is destitute of independence of opinion. He is not interested in contriving an opinion of his own, by study and reflection, but is only anxious to find out what his neighbor's opinion is and slavishly adopt it. A generation ago, I found out that the latest review of a book was pretty sure to be just a reflection of the *earliest* review of it; that whatever the first reviewer found to praise or censure in the book would be repeated in the latest reviewer's report, with nothing fresh added. Therefore more than once I took the precaution of sending my book, in manuscript, to Mr. Howells, when he was editor of the "Atlantic Monthly," so that he could prepare a review of it at leisure. I knew he would say the truth about the book—I also knew that he would find more merit than demerit in it, because I already knew that that was the condition of the book. I allowed no copy of it to go out to the press until after Mr. Howells's notice of it had appeared. That book was always safe. There wasn't a man behind a pen in all America that had the courage to find anything in the book which Mr. Howells had not found— there wasn't a man behind a pen in America that had spirit enough to say a brave and original thing about the book on his own responsibility.

I believe that the trade of critic, in literature, music, and the drama, is the most degraded of all trades, and that it has no real value—certainly no large value. When Charles Dudley Warner and I were about to bring out "The Gilded Age," the editor of the "Daily Graphic" persuaded me to let him have an advance copy, he giving me his word of honor that no notice of it would appear in his paper until after the "Atlantic Monthly" notice should have appeared. This reptile published a review of the book within three days afterward. I could not really complain, because he had only given me his word of honor as security; I ought to have required of him something substantial. I believe his notice did not deal mainly with the merit of the book, or the lack of it, but with my moral attitude toward the public. It was charged that 1 had used my reputation to play a swindle upon the public; that Mr. Warner had written as much as half of the book, and that I had used my name to float it and give it currency; a currency—so the critic averred—which it could not have acquired without my name, and that this conduct of mine was a grave fraud upon the people. The " Graphic " was not an authority upon any subject whatever. It had a sort of distinction, in that it was the first and only illustrated daily newspaper that the world had seen; but it was without character; it was poorly and cheaply edited; its opinion of a book or of any other work of art was of no consequence. Everybody knew this, yet all the critics in America, one after the other, copied the " Graphic's " criticism, merely changing the phraseology, and left me under that charge of dishonest conduct. Even the great Chicago " Tribune," the most important journal in the Middle West, was not able to invent anything fresh, but adopted the view of the humble " Daily Graphic," dishonesty-charge and all.

However, let it go. It is the will of God that we must have critics, and missionaries, and Congressmen, and humorists, and we must bear the burden. Meantime, I seem to have been drifting into criticism myself. But that is nothing. At the worst, criticism is nothing more than a crime, and I am not unused to that.

What I have been travelling toward all this time is this: the first critic that ever had occasion to describe my personal appearance littered his description with foolish and inexcusable errors whose aggregate furnished the result that I was distinctly and distressingly unhandsome. That description floated around the country in the papers, and was in constant use and wear for a quarter of a century. It seems strange to me that apparently no critic in the country could be found who could look at me and have the courage to take up his pen and destroy that lie. That lie began its course on the Pacific coast, in 1864, and it likened me in personal appearance to Petroleum V. Nasby, who had been out there lecturing. For twenty-five years afterward, no critic could furnish a description of me without fetching in Nasby to help out my portrait. I knew Nasby well, and he was a good fellow, but in my life I have not felt malignant enough about any more than three persons to charge those persons with resembling Nasby. It hurts me to the heart. I was always hand-

some.  Anybody but a critic could have seen it.  And it had
long been a distress to my family — including Susy — that the
critics should go on making this wearisome mistake, year after
year, when there was no foundation for it.  Even when a critic
wanted to be particularly friendly and complimentary to me, he
didn't dare to go beyond my clothes.  He never ventured beyond
that old safe frontier.  When he had finished with my clothes
he had said all the kind things, the pleasant things, the complimentary things he could risk.  Then he dropped back on Nasby.

Yesterday I found this clipping in the pocket of one of those
ancient memorandum-books of mine.  It is of the date of thirty-
nine years ago, and both the paper and the ink are yellow with
the bitterness that I felt in that old day when I clipped it out
to preserve it and brood over it, and grieve about it.  I will copy
it here, to wit:

A correspondent of the Philadelphia " Press," writing of one of
Schuyler Colfax's receptions, says of our Washington correspondent:
" Mark Twain, the delicate humorist, was present; quite a lion, as he
deserves to be.  Mark is a bachelor, faultless in taste, whose snowy
vest is suggestive of endless quarrels with Washington washerwomen;
but the heroism of Mark is settled for all time, for such purity and
smoothness were never seen before.  His lavender gloves might have
been stolen from some Turkish harem, so delicate were they in size;
but more likely—anything else were more likely than that.  In form
and feature he bears some resemblance to the immortal Nasby; but
whilst Petroleum is brunette to the core, Twain is golden, amber-hued,
melting, blonde."

Let us return to Susy's biography now, and get the opinion of
one who is unbiassed:

### From Susy's Biography.

Papa's appearance has been described many times, but very incorrectly.  He has beautiful gray hair, not any too thick or any too long,
but just right; a Roman nose, which greatly improves the beauty of
his features; kind blue eyes and a small mustache.  He has a wonderfully shaped head and profile.  He has a very good figure—in short,
he is an extrodinarily fine looking man.  All his features are perfect,
except that he hasn't extrodinary teeth.  His complexion is very fair,
and he doesn't ware a beard.  He is a very good man and a very funny
one.  He *has* got a temper, but we all of us have in this family.  He
is the loveliest man I ever saw or ever hope to see—and oh, so absent-
minded.  He does tell perfectly delightful stories.  Clara and I used
to sit on each arm of his chair and listen while he told us stories about
the pictures on the wall.

I remember the story-telling days vividly. They were a difficult and exacting audience—those little creatures.

Along one side of the library, in the Hartford home, the bookshelves joined the mantelpiece—in fact there were shelves on both sides of the mantelpiece. On these shelves, and on the mantelpiece, stood various ornaments. At one end of the procession was a framed oil-painting of a cat's head, at the other end was a head of a beautiful young girl, life-size—called Emmeline, because she looked just about like that—an impressionist watercolor. Between the one picture and the other there were twelve or fifteen of the bric-à-brac things already mentioned; also an oil-painting by Elihu Vedder, "The Young Medusa." Every now and then the children required me to construct a romance—always impromptu—not a moment's preparation permitted—and into that romance I had to get all that bric-à-brac and the three pictures. I had to start always with the cat and finish with Emmeline. I was never allowed the refreshment of a change, end-for-end. It was not permissible to introduce a bric-à-brac ornament into the story out of its place in the procession.

These bric-à-bracs were never allowed a peaceful day, a reposeful day, a restful Sabbath. In their lives there was no Sabbath, in their lives there was no peace; they knew no existence but a monotonous career of violence and bloodshed. In the course of time, the bric-à-brac and the pictures showed wear. It was because they had had so many and such tumultuous adventures in their romantic careers.

As romancer to the children I had a hard time, even from the beginning. If they brought me a picture, in a magazine, and required me to build a story to it, they would cover the rest of the page with their pudgy hands to keep me from stealing an idea from it. The stories had to come hot from the bat, always. They had to be absolutely original and fresh. Sometimes the children furnished me simply a character or two, or a dozen, and required me to start out at once on that slim basis and deliver those characters up to a vigorous and entertaining life of crime. If they heard of a new trade, or an unfamiliar animal, or anything like that, I was pretty sure to have to deal with those things in the next romance. Once Clara required me to build a sudden tale out of a plumber and a " bawgunstrictor," and I had to do it. She didn't know what a boa-constrictor was, until he developed in the tale—then she was better satisfied with it than ever.

### From Susy's Biography.

Papa's favorite game is billiards, and when he is tired and wishes to rest himself he stays up all night and plays billiards, it seems to rest his head. He smokes a great deal almost incessantly. He has the mind of an author exactly, some of the simplest things he cant understand. Our burglar-alarm is often out of order, and papa had been obliged to take the mahogany-room off from the alarm altogether for a time, because the burglar-alarm had been in the habit of ringing even when the mahogany-room was closed. At length he thought that perhaps the burglar-alarm might be in order, and he decided to try and see; accordingly he put it on and then went down and opened the window; consequently the alarm bell rang, it would even if the alarm had been in order. Papa went despairingly upstairs and said to mamma, "Livy the mahogany-room won't go on. I have just opened the window to see."

"Why, Youth," mamma replied "if you've opened the window, why of coarse the alarm will ring!"

"That's what I've opened it for, why I just went down to see if it would ring!"

Mamma tried to explain to papa that when he wanted to go and see whether the alarm would ring while the window was closed he *mustn't* go and open the window—but in vain, papa couldn't understand, and got very impatient with mamma for trying to make him believe an impossible thing true.

This is a frank biographer, and an honest one; she uses no sand-paper on me. I have, to this day, the same dull head in the matter of conundrums and perplexities which Susy had discovered in those long-gone days. Complexities annoy me; they irritate me; then this progressive feeling presently warms into anger. I cannot get far in the reading of the commonest and simplest contract—with its " parties of the first part," and " parties of the second part," and " parties of the third part,"—before my temper is all gone. Ashcroft comes up here every day and pathetically tries to make me understand the points of the lawsuit which we are conducting against Henry Butters, Harold Wheeler, and the rest of those Plasmon buccaneers, but daily he has to give it up. It is pitiful to see, when he bends his earnest and appealing eyes upon me and says, after one of his efforts, " Now you *do* understand *that,* don't you?"

I am always obliged to say, " I *don't,* Ashcroft. I wish I could understand it, but I don't. Send for the cat."

In the days which Susy is talking about, a perplexity fell to my lot one day. F. G. Whitmore was my business agent, and he brought me out from town in his buggy. We drove by the *porte-cochère* and toward the stable. Now this was a *single* road, and was like a spoon whose handle stretched from the gate to a great round flower-bed in the neighborhood of the stable. At the approach to the flower-bed the road divided and circumnavigated it, making a loop, which I have likened to the bowl of the spoon. As we neared the loop, I saw that Whitmore was laying his course to port, (I was sitting on the starboard side—the side the house was on), and was going to start around that spoon-bowl on that left-hand side. I said,

"Don't do that, Whitmore; take the right-hand side. Then I shall be next to the house when we get to the door."

He said, "*That* will not happen in *any case,* it doesn't make any difference which way I go around this flower-bed."

I explained to him that he was an ass, but he stuck to his proposition, and I said,

"Go on and try it, and see."

He went on and tried it, and sure enough he fetched me up at the door on the very side that he had said I would be. I was not able to believe it then, and I don't believe it yet.

I said, "Whitmore, that is merely an accident. You can't do it again."

He said he could—and he drove down into the street, fetched around, came back, and actually did it again. I was stupefied, paralyzed, petrified, with these strange results, but they did not convince me. I didn't believe he could do it another time, but he did. He said he could do it all day, and fetch up the same way every time. By that time my temper was gone, and I asked him to go home and apply to the Asylum and I would pay the expenses; I didn't want to see him any more for a week.

I went up-stairs in a rage and started to tell Livy about it, expecting to get her sympathy for me and to breed aversion in her for Whitmore; but she merely burst into peal after peal of laughter, as the tale of my adventure went on, for her head was like Susy's: riddles and complexities had no terrors for it. Her mind and Susy's were analytical; I have tried to make it appear that mine was different. Many and many a time I have told that buggy experiment, hoping against hope that I would some time or other find somebody who would be on my side, but it has never happened. And I am never able to go glibly forward and state the circumstances of that buggy's progress without having to halt and consider, and call up in my mind the spoon-handle, the bowl of the spoon, the buggy and the horse, and my position in the buggy: and the minute I have got that far and try to turn it to the left it goes to ruin; I can't see how it is ever going to fetch me out right when we get to the door. Susy is right in her estimate. I can't understand things.

That burglar-alarm which Susy mentions led a gay and careless life, and had no principles. It was generally out of order at one point or another; and there was plenty of opportunity, because all the windows and doors in the house, from the cellar up to the top floor, were connected with it. However, in its seasons of being out of order it could trouble us for only a very little while: we quickly found out that it was fooling us, and that it was buzzing its blood-curdling alarm merely for its own amusement. Then we would shut it off, and send to New York for the electrician—there not being one in all Hartford in those days. When the repairs were finished we would set the alarm again and reestablish our confidence in it. It never did any real business except upon one single occasion. All the rest of its expensive career was frivolous and without purpose. Just that one time it performed its duty, and its whole duty—gravely, seriously, admirably. It let fly about two o'clock one black and dreary March morning, and I turned out promptly, because I knew that it was not fooling, this time. The bath-room door was on my side of the bed. I stepped in there, turned up the gas, looked at the annunciator, and turned off the alarm—so far as the door indicated was concerned—thus stopping the racket. Then I came back to bed. Mrs. Clemens opened the debate:

" What was it?"

" It was the cellar door."

" Was it a burglar, do you think?"

" Yes," I said, " of course it was. Did you suppose it was a Sunday-school superintendent?"

" No. What do you suppose he wants?"

" I suppose he wants jewelry, but he is not acquainted with the house and he thinks it is in the cellar. I don't like to disappoint a burglar whom I am not acquainted with, and who has done me no harm, but if he had had common sagacity enough to inquire, I could have told him we kept nothing down there but coal and vegetables. Still it may be that he *is* acquainted with the place, and that what he really wants is coal and vegetables. On the whole, I think it is vegetables he is after."

" Are you going down to see ?"

" No; I could not be of any assistance. Let him select for himself; I don't know where the things are."

Then she said, " But suppose he comes up to the ground floor !"

" That's all right. We shall know it the minute he opens a door on that floor. It will set off the alarm."

Just then the terrific buzzing broke out again. I said,

" He has arrived. I told you he would. I know all about burglars and their ways. They are systematic people."

I went into the bath-room to see if I was right, and I was. I shut off the dining-room and stopped the buzzing, and came back to bed. My wife said,

" What do you suppose he is after now ?"

I said, " I think he has got all the vegetables he wants and is coming up for napkin-rings and odds and ends for the wife and children. They all have families—burglars have—and they are always thoughtful of them, always take a few necessaries of life for themselves, and fill out with tokens of remembrance for the family. In taking them they do not forget us: those very things represent tokens of his remembrance of us, and also of our remembrance of him. We never get them again; the memory of the attention remains embalmed in our hearts."

" Are you going down to see what it is he wants now ?"

" No," I said, " I am no more interested than I was before. They are experienced people,—burglars; *they* know what they want; I should be no help to him. I *think* he is after ceramics and bric-à-brac and such things. If he knows the house he knows that that is all that he can find on the dining-room floor."

She said, with a strong interest perceptible in her tone, " Suppose he comes up here !"

I said, " It is all right. He will give us notice."

" What shall we do then ?"

" Climb out of the window."

She said, a little restively, " Well, what is the use of a burglar-alarm for us ?"

" You have seen, dear heart, that it has been useful up to the present moment, and I have explained to you how it will be continuously useful after he gets up here."

That was the end of it. He didn't ring any more alarms. Presently I said,

" He is disappointed, I think. He has gone off with the vegetables and the bric-à-brac, and I think he is dissatisfied."

We went to sleep, and at a quarter before eight in the morning I was out, and hurrying, for I was to take the 8.29 train for New York. I found the gas burning brightly—full head—all over the first floor. My new overcoat was gone; my old umbrella was gone; my new patent-leather shoes, which I had never worn, were gone. The large window which opened into the *ombra* at the rear of the house was standing wide. I passed out through it and tracked the burglar down the hill through the trees; tracked him without difficulty, because he had blazed his progress with imitation silver napkin-rings, and my umbrella, and various other things which he had disapproved of; and I went back in triumph and proved to my wife that he *was* a disappointed burglar. I had suspected he would be, from the start, and from his not coming up to our floor to get human beings.

Things happened to me that day in New York. I will tell about them another time.

### From Susy's Biography.

Papa has a peculiar gait we like, it seems just to sute him, but most people do not; he always walks up and down the room while thinking and between each coarse at meals.

A lady distantly related to us came to visit us once in those days. She came to stay a week, but all our efforts to make her happy failed, we could not imagine why, and she got up her anchor and sailed the next morning. We did much guessing, but could not solve the mystery. Later we found out what the trouble was. It was my tramping up and down between the courses. She conceived the idea that I could not stand her society.

That word " Youth," as the reader has perhaps already guessed, was my wife's pet name for me. It was gently satirical, but also affectionate. I had certain mental and material peculiarities and customs proper to a much younger person than I was.

### From Susy's Biography.

Papa is very fond of animals particularly of cats, we had a dear little gray kitten once that he named "Lazy" (papa always wears gray to match his hair and eyes) and he would carry him around on his shoulder, it was a mighty pretty sight! the gray cat sound asleep against papa's gray coat and hair. The names that he has given our different cats, are realy remarkably funny, they are namely Stray Kit, Abner, Motley, Fraeulein, Lazy, Bufalo Bill, Cleveland, Sour Mash, and Pestilence and Famine.

At one time when the children were small, we had a very black mother-cat named Satan, and Satan had a small black offspring named Sin. Pronouns were a difficulty for the children. Little Clara came in one day, her black eyes snapping with indignation, and said,

"Papa, Satan ought to be punished. She is out there at the greenhouse and there she stays and stays, and his kitten is downstairs crying."

### From Susy's Biography.

Papa uses very strong language, but I have an idea not nearly so strong as when he first maried mamma. A lady acquaintance of his is rather apt to interupt what one is saying, and papa told mamma that he thought he should say to the lady's husband "I am glad your wife wasn't present when the Deity said 'Let there be light.'"

It is as I have said before. This is a frank historian. She doesn't cover up one's deficiencies, but gives them an equal showing with one's handsomer qualities. Of course I made the remark which she has quoted—and even at this distant day I am still as much as half persuaded that if that lady had been present when the Creator said, "Let there be light," she would have interrupted Him and we shouldn't ever have got it.

### From Susy's Biography.

Papa said the other day, "I am a mugwump and a mugwump is pure from the marrow out. (Papa knows that I am writing this biography of him, and he said this for it.) He doesn't like to go to church at all, why I never understood, until just now, he told us the other day that he couldn't bear to hear any one talk but himself, but that he could listen to himself talk for hours without getting tired, of course he said this in joke, but I've no dought it was founded on truth.

MARK TWAIN.

*(To be Continued.)*

# Chapter V

## November 2, 1906. Pages 833–44.

PREFATORY NOTE.—Mr. Clemens began to write his autobiography many years ago, and he continues to add to it day by day. It was his original intention to permit no publication of his memoirs until after his death; but, after leaving "Pier No. 70," he concluded that a considerable portion might now suitably be given to the public. It is that portion, garnered from the quarter-million of words already written, which will appear in this REVIEW during the coming year. No part of the autobiography will be published in book form during the lifetime of the author.—EDITOR N. A. R.

SUSY's remark about my strong language troubles me, and I must go back to it. All through the first ten years of my married life I kept a constant and discreet watch upon my tongue while in the house, and went outside and to a distance when circumstances were too much for me and I was obliged to seek relief. I prized my wife's respect and approval above all the rest of the human race's respect and approval. I dreaded the day when she should discover that I was but a whited sepulchre partly freighted with suppressed language. I was so careful, during ten years, that I had not a doubt that my suppressions had been successful. Therefore I was quite as happy in my guilt as I could have been if I had been innocent.

But at last an accident exposed me. I went into the bathroom one morning to make my toilet, and carelessly left the door two or three inches ajar. It was the first time that I had ever failed to take the precaution of closing it tightly. I knew the necessity of being particular about this, because shaving was always a trying ordeal for me, and I could seldom carry it through to a finish without verbal helps. Now this time I was unprotected, but did not suspect it. I had no extraordinary trouble with my razor on this occasion, and was able to worry through with mere mutterings and growlings of an improper sort, but with nothing noisy or emphatic about them—no snapping and barking. Then I put on a shirt. My shirts are an invention of my own. They open in the back, and are buttoned there— when there are buttons. This time the button was missing. My temper jumped up several degrees in a moment, and my remarks rose accordingly, both in loudness and vigor of expression. But I was not troubled, for the bath-room door was a solid one and I supposed it was firmly closed. I flung up the window and threw the shirt out. It fell upon the shrubbery where the people on their way to church could admire it if they wanted to; there was merely fifty feet of grass between the shirt and the passer-by. Still rumbling and thundering distantly, I put on another shirt. Again the button was absent. I augmented my language to meet the emergency, and threw that shirt out of the window. I was too angry—too insane—to examine the third shirt, but put it furiously on. Again the button was absent, and that shirt followed its comrades out of the window. Then I straightened up, gathered my reserves, and let myself go like a cavalry charge. In the midst of that great assault, my eye fell upon that gaping door, and I was paralyzed.

It took me a good while to finish my toilet. I extended the time unnecessarily in trying to make up my mind as to what I would best do in the circumstances. I tried to hope that Mrs. Clemens was asleep, but I knew better. I could not escape by the window. It was narrow, and suited only to shirts. At last I made up my mind to boldly loaf through the bedroom with the air of a person who had not been doing anything. I made half the journey successfully. I did not turn my eyes in her

direction, because that would not be safe. It is very difficult to
look as if you have not been doing anything when the facts are
the other way, and my confidence in my performance oozed steadily
out of me as I went along. I was aiming for the left-hand door
because it was furthest from my wife. It had never been opened
from the day that the house was built, but it seemed a blessed
refuge for me now. The bed was this one, wherein I am lying
now, and dictating these histories morning after morning with
so much serenity. It was this same old elaborately carved black
Venetian bedstead—the most comfortable bedstead that ever was,
with space enough in it for a family, and carved angels enough
surmounting its twisted columns and its headboard and footboard
to bring peace to the sleepers, and pleasant dreams. I had to
stop in the middle of the room. I hadn't the strength to go on.
I believed that I was under accusing eyes—that even the carved
angels were inspecting me with an unfriendly gaze. You know
how it is when you are convinced that somebody behind you is
looking steadily at you. You *have* to turn your face—you can't
help it. I turned mine. The bed was placed as it is now, with the
foot where the head ought to be. If it had been placed as it
should have been, the high headboard would have sheltered me.
But the footboard was no sufficient protection, for I could be
seen over it. I was exposed. I was wholly without protection. I
turned, because I couldn't help it—and my memory of what I
saw is still vivid, after all these years.

Against the white pillows I saw the black head—I saw that
young and beautiful face; and I saw the gracious eyes with a
something in them which I had never seen there before. They
were snapping and flashing with indignation. I felt myself
crumbling; I felt myself shrinking away to nothing under that
accusing gaze. I stood silent under that desolating fire for as
much as a minute, I should say—it seemed a very, very long
time. Then my wife's lips parted, and from them issued—
*my latest bath-room remark.* The language perfect, but the
expression velvety, unpractical, apprenticelike, ignorant, inex-
perienced, comically inadequate, absurdly weak and unsuited to
the great language. In my lifetime I had never heard anything
so out of tune, so inharmonious, so incongruous, so ill-suited to
each other as were those mighty words set to that feeble music.
I tried to keep from laughing, for I was a guilty person in deep

need of charity and mercy. I tried to keep from bursting, and I succeeded—until she gravely said, " There, now you know how it sounds."

Then I exploded; the air was filled with my fragments, and you could hear them whiz. I said, " Oh Livy, if it sounds like *that* I will never do it again !"

Then she had to laugh herself. Both of us broke into convulsions, and went on laughing until we were physically exhausted and spiritually reconciled.

The children were present at breakfast—Clara aged six and Susy eight—and the mother made a guarded remark about strong language; guarded because she did not wish the children to suspect anything—a guarded remark which censured strong language. Both children broke out in one voice with this comment, " Why, mamma, papa uses it !"

I was astonished. I had supposed that that secret was safe in my own breast, and that its presence had never been suspected. I asked,

" How did you know, you little rascals ?"

" Oh," they said, " we often listen over the balusters when you are in the hall explaining things to George."

### From Susy's Biography.

One of papa's latest books is " The Prince and the Pauper " and it is unquestionably the best book he has ever written, some people want him to keep to his old style, some gentleman wrote him, " I enjoyed Huckleberry Finn immensely and am glad to see that you have returned to your old style." That enoyed me that enoyed me greatly, because it trobles me [Susy was troubled by that word, and uncertain; she wrote a *u* above it in the proper place, but reconsidered the matter and struck it out] to have so few people know papa, I mean realy know him, they think of Mark Twain as a humorist joking at everything; " And with a mop of reddish brown hair which sorely needs the barbars brush a roman nose, short stubby mustache, a sad careworn face, with maney crow's feet " etc. That is the way people picture papa, I have wanted papa to write a book that would reveal something of his kind sympathetic nature, and " The Prince and the Pauper " partly does it. The book is full of lovely charming ideas, and oh the language! It is *perfect*. I think that one of the most touching scenes in it, is where the pauper is riding on horseback with his nobles in the " recognition procession " and he sees his mother oh and then what followed! How she runs to his side, when she sees him throw up his hand palm outward, and is rudely pushed off by one of the King's officers, and then how the little pauper's consceince

troubles him when he remembers the shameful words that were falling
from his lips, when she was turned from his side "I know you not
woman" and how his grandeurs were stricken valueless, and his pride
consumed to ashes.    It is a wonderfully beautiful and touching little
scene, and papa has described it so wonderfully.    I never saw a man
with so much variety of feeling as papa has; now the "Prince and
the Pauper" is full of touching places; but there is most always a
streak of humor in them somewhere.    Now in the coronation—in the
stirring coronation, just after the little king has got his crown back
again papa brings that in about the Seal, where the pauper says he
used the Seal "to crack nuts with."   Oh it is so funny and nice!
Papa very seldom writes a passage without some humor in it somewhere, and I dont think he ever will.

The children always helped their mother to edit my books in
manuscript.   She would sit on the porch at the farm and read
aloud, with her pencil in her hand, and the children would keep
an alert and suspicious eye upon her right along, for the belief
was well grounded in them that whenever she came across a
particularly satisfactory passage she would strike it out.   Their
suspicions were well founded.   The passages which were so satisfactory to them always had an element of strength in them
which sorely needed modification or expurgation, and were always
sure to get it at their mother's hand.   For my own entertainment,
and to enjoy the protests of the children, I often abused my
editor's innocent confidence.   I often interlarded remarks of a
studied and felicitously atrocious character purposely to achieve
the children's brief delight, and then see the remorseless pencil
do its fatal work.   I often joined my supplications to the children's for mercy, and strung the argument out and pretended to
be in earnest.   They were deceived, and so was their mother.   It
was three against one, and most unfair.   But it was very delightful, and I could not resist the temptation.   Now and then we
gained the victory and there was much rejoicing.   Then I
privately struck the passage out myself.   It had served its purpose.   It had furnished three of us with good entertainment, and
in being removed from the book by me it was only suffering the
fate originally intended for it.

*From Susy's Biography.*

Papa was born in Missouri.   His mother is Grandma Clemens
(Jane Lampton Clemens) of Kentucky.   Grandpa Clemens was of the
F.F.V's of Virginia.

Without doubt it was I that gave Susy that impression. I cannot imagine why, because I was never in my life much impressed by grandeurs which proceed from the accident of birth. I did not get this indifference from my mother. She was always strongly interested in the ancestry of the house. She traced her own line back to the Lambtons of Durham, England—a family which had been occupying broad lands there since Saxon times. I am not sure, but I think that those Lambtons got along without titles of nobility for eight or nine hundred years, then produced a great man, three-quarters of a century ago, and broke into the peerage. My mother knew all about the Clemenses of Virginia, and loved to aggrandize them to me, but she has long been dead. There has been no one to keep those details fresh in my memory, and they have grown dim.

There was a Jere. Clemens who was a United States Senator, and in his day enjoyed the usual Senatorial fame—a fame which perishes whether it spring from four years' service or forty. After Jere. Clemens's fame as a Senator passed away, he was still remembered for many years on account of another service which he performed. He shot old John Brown's Governor Wise in the hind leg in a duel. However, I am not very clear about this. It may be that Governor Wise shot *him* in the hind leg. However, I don't think it is important. I think that the only thing that is really important is that one of them got shot in the hind leg. It would have been better and nobler and more historical and satisfactory if both of them had got shot in the hind leg— but it is of no use for me to try to recollect history. I never had a historical mind. Let it go. Whichever way it happened I am glad of it, and that is as much enthusiasm as I can get up for a person bearing my name. But I am forgetting the first Clemens—the one that stands furthest back toward the really original *first* Clemens, which was Adam.

*From Susy's Biography.*

Clara and I are sure that papa played the trick on Grandma, about the whipping, that is related in " The Adventures of Tom Sayer "; " Hand me that switch." The switch hovered in the air, the peril was desperate—" My, look behind you Aunt!" The old lady whirled around and snatched her skirts out of danger. The lad fled on the instant, scrambling up the high board fence and dissapeared over it.

Susy and Clara were quite right about that.

Then Susy says:

And we know papa played " Hookey " all the time.  And how readily would papa pretend to be dying so as not to have to go to school!

These revelations and exposures are searching, but they are just.  If I am as transparent to other people as I was to Susy, I have wasted much effort in this life.

Grandma couldn't make papa go to school, so she let him go into a printing-office to learn the trade.  He did so, and gradually picked up enough education to enable him to do about as well as those who were more studious in early life.

It is noticeable that Susy does not get overheated when she is complimenting me, but maintains a proper judicial and biographical calm.  It is noticeable, also, and it is to her credit as a biographer, that she distributes compliment and criticism with a fair and even hand.

My mother had a good deal of trouble with me, but I think she enjoyed it.  She had none at all with my brother Henry, who was two years younger than I, and I think that the unbroken monotony of his goodness and truthfulness and obedience would have been a burden to her but for the relief and variety which I furnished in the other direction.  I was a tonic.  I was valuable to her.  I never thought of it before, but now I see it.  I never knew Henry to do a vicious thing toward me, or toward any one else—but he frequently did righteous ones that cost me as heavily.  It was his duty to report me, when I needed reporting and neglected to do it myself, and he was very faithful in discharging that duty.  He is " Sid " in " Tom Sawyer."  But Sid was not Henry.  Henry was a very much finer and better boy than ever Sid was.

It was Henry who called my mother's attention to the fact that the thread with which she had sewed my collar together to keep me from going in swimming, had changed color.  My mother would not have discovered it but for that, and she was manifestly piqued when she recognized that that prominent bit of circumstantial evidence had escaped her sharp eye.  That detail probably added a detail to my punishment.  It is human.  We generally visit our shortcomings on somebody else when there is a possible excuse for it—but no matter, I took it out of Henry.  There is always compensation for such as are unjustly used.  I often took it out of him—sometimes as an advance payment for something which I hadn't yet done. These were occasions when the opportunity was too strong a temptation, and I· had to draw on the future. I did not need to copy this idea from my mother, and probably didn't. Still she wrought upon that principle upon occasion.

If the incident of the broken sugar-bowl is in " Tom Sawyer " —I don't remember whether it is or not—that is an example of it. Henry never stole sugar. He took it openly from the bowl. His mother knew he wouldn't take sugar when she wasn't looking, but she had her doubts about me. Not exactly doubts, either. She knew very well I *would*. One day when she was not present, Henry took sugar from her prized and precious old English sugar-bowl, which was an heirloom in the family—and he managed to break the bowl. It was the first time I had ever had a chance to tell anything on him, and I was inexpressibly glad. I told him I was going to tell on ·him, but he was not disturbed. When my mother came in and saw the bowl lying on the floor in fragments, she was speechless for a minute. I allowed that silence to work; I judged it would increase the effect. I was waiting for her to ask " Who did that?"—so that I could fetch out my news. But it was an error of calculation. When she got through with her silence she didn't ask anything about it—she merely gave me a crack on the skull with her thimble that I felt all the way down to my heels. Then I broke out with my injured innocence, expecting to make her very sorry that she had punished the wrong one. I expected her to do something remorseful and pathetic. I told her that I was not the one—it was Henry. But there was no upheaval. She said, without emotion, " It's all right. It isn't any matter. You deserve it for something you've done that I didn't know about; and if you haven't done it, why then you deserve it for something that you are going to do, that I sha'n't hear about."

There was a stairway outside the house, which led up to the rear part of the second story. One day Henry was sent on an errand, and he took a tin bucket along. I knew he would have to ascend those stairs, so I went up and locked the door on the inside, and came down into the garden, which had been newly ploughed and was rich in choice firm clods of black mold. I gathered a generous equipment of these, and ambushed him. I

waited till he had climbed the stairs and was near the landing
and couldn't escape. Then I bombarded him with clods, which
he warded off with his tin bucket the best he could, but without
much success, for I was a good marksman. The clods smashing
against the weather-boarding fetched my mother out to see what
was the matter, and I tried to explain that I was amusing Henry.
Both of them were after me in a minute, but I knew the way
over that high board fence and escaped for that time. After
an hour or two, when I ventured back, there was no one around
and I thought the incident was closed. But it was not. Henry
was ambushing me. With an unusually competent aim for him,
he landed a stone on the side of my head which raised a bump
there that felt like the Matterhorn. I carried it to my mother
straightway for sympathy, but she was not strongly moved. It
seemed to be her idea that incidents like this would eventually
reform me if I harvested enough of them. So the matter was
only educational. I had had a sterner view of it than that, before.

It was not right to give the cat the " Pain-Killer "; I realize
it now. I would not repeat it in these days. But in those " Tom
Sawyer " days it was a great and sincere satisfaction to me to
see Peter perform under its influence—and if actions *do* speak
as loud as words, he took as much interest in it as I did. It was
a most detestable medicine, Perry Davis's Pain-Killer. Mr.
Pavey's negro man, who was a person of good judgment and considerable curiosity, wanted to sample it, and I let him. It was
his opinion that it was made of hell-fire.

Those were the cholera days of '49. The people along the
Mississippi were paralyzed with fright. Those who could run
away, did it. And many died of fright in the flight. Fright
killed three persons where the cholera killed one. Those who
couldn't flee kept themselves drenched with cholera preventives,
and my mother chose Perry Davis's Pain-Killer for me. She
was not distressed about herself. She avoided that kind of pre-
ventive. But she made me promise to take a teaspoonful of
Pain-Killer every day. Originally it was my intention to keep
the promise, but at that time I didn't know as much about Pain-
Killer as I knew after my first experiment with it. She didn't
watch Henry's bottle—she could trust Henry. But she marked
my bottle with a pencil, on the label, every day, and examined it

to see if the teaspoonful had been removed. The floor was not carpeted. It had cracks in it, and I fed the Pain-Killer to the cracks with very good results—no cholera occurred down below.

It was upon one of these occasions that that friendly cat came waving his tail and supplicating for Pain-Killer—which he got— and then went into those hysterics which ended with his colliding with all the furniture in the room and finally going out of the open window and carrying the flower-pots with him, just in time for my mother to arrive and look over her glasses in petrified astonishment and say, " What in the world is the matter with Peter ?"

I don't remember what my explanation was, but if it is recorded in that book it may not be the right one.

Whenever my conduct was of such exaggerated impropriety that my mother's extemporary punishments were inadequate, she saved the matter up for Sunday, and made me go to church Sunday night—which was a penalty sometimes bearable, perhaps, but as a rule it was not, and I avoided it for the sake of my constitution. She would never believe that I had been to church until she had applied her test: she made me tell her what the text was. That was a simple matter, and caused me no trouble. I didn't have to go to church to get a text. I selected one for myself. This worked very well until one time when my text and the one furnished by a neighbor, who had been to church, didn't tally. After that my mother took other methods. I don't know what they were now.

In those days men and boys wore rather long cloaks in the winter-time. They were black, and were lined with very bright and showy Scotch plaids. One winter's night when I was starting to church to square a crime of some kind committed during the week, I hid my cloak near the gate and went off and played with the other boys until church was over. Then I returned home. But in the dark I put the cloak on wrong side out, entered the room, threw the cloak aside, and then stood the usual examination. I got along very well until the temperature of the church was mentioned. My mother said,

" It must have been impossible to keep warm there on such a night."

I didn't see the art of that remark, and was foolish enough to explain that I wore my cloak all the time that I was in church.

She asked if I kept it on from church home, too. I didn't see
the bearing of that remark. I said that that was what I had
done. She said,

"You wore it in church with that red Scotch plaid outside
and glaring? Didn't that attract any attention?"

Of course to continue such a dialogue would have been tedious
and unprofitable, and I let it go, and took the consequences.

That was about 1849. Tom Nash was a boy of my own age
—the postmaster's son. The Mississippi was frozen across, and
he and I went skating one night, probably without permission.
I cannot see why we should go skating in the night unless without
permission, for there could be no considerable amusement to be
gotten out of skating at night if nobody was going to object to
it. About midnight, when we were more than half a mile out
toward the Illinois shore, we heard some ominous rumbling and
grinding and crashing going on between us and the home side
of the river, and we knew what it meant—the ice was breaking up.
We started for home, pretty badly scared. We flew along at full
speed whenever the moonlight sifting down between the clouds
enabled us to tell which was ice and which was water. In the
pauses we waited; started again whenever there was a good bridge
of ice; paused again when we came to naked water and waited
in distress until a floating vast cake should bridge that place.
It took us an hour to make the trip—a trip which we made in a
misery of apprehension all the time. But at last we arrived
within a very brief distance of the shore. We waited again;
there was another place that needed bridging. All about us
the ice was plunging and grinding along and piling itself up in
mountains on the shore, and the dangers were increasing, not
diminishing. We grew very impatient to get to solid ground, so
we started too early and went springing from cake to cake. Tom
made a miscalculation, and fell short. He got a bitter bath, but
he was so close to shore that he only had to swim a stroke or two
—then his feet struck hard bottom and he crawled out. I arrived
a little later, without accident. We had been in a drenching
perspiration, and Tom's bath was a disaster for him. He took
to his bed sick, and had a procession of diseases. The closing one
was scarlet-fever, and he came out of it stone deaf. Within a
year or two speech departed, of course. But some years later he
was taught to talk, after a fashion—one couldn't always make out

what it was he was trying to say. Of course he could not modulate his voice, since he couldn't hear himself talk. When he supposed he was talking low and confidentially, you could hear him in Illinois.

Four years ago (1902) I was invited by the University of Missouri to come out there and receive the honorary degree of LL.D. I took that opportunity to spend a week in Hannibal— a city now, a village in my day. It had been fifty-three years since Tom Nash and I had had that adventure. When I was at the railway station ready to leave Hannibal, there was a crowd of citizens there. I saw Tom Nash approaching me across a vacant space, and I walked toward him, for I recognized him at once. He was old and white-headed, but the boy of fifteen was still visible in him. He came up to me, made a trumpet of his hands at my ear, nodded his head toward the citizens and said confidentially—in a yell like a fog-horn—

" Same damned fools, Sam !"

*From Susy's Biography.*

Papa was about twenty years old when he went on the Mississippi as a pilot. Just before he started on his tripp Grandma Clemens asked him to promise her on the Bible not to touch intoxicating liquors or swear, and he said " Yes, mother, I will," and he kept that promise seven years when Grandma released him from it.

Under the inspiring influence of that remark, what a garden of forgotten reforms rises upon my sight !

MARK TWAIN.

*(To be Continued.)*

# Chapter VI

## November 16, 1906. Pages 961–70.

PREFATORY NOTE.—Mr. Clemens began to write his autobiography many years ago, and he continues to add to it day by day. It was his original intention to permit no publication of his memoirs until after his death; but, after leaving "Pier No. 70," he concluded that a considerable portion might now suitably be given to the public. It is that portion, garnered from the quarter-million of words already written, which will appear in this REVIEW during the coming year. No part of the autobiography will be published in book form during the lifetime of the author.—EDITOR N. A. R.

### *From Susy's Biography.*

Papa made arrangements to read at Vassar College the 1st of May, and I went with him. We went by way of New York City. Mamma went with us to New York and stayed two days to do some shopping. We started Tuesday, at ½ past two o'clock in the afternoon, and reached New York about ¼ past six. Papa went right up to General Grants from the station and mamma and I went to the Everett House. Aunt Clara came to supper with us up in our room. . . .

We and Aunt Clara were going were going to the theatre right after supper, and we expected papa to take us there and to come home as early as he could. But we got through dinner and he didn't come, and didn't come, and mamma got more perplexed and worried, but at last we thought we would have to go without him. So we put on our things and started down stairs but before we'd goten half down we met papa coming up with a great bunch of roses in his hand. He explained that the reason he was so late was that his watch stopped and he didn't notice and kept thinking it an hour earlier than it really was. The roses he carried were some Col. Fred Grant sent to mamma. We went to the theatre and enjoyed " Adonis " [word illegible] acted very much. We reached home about ½ past eleven o'clock and went right to bed. Wednesday morning we got up rather late and had breakfast about ½ past nine o'clock. After breakfast mamma went out shopping and papa and I went to see papa's agent about some business matters. After papa had gotten through talking to Cousin Charlie, [Webster] papa's agent, we went to get a friend of papa's, Major Pond, to go and see a Dog Show with us. Then we went to see the dogs with Major Pond and we had a delightful time seeing so many dogs together; when we got through seeing the dogs papa thought he would go and see General Grant and I went with him—this was April 29, 1885. Papa went up into General Grant's room and he took me with him, I felt greatly honored and delighted when papa took me into General Grant's room and let me see the General and Col. Grant, for General Grant is a man I shall be glad all my life that I have seen. Papa and General Grant had a long talk together and papa has written an account of his talk and visit with General Grant for me to put into this biography.

Susy has inserted in this place that account of mine—as follows:

April 29, 1885.

I called on General Grant and took Susy with me. The General was looking and feeling far better than he had looked or felt for some months. He had ventured to work again on his book that morning—the first time he had done any work for perhaps a month. This morning's work was his first attempt at dictating, and it was a thorough success, to his great delight. He had always said that it would be impossible for him to dictate anything, but I had said that he was noted for clearness of statement, and as a narrative was simply a statement of consecutive facts, he was consequently peculiarly qualified and equipped for dictation. This turned out to be true. For he had dictated two hours that morning to a shorthand writer, had never hesitated for words, had not repeated himself, and the manuscript when finished needed no revision. The two hours' work was an account of Appomattox —and this was such an extremely important feature that his book would necessarily have been severely lame without it. Therefore I had taken a shorthand writer there before, to see if I could not get him to write at least a few lines about Appomattox.* But he was at that time not well enough to undertake it. I was aware that of all the hundred ver-

* I was his publisher. I was putting his " Personal Memoirs " to press at the time.—S. L. C.

sions of Appomattox, not one was really correct. Therefore I was extremely anxious that he should leave behind him the truth. His throat was not distressing him, and his voice was much better and stronger than usual. He was so delighted to have gotten Appomattox accomplished once more in his life—to have gotten the matter off his mind—that he was as talkative as his old self. He received Susy very pleasantly, and then fell to talking about certain matters which he hoped to be able to dictate next day; and he said in substance that, among other things, he wanted to settle once for all a question that had been bandied about from mouth to mouth and from newspaper to newspaper. That question was, "With whom originated the idea of the march to the sea? Was it Grant's, or was it Sherman's idea?" Whether I, or some one else (being anxious to get the important fact settled) asked him with whom the idea originated, I don't remember. But I remember his answer. I shall always remember his answer. General Grant said:

"Neither of us originated the idea of Sherman's march to the sea. The enemy did it."

He went on to say that the enemy, however, necessarily originated a great many of the plans that the general on the opposite side gets the credit for; at the same time that the enemy is doing that, he is laying open other moves which the opposing general sees and takes advantage of. In this case, Sherman had a plan all thought out, of course. He meant to destroy the two remaining railroads in that part of the country, and that would finish up that region. But General Hood did not play the military part that he was expected to play. On the contrary, General Hood made a dive at Chattanooga. This left the march to the sea open to Sherman, and so after sending part of his army to defend and hold what he had acquired in the Chattanooga region, he was perfectly free to proceed, with the rest of it, through Georgia. He saw the opportunity, and he would not have been fit for his place if he had not seized it.

"He wrote me" (the General is speaking) "what his plan was, and I sent him word to go ahead. My staff were opposed to the movement." (I think the General said they tried to persuade him to stop Sherman. The chief of his staff, the General said, even went so far as to go to Washington without the General's knowledge and get the ear of the authorities, and he succeeded in arousing their fears to such an extent that they telegraphed General Grant to stop Sherman.)

Then General Grant said, "Out of deference to the Government, I telegraphed Sherman and stopped him twenty-four hours; and then considering that that was deference enough to the Government, I telegraphed him to go ahead again."

I have not tried to give the General's language, but only the general idea of what he said. The thing that mainly struck me was his terse remark that the enemy originated the idea of the march to the sea. It struck me because it was so suggestive of the General's epigrammatic fashion—saying a great deal in a single crisp sentence. (This is my account, and signed "Mark Twain.")

*Susy Resumes.*

After papa and General Grant had had their talk, we went back to the hotel where mamma was, and papa told mamma all about his interview with General Grant. Mamma and I had a nice quiet afternoon together.

That pair of devoted comrades were always shutting themselves up together when there was opportunity to have what Susy called " a cozy time." From Susy's nursery days to the end of her life, she and her mother were close friends; intimate friends, passionate adorers of each other. Susy's was a beautiful mind, and it made her an interesting comrade. And with the fine mind she had a heart like her mother's. Susy never had an interest or an occupation which she was not glad to put aside for that something which was in all cases more precious to her— a visit with her mother. Susy died at the right time, the fortunate time of life; the happy age—twenty-four years. At twenty-four, such a girl has seen the best of life—life as a happy dream. After that age the risks begin; responsibility comes, and with it the cares, the sorrows, and the inevitable tragedy. For her mother's sake I would have brought her back from the grave if I could, but I would not have done it for my own.

*From Susy's Biography.*

Then papa went to read in public; there were a great many authors that read, that Thursday afternoon, beside papa; I would have liked to have gone and heard papa read, but papa said he was going to read in Vassar just what he was planning to read in New York, so I stayed at home with mamma.

The next day mamma planned to take the four o'clock car back to Hartford. We rose quite early that morning and went to the Vienna Bakery and took breakfast there. From there we went to a German bookstore and bought some German books for Clara's birthday.

Dear me, the power of association to snatch mouldy dead memories out of their graves and make them walk! That remark about buying foreign books throws a sudden white glare upon the distant past; and I see the long stretch of a New York street with an unearthly vividness, and John Hay walking down it, grave and remorseful. I was walking down it too, that morning, and I overtook Hay and asked him what the trouble was. He turned a lustreless eye upon me and said:

" My case is beyond cure. In the most innocent way in the world I have committed a crime which will never be forgiven

by the sufferers, for they will never believe—oh, well, no, I was
going to say they would never believe that I did the thing innocently. The truth is they will know that I acted innocently,
because they are rational people; but what of that? I never
can look them in the face again—nor they me, perhaps."

Hay was a young bachelor, and at that time was on the
"Tribune" staff. He explained his trouble in these words, substantially:

"When I was passing along here yesterday morning on my
way down-town to the office, I stepped into a bookstore where I
am acquainted, and asked if they had anything new from the
other side. They handed me a French novel, in the usual yellow
paper cover, and I carried it away. I didn't even look at the
title of it. It was for recreation reading, and I was on my way
to my work. I went mooning and dreaming along, and I think I
hadn't gone more than fifty yards when I heard my name called.
I stopped, and a private carriage drew up at the sidewalk and
I shook hands with the inmates—mother and young daughter,
excellent people. They were on their way to the steamer to sail
for Paris. The mother said,

"'I saw that book in your hand and I judged by the look of
it that it was a French novel. Is it?'

"I said it was.

"She said, 'Do let me have it, so that my daughter can practise her French on it on the way over.'

"Of course I handed her the book, and we parted. Ten minutes ago I was passing that bookstore again, and I stepped in
and fetched away another copy of that book. Here it is. Read
the first page of it. That is enough. You will know what the
rest is like. I think it must be the foulest book in the French
language--one of the foulest, anyway. I would be ashamed to
offer it to a harlot—but, oh dear, I gave it to that sweet young
girl without shame. Take my advice; don't give away a book
until you have examined it."

*From Susy's Biography.*

Then mamma and I went to do some shopping and papa went to see
General Grant. After we had finnished doing our shopping we went
home to the hotel together. When we entered our rooms in the hotel
we saw on the table a vase full of exquisett red roses. Mamma who is
very fond of flowers exclaimed "Oh I wonder who could have sent

them." We both looked at the card in the midst of the roses and saw
that it was written on in papa's handwriting, it was written in German. 'Liebes Geshchenk on die mamma.' [I am sure I didn't say
"on"—that is Susy's spelling, not mine; also I am sure I didn't spell
Geschenk so liberally as all that.—S. L. C.] Mamma was delighted. Papa came home and gave mamma her ticket; and after visiting a while with her went to see Major Pond and mamma and I sat down
to our lunch. After lunch most of our time was taken up with packing, and at about three o'clock we went to escort mamma to the train.
We got on board the train with her and stayed with her about five
minutes and then we said good-bye to her and the train started for
Hartford. It was the first time I had ever beene away from home without mamma in my life, although I was 13 yrs. old. Papa and I drove
back to the hotel and got Major Pond and then went to see the Brooklyn Bridge we went across it to Brooklyn on the cars and then walked
back across it from Brooklyn to New York. We enjoyed looking at the
beautiful scenery and we could see the bridge moove under the intense
heat of the sun. We had a perfectly delightful time, but weer pretty
tired when we got back to the hotel.

The next morning we rose early, took our breakfast and took an early
train to Poughkeepsie. We had a very pleasant journey to Poughkeepsie. The Hudson was magnificent—shrouded with beautiful mist. When
we arived at Poughkeepsie it was raining quite hard; which fact greatly
dissapointed me because I very much wanted to see the outside of the
buildings of Vassar College and as it rained that would be impossible.
It was quite a long drive from the ᵉᵗᵃᵗion to Vasser College and papa
and I had a nice long time to discuss and laugh over German profanity.
One of the German phrases papa particularly enjoys is " O heilige maria
Mutter Jesus!" Jean has a German nurse, and this was one of her
phrases, there was a time when Jean exclaimed " Ach Gott!" to every
trifle, but when mamma found it out she was shocked and instantly put
a stop to it.

It brings that pretty little German girl vividly before me—
a sweet and innocent and plump little creature with peachy
cheeks; a clear-souled little maiden and without offence, notwithstanding her profanities, and she was loaded to the eyebrows
with them. She was a mere child. She was not fifteen yet.
She was just from Germany, and knew no English. She was
always scattering her profanities around, and they were such a
satisfaction to me that I never dreamed of such a thing as modi-
fying her. For my own sake, I had no disposition to tell on her.
Indeed I took pains to keep her from being found out. I told
her to confine her religious exercises to the children's quarters,
and urged her to remember that Mrs. Clemens was prejudiced
against pieties on week-days. To the children, the little maid's

profanities sounded natural and proper and right, because they had been used to that kind of talk in Germany, and they attached no evil importance to it. It grieves me that I have forgotten those vigorous remarks. I long hoarded them in my memory as a treasure. But I remember one of them still, because I heard it so many times. The trial of that little creature's life was the children's hair. She would tug and strain with her comb, accompanying her work with her misplaced pieties. And when finally she was through with her triple job she always fired up and exploded her thanks toward the sky, where they belonged, in this form: " *Gott sei Dank ich bin fertig mit'm Gott verdammtes Haar!*" (I believe I am not quite brave enough to translate it.)

### From Susy's Biography.

We at length reached Vassar College and she looked very finely, her buildings and her grounds being very beautiful. We went to the front doore and range the bell. The young girl who came to the doore wished to know who we wanted to see. Evidently we were not expected. Papa told her who we wanted to see and she showed us to the parlor. We waited, no one came; and waited, no one came, still no one came. It was beginning to seem pretty awkward, " Oh well this is a pretty piece of business," papa exclaimed. At length we heard footsteps coming down the long corridor and Miss C, (the lady who had invited papa) came into the room. She greeted papa very pleasantly and they had a nice little chatt together. Soon the lady principal also entered and she was very pleasant and agreable. She showed us to our rooms and said she would send for us when dinner was ready. We went into our rooms, but we had nothing to do for half an hour exept to watch the rain drops as they fell upon the window panes. At last we were called to dinner, and I went down without papa as he never eats anything in the middle of the day. I sat at the table with the lady principal and enjoyed very much seeing all the young girls trooping into the dining-room. After dinner I went around the College with the young ladies and papa stayed in his room and smoked. When it was supper time papa went down and ate supper with us and we had a very delightful supper. After supper the young ladies went to their rooms to dress for the evening. Papa went to his room and I went with the lady principal. At length the guests began to arive, but papa still remained in his room until called for. Papa read in the chapell. It was the first time I had ever heard him read in my life—that is in public. When he came out on to the stage I remember the people behind me exclaimed " Oh how queer he is! Isn't he funny!" I thought papa was very funny, although I did not think him queer. He read " A Trying Situation " and " The Golden Arm," a ghost story that he heard down South when he was a little boy. " The Golden Arm " papa had told me before, but he had startled me so that

I did not much wish to hear it again.  But I had resolved this time to be prepared and not to let myself be startled, but still papa did, and very very much; he startled the whole roomful of people and they jumped as one man.  The other story was also very funny and interesting and I enjoyed the evening inexpressibly much.  After papa had finished reading we all went down to the collation in the dining-room and after that there was dancing and singing.  Then the guests went away and papa and I went to bed.  The next morning we rose early, took an early train for Hartford and reached Hartford at ½ past 2 o'clock.  We were very glad to get back.

How charitably she treats that ghastly experience!  It is a dear and lovely disposition, and a most valuable one, that can brush away indignities and discourtesies and seek and find the pleasanter features of an experience.  Susy had that disposition, and it was one of the jewels of her character that had come to her straight from her mother.  It is a feature that was left out of me at birth.  And, at seventy, I have not yet acquired it.  I did not go to Vassar College professionally, but as a guest—as a guest, and gratis.  Aunt Clara (now Mrs. John B. Stanchfield) was a graduate of Vassar and it was to please her that I inflicted that journey upon Susy and myself.  The invitation had come to me from both the lady mentioned by Susy and the President of the College—a sour old saint who has probably been gathered to his fathers long ago; and I hope they enjoy him; I hope they value his society.  I think I can get along without it, in either end of the next world.

We arrived at the College in that soaking rain, and Susy has described, with just a suggestion of dissatisfaction, the sort of reception we got.  Susy had to sit in her damp clothes half an hour while we waited in the parlor; then she was taken to a fireless room and left to wait there again, as she has stated.  I do not remember that President's name, and I am sorry.  He did not put in an appearance until it was time for me to step upon the platform in front of that great garden of young and lovely blossoms.  He caught up with me and advanced upon the platform with me and was going to introduce me.  I said in substance:

" You have allowed me to get along without your help thus far, and if you will retire from the platform I will try to do the rest without it."

I did not see him any more, but I detest his memory.  Of

course my resentment did not extend to the students, and so I had an unforgettable good time talking to them. And I think they had a good time too, for they responded " as one man," to use Susy's unimprovable phrase.

Girls are charming creatures. I shall have to be twice seventy years old before I change my mind as to that. I am to talk to a crowd of them this afternoon, students of Barnard College (the sex's annex to Columbia University), and I think I shall have as pleasant a time with those lasses as I had with the Vassar girls twenty-one years ago.

*From Susy's Biography.*

I stopped in the middle of mamma's early history to tell about our tripp to Vassar because I was afraid I would forget about it, now I will go on where I left off. Some time after Miss Emma Nigh died papa took mamma and little Langdon to Elmira for the summer. When in Elmira Langdon began to fail but I think mamma did not know just what was the matter with him.

I was the cause of the child's illness. His mother trusted him to my care and I took him a long drive in an open barouche for an airing. It was a raw, cold morning, but he was well wrapped about with furs and, in the hands of a careful person, no harm would have come to him. But I soon dropped into a reverie and forgot all about my charge. The furs fell away and exposed his bare legs. By and by the coachman noticed this, and I arranged the wraps again, but it was too late. The child was almost frozen. I hurried home with him. I was aghast at what I had done, and I feared the consequences. I have always felt shame for that treacherous morning's work and have not allowed myself to think of it when I could help it. I doubt if I had the courage to make confession at that time. I think it most likely that I have never confessed until now.

*From Susy's Biography.*

At last it was time for papa to return to Hartford, and Langdon was real sick at that time, but still mamma decided to go with him, thinking the journey might do him good. But after they reached Hartford he became very sick, and his trouble prooved to be diptheeria. He died about a week after mamma and papa reached Hartford. He was burried by the side of grandpa at Elmira, New York. [Susy rests there with them.—S. L. C.] After that, mamma became very very ill, so ill that there seemed great danger of death, but with a great deal of good care she recovered. Some months afterward mamma and papa [and Susy, who was perhaps fourteen or fifteen months old at the time.— S. L. C.] went to Europe and stayed for a time in Scotland and England. In Scotland mamma and papa became very well equanted with Dr. John Brown, the author of " Rab and His Friends," and he mett, but was not so well equanted with, Mr. Charles Kingsley, Mr. Henry M. Stanley, Sir Thomas Hardy grandson of the Captain Hardy to whom Nellson said " Kiss me Hardy," when dying on shipboard, Mr. Henry Irving, Robert Browning, Sir Charles Dilke, Mr. Charles Reade, Mr. William Black, Lord Houghton, Frank Buckland, Mr. Tom Hughes, Anthony Trollope, Tom Hood, son of the poet—and mamma and papa were quite well equanted with Dr. Macdonald and family, and papa met Harrison Ainsworth.

I remember all these men very well indeed, except the last one. I do not recall Ainsworth. By my count, Susy mentions fourteen men. They are all dead except Sir Charles Dilke.

We met a great many other interesting people, among them Lewis Carroll, author of the immortal " Alice "—but he was only interesting to look at, for he was the stillest and shyest full-grown man I have ever met except " Uncle Remus." Dr. Macdonald and several other lively talkers were present, and the talk went briskly on for a couple of hours, but Carroll sat still all the while except that now and then he answered a question. His answers were brief. I do not remember that he elaborated any of them.

At a dinner at Smalley's we met Herbert Spencer. At a large luncheon party at Lord Houghton's we met Sir Arthur Helps, who was a celebrity of world-wide fame at the time, but is quite forgotten now. Lord Elcho, a large vigorous man, sat at some distance down the table. He was talking earnestly about Godalming. It was a deep and flowing and unarticulated rumble, but I got the Godalming pretty clearly every time it broke free of the rumble, and as all the strength was on the first end of the word it startled me every time, because it sounded so like swearing. In the middle of the luncheon Lady Houghton rose, remarked to the guests on her right and on her left in a matter-of-fact way, " Excuse me, I have an engagement," and without further ceremony she went off to meet it. This would have been doubtful etiquette in America. Lord Houghton told a number of delightful stories. He told them in French, and I lost nothing of them but the nubs.                    MARK TWAIN.

*(To be Continued.)*

# Chapter VII

December 7, 1906. Pages 1089–95.

PREFATORY NOTE.—Mr. Clemens began to write his autobiography many years ago, and he continues to add to it day by day. It was his original intention to permit no publication of his memoirs until after his death; but, after leaving "Pier No. 70," he concluded that a considerable portion might now suitably be given to the public. It is that portion, garnered from the quarter-million of words already written, which will appear in this REVIEW during the coming year. No part of the autobiography will be published in book form during the lifetime of the author.—EDITOR N. A. R.

I WAS always heedless. I was born heedless; and therefore I was constantly, and quite unconsciously, committing breaches of the minor proprieties, which brought upon me humiliations which ought to have humiliated me but didn't, because I didn't know anything had happened. But Livy knew; and so the humiliations fell to her share, poor child, who had not earned them and did not deserve them. She always said I was the most difficult child she had. She was very sensitive about me. It distressed her to see me do heedless things which could bring me under criticism, and so she was always watchful and alert to protect me from the kind of transgressions which I have been speaking of.

When I was leaving Hartford for Washington, upon the occasion referred to, she said: " I have written a small warning and put it in a pocket of your dress-vest. When you are dressing to go to the Authors' Reception at the White House you will naturally put your fingers in your vest pockets, according to your custom, and you will find that little note there. Read it carefully, and do as it tells you. I cannot be with you, and so I delegate my sentry duties to this little note. If I should give you the warning by word of mouth, now, it would pass from your head and be forgotten in a few minutes."

It was President Cleveland's first term. I had never seen his wife—the young, the beautiful, the good-hearted, the sympathetic, the fascinating. Sure enough, just as I had finished dressing to go to the White House I found that little note, which I had long ago forgotten. It was a grave little note, a serious little note, like its writer, but it made me laugh. Livy's gentle gravities often produced that effect upon me, where the expert humorist's best joke would have failed, for I do not laugh easily.

When we reached the White House and I was shaking hands with the President, he started to say something, but I interrupted him and said:

" If your Excellency will excuse me, I will come back in a moment; but now I have a very important matter to attend to, and it must be attended to at once."

I turned to Mrs. Cleveland, the young, the beautiful, the fascinating, and gave her my card, on the back of which I had written " *He didn't* "—and I asked her to sign her name below those words.

She said: " He didn't? He didn't what?"

" Oh," I said, " never mind. We cannot stop to discuss that now. This is urgent. Won't you please sign your name?" (I handed her a fountain-pen.)

" Why," she said, " I cannot commit myself in that way. Who is it that didn't?—and what is it that he didn't?"

" Oh," I said, " time is flying, flying, flying. Won't you take me out of my distress and sign your name to it? It's all right. I give you my word it's all right."

She looked nonplussed; but hesitatingly and mechanically she took the pen and said:

" I will sign it. I will take the risk. But you must tell me

all about it, right afterward, so that you can be arrested before
you get out of the house in case there should be anything criminal
about this."

Then she signed; and I handed her Mrs. Clemens's note, which
was very brief, very simple, and to the point. It said: "*Don't
wear your arctics in the White House.*" It made her shout; and
at my request she summoned a messenger and we sent that card
at once to the mail on its way to Mrs. Clemens in Hartford.

When the little Ruth was about a year or a year and a half
old, Mason, an old and valued friend of mine, was consul-general
at Frankfort-on-the-Main. I had known him well in 1867, '68
and '69, in America, and I and mine had spent a good deal of
time with him and his family in Frankfort in '78. He was a
thoroughly competent, diligent, and conscientious official. Indeed he possessed these qualities in so large a degree that among
American consuls he might fairly be said to be monumental, for
at that time our consular service was largely—and I think I
may say mainly—in the hands of ignorant, vulgar, and incapable
men who had been political heelers in America, and had been
taken care of by transference to consulates where they could be
supported at the Government's expense instead of being transferred to the poor house, which would have been cheaper and
more patriotic. Mason, in '78, had been consul-general in Frankfort several years—four, I think. He had come from Marseilles
with a great record. He had been consul there during thirteen
years, and one part of his record was heroic. There had been a
desolating cholera epidemic, and Mason was the only representative of any foreign country who stayed at his post and saw it
through. And during that time he not only represented his own
country, but he represented all the other countries in Christendom and did their work, and did it well·and was praised for it
by them in words of no uncertain sound. This great record of
Mason's had saved him from official decapitation straight along
while Republican Presidents occupied the chair, but now it was
occupied by a Democrat. Mr. Cleveland was not seated in it—
he was not yet inaugurated—before he was deluged with appli-
cations from Democratic politicians desiring the appointment
of a thousand or so politically useful Democrats to Mason's place.
A year or two later Mason wrote me and asked me if I couldn't
do something to save him from destruction.

I was very anxious to keep him in his place, but at first I could not think of any way to help him, for I was a mugwump. We, the mugwumps, a little company made up of the unenslaved of both parties, the very best men to be found in the two great parties — that was our idea of it — voted sixty thousand strong for Mr. Cleveland in New York and elected him. Our principles were high, and very definite. We were not a party; we had no candidates; we had no axes to grind. Our vote laid upon the man we cast it for no obligation of any kind. By our rule we could not ask for office; we could not accept office. When voting, it was our duty to vote for the best man, regardless of his party name. We had no other creed. Vote for the best man— that was creed enough.

Such being my situation, I was puzzled to know how to try to help Mason, and, at the same time, save my mugwump purity undefiled. It was a delicate place. But presently, out of the ruck of confusions in my mind, rose a sane thought, clear and bright—to wit: since it was a mugwump's duty to do his best to put the best man in office, necessarily it must be a mugwump's duty to try to *keep* the best man in when he was already there. My course was easy now. It might not be quite delicate for a mugwump to approach the President directly, but I could approach him indirectly, with all delicacy, since in that case not even courtesy would require him to take notice of an application which no one could prove had ever reached him.

Yes, it was easy and simple sailing now. I could lay the matter before Ruth, in her cradle, and wait for results. I wrote the little child, and said to her all that I have just been saying about mugwump principles and the limitations which they put upon me. I explained that it would not be proper for me to apply to her father in Mr. Mason's behalf, but I detailed to her Mr. Mason's high and honorable record and suggested that she take the matter in her own hands and do a patriotic work which I felt some delicacy about venturing upon myself. I asked her to forget that her father was only President of the United States, and her subject and servant; I asked her not to put her application in the form of a command, but to modify it, and give it the fictitious and pleasanter form of a mere request—that it would be no harm to let him gratify himself with the superstition that he was independent and could do as he pleased in the matter. I begged her to put stress, and plenty of it, upon the proposition that to keep Mason in his place would be a benefaction to the nation; to enlarge upon that, and keep still about all other considerations.

In due time I received a letter from the President, written with his own hand, signed by his own hand, acknowledging Ruth's intervention and thanking me for enabling him to save to the country the services of so good and well - tried a servant as Mason, and thanking me, also, for the detailed fulness of Mason's record, which could leave no doubt in any one's mind that Mason was in his right place and ought to be kept there. Mason has remained in the service ever since, and is now consul-general at Paris.

During the time that we were living in Buffalo in '70-'71, Mr. Cleveland was sheriff, but I never happened to make his acquaintance, or even see him. In fact, I suppose I was not even aware of his existence. Fourteen years later, he was become the greatest man in the State. I was not living in the State at the time. He was Governor, and was about to step into the post of President of the United States. At that time I was on the public highway in company with another bandit, George W. Cable. We were robbing the public with readings from our works during four months—and in the course of time we went to Albany to levy tribute, and I said, " We ought to go and pay our respects to the Governor."

So Cable and I went to that majestic Capitol building and stated our errand. We were shown into the Governor's private office, and I saw Mr. Cleveland for the first time. We three stood chatting together. I was born lazy, and I comforted myself by turning the corner of a table into a sort of seat. Presently the Governor said:

" Mr. Clemens, I was a fellow citizen of yours in Buffalo a good many months, a good while ago, and during those months you burst suddenly into a mighty fame, out of a previous long-continued and no doubt proper obscurity—but I was a nobody, and you wouldn't notice me nor have anything to do with me. But now that I have become somebody, you have changed your style, and you come here to shake hands with me and be sociable. How do you explain this kind of conduct?"

" Oh," I said, " it is very simple, your Excellency. In Buffalo you were nothing but a sheriff. I was in society. I couldn't afford to associate with sheriffs. But you are a Governor now, and you are on your way to the Presidency. It is a great difference, and it makes you worth while."

There appeared to be about sixteen doors to that spacious room. From each door a young man now emerged, and the sixteen lined up and moved forward and stood in front of the Governor with an aspect of respectful expectancy in their attitude. No one spoke for a moment. Then the Governor said:

"You are dismissed, gentlemen. Your services are not required. Mr. Clemens is sitting on the bells."

There was a cluster of sixteen bell buttons on the corner of the table; my proportions at that end of me were just right to enable me to cover the whole of that nest, and that is how I came to hatch out those sixteen clerks.

In accordance with the suggestion made in Gilder's letter recently received I have written the following note to ex-President Cleveland upon his sixty-ninth birthday:

HONORED SIR:—

Your patriotic virtues have won for you the homage of half the nation and the enmity of the other half. This places your character as a citizen upon a summit as high as Washington's. The verdict is unanimous and unassailable. The votes of both sides are necessary in cases like these, and the votes of the one side are quite as valuable as are the votes of the other. Where the votes are all in a man's favor the verdict is against him. It is sand, and history will wash it away. But the verdict for you is rock, and will stand.

                                                            S. L. CLEMENS.

As of date March 18, 1906. . . .

In a diary which Mrs. Clemens kept for a little while, a great many years ago, I find various mentions of Mrs. Harriet Beecher Stowe, who was a near neighbor of ours in Hartford, with no fences between. And in those days she made as much use of our grounds as of her own, in pleasant weather. Her mind had decayed, and she was a pathetic figure. She wandered about all the day long in the care of a muscular Irishwoman. Among the colonists of our neighborhood the doors always stood open in pleasant weather. Mrs. Stowe entered them at her own free will, and as she was always softly slippered and generally full of animal spirits, she was able to deal in surprises, and she liked to do it. She would slip up behind a person who was deep in dreams and musings and fetch a war-whoop that would jump that person out of his clothes. And she had other moods. Sometimes we would hear gentle music in the drawing - room and would find her there at the piano singing ancient and melancholy songs with infinitely touching effect.

Her husband, old Professor Stowe, was a picturesque figure. He wore a broad slouch hat. He was a large man, and solemn. His beard was white and thick and hung far down on his breast. The first time our little Susy ever saw him she encountered him on the street near our house and came flying wide-eyed to her mother and said, " Santa Claus has got loose !"

Which reminds me of Rev. Charley Stowe's little boy—a little boy of seven years. I met Rev. Charley crossing his mother's grounds one morning and he told me this little tale. He had been out to Chicago to attend a Convention of Congregational clergymen, and had taken his little boy with him. During the trip he reminded the little chap, every now and then, that he must be on his very best behavior there in Chicago. He said: " We shall be the guests of a clergyman, there will be other guests—clergymen and their wives—and you must be careful to let those people see by your walk and conversation that you are of a godly household. Be very careful about this." The admonition bore fruit. At the first breakfast which they ate in the Chicago clergyman's house he heard his little son say in the meekest and most reverent way to the lady opposite him,

" Please, won't you, for Christ's sake, pass the butter?"

MARK TWAIN.

*(To be Continued.)*

# Chapter VIII

December 21, 1906. Pages 1217–24.

PREFATORY NOTE.—Mr. Clemens began to write his autobiography many years ago, and he continues to add to it day by day. It was his original intention to permit no publication of his memoirs until after his death; but, after leaving " Pier No. 70," he concluded that a considerable portion might now suitably be given to the public. It is that portion, garnered from the quarter-million of words already written, which will appear in this REVIEW during the coming year. No part of the autobiography will be published in book form during the lifetime of the author.—EDITOR N. A. R.

[*Dictated in 1906.*] In those early days duelling suddenly became a fashion in the new Territory of Nevada, and by 1864 everybody was anxious to have a chance in the new sport, **(1864.)** mainly for the reason that he was not able to thoroughly respect himself so long as he had not killed or crippled somebody in a duel or been killed or crippled in one himself.

At that time I had been serving as city editor on Mr. Goodman's Virginia City " Enterprise " for a matter of two years. I was twenty-nine years old. I was ambitious in several ways, but

I had entirely escaped the seductions of that particular craze.
I had had no desire to fight a duel; I had no intention of pro-
voking one. I did not feel respectable, but I got a certain
amount of satisfaction out of feeling safe. I was ashamed of
myself; the rest of the staff were ashamed of me—but I got along
well enough. I had always been accustomed to feeling ashamed
of myself, for one thing or another, so there was no novelty for
me in the situation. I bore it very well. Plunkett was on the
staff; R. M. Daggett was on the staff. These had tried to get
into duels, but for the present had failed, and were waiting.
Goodman was the only one of us who had done anything to shed
credit upon the paper. The rival paper was the Virginia
"Union." Its editor for a little while was Tom Fitch, called the
"silver-tongued orator of Wisconsin"—that was where he came
from. He tuned up his oratory in the editorial columns of the
"Union," and Mr. Goodman invited him out and modified him
with a bullet. I remember the joy of the staff when Goodman's
challenge was accepted by Fitch. We ran late that night, and
made much of Joe Goodman. He was only twenty-four years
old; he lacked the wisdom which a person has at twenty-nine,
and he was as glad of being *it* as I was that I wasn't. He chose
Major Graves for his second (that name is not right, but it's
close enough; I don't remember the Major's name). Graves
came over to instruct Joe in the duelling art. He had been a
Major under Walker, the "gray-eyed man of destiny," and had
fought all through that remarkable man's filibustering campaign
in Central America. That fact gauges the Major. To say that
a man was a Major under Walker, and came out of that struggle
ennobled by Walker's praise, is to say that the Major was not
merely a brave man but that he was brave to the very utmost
limit of that word. All of Walker's men were like that. I knew
the Gillis family intimately. The father made the campaign
under Walker, and with him one son. They were in the memorable Plaza fight, and stood it out to the last against over-
whelming odds, as did also all of the Walker men. The son was
killed at the father's side. The father received a bullet through
the eye. The old man—for he was an old man at the time—
wore spectacles, and the bullet and one of the glasses went into
his skull and remained there. There were some other sons:
Steve, George, and Jim, very young chaps—the merest lads—

who wanted to be in the Walker expedition, for they had their father's dauntless spirit. But Walker wouldn't have them; he said it was a serious expedition, and no place for children.

The Major was a majestic creature, with a most stately and dignified and impressive military bearing, and he was by nature and training courteous, polite, graceful, winning; and he had that quality which I think I have encountered in only one other man—Bob Howland—a mysterious quality which resides in the eye; and when that eye is turned upon an individual or a squad, in warning, that is enough. The man that has that eye doesn't need to go armed; he can move upon an armed desperado and quell him and take him prisoner without saying a single word. I saw Bob Howland do that, once—a slender, good-natured, amiable, gentle, kindly little skeleton of a man, with a sweet blue eye that would win your heart when it smiled upon you, or turn cold and freeze it, according to the nature of the occasion.

The Major stood Joe up straight; stood Steve Gillis up fifteen paces away; made Joe turn right side towards Steve, cock his navy six-shooter—that prodigious weapon—and hold it straight down against his leg; told him that *that* was the correct position for the gun—that the position ordinarily in use at Virginia City (that is to say, the gun straight up in the air, then brought slowly down to your man) was all wrong. At the word " *One,*" you must raise the gun slowly and steadily to the place on the other man's body that you desire to convince. Then, after a pause, *"two, three—fire—Stop!"* At the word " stop," you may fire—but not earlier. You may give yourself as much time as you please *after* that word. Then, when you fire, you may advance and go on firing at your leisure and pleasure, if you can get any pleasure out of it. And, in the meantime, the other man, if he has been properly instructed and is alive to his privileges, is advancing on *you,* and firing—and it is always likely that more or less trouble will result.

Naturally, when Joe's revolver had risen to a level it was pointing at Steve's breast, but the Major said " No, that is not wise. Take all the risks of getting murdered yourself, but don't run any risk of murdering the other man. If you survive a duel you want to survive it in such a way that the memory of it will not linger along with you through the rest of your life and interfere with your sleep. Aim at your man's leg; not at the knee, not above the knee; for those are dangerous spots. Aim below the knee; cripple him, but leave the rest of him to his mother."

By grace of these truly wise and excellent instructions, Joe tumbled Fitch down next morning with a bullet through his lower leg, which furnished him a permanent limp. And Joe lost nothing but a lock of hair, which he could spare better then than he could now. For when I saw him here in New York a year ago, his crop was gone; he had nothing much left but a fringe, with a dome rising above.

About a year later I got *my* chance. But I was not hunting for it. Goodman went off to San Francisco for a week's holiday, and left me to be chief editor. I had supposed that that was an easy berth, there being nothing to do but write one editorial per day; but I was disappointed in that superstition. I couldn't find anything to write an article about, the first day. Then it occurred to me that inasmuch as it was the 22nd of April, 1864, the **(1864.)** next morning would be the three-hundredth anniversary of Shakespeare's birthday—and what better theme could I want than that? I got the Cyclopædia and examined it, and found out who Shakespeare was and what he had done, and I borrowed all that and laid it before a community that couldn't have been better prepared for instruction about Shakespeare than if they had been prepared by art. There wasn't enough of what Shakespeare had done to make an editorial of the necessary length, but I filled it out with what he hadn't done—which in many respects was more important and striking and readable than the handsomest things he had really accomplished. But next day I was in trouble again. There were no more Shakespeares to work up. There was nothing in past history, or in the world's future possibilities, to make an editorial out of, suitable to that community; so there was but one theme left. That theme was Mr. Laird, proprietor of the Virginia "Union." *His* editor had gone off to San Francisco too, and Laird was trying his hand at editing. I woke up Mr. Laird with some courtesies of the kind that were fashionable among newspaper editors in that region, and he came back at me the next day in a most vitriolic way. He was hurt by something I had said about him—some little thing —I don't remember what it was now — probably called him a horse-thief, or one of those little phrases customarily used to describe another editor. They were no doubt just, and accurate, but Laird was a very sensitive creature. and he didn't like it. So we expected a challenge from Mr. Laird, because according to the rules — according to the etiquette of duelling as reconstructed and reorganized and improved by the duellists of that region—whenever you said a thing about another person that he didn't like, it wasn't sufficient for him to talk back in the same offensive spirit: etiquette required him to send a challenge; so we waited for a challenge—waited all day. It didn't come. And as the day wore along, hour after hour, and no challenge came, the boys grew depressed. They lost heart. But I was cheerful; I felt better and better all the time. They couldn't understand it, but *I* could understand it. It was my *make* that enabled me to be cheerful when other people were despondent. So then it became necessary for us to waive etiquette and challenge Mr. Laird. When we reached that decision, they began to cheer up, but I began to lose some of my animation. However, in enterprises of this kind you are in the hands of your friends; there is nothing for you to do but to abide by what they consider to be the best course. Daggett wrote a challenge for me, for Daggett had the language — the right language — the convincing language—and I lacked it. Daggett poured out a stream of unsavory epithets upon Mr. Laird, charged with a vigor and venom of a strength calculated to persuade him; and Steve Gillis, my second, carried the challenge and came back to wait for the return. It didn't come. The boys were exasperated, but I kept my temper. Steve carried another challenge, hotter than the other, and we waited again. Nothing came of it. I began to feel quite comfortable. I began to take an interest in the challenges myself. I had not felt any before; but it seemed to me that I was accumulating a great and valuable reputation at no expense, and my delight in this grew and grew, as challenge after challenge was declined, until by midnight I was beginning to think that there was nothing in the world so much to be desired as a chance to fight a duel. So I hurried Daggett up; made him keep on sending challenge after challenge. Oh, well, I overdid it; Laird accepted. I might have known that that would happen—Laird was a man you couldn't depend on.

The boys were jubilant beyond expression. They helped me make my will, which was another discomfort—and I already had enough. Then they took me home. I didn't sleep any—didn't want to sleep. I had plenty of things to think about, and less than four hours to do it in—because five o'clock was the hour appointed for the tragedy, and I should have to use up one hour —beginning at four—in practising with the revolver and finding out which end of it to level at the adversary. At four we went down into a little gorge, about a mile from town, and borrowed a barn door for a mark—borrowed it of a man who was over in California on a visit—and we set the barn door up and stood a fence-rail up against the middle of it, to represent Mr. Laird. But the rail was no proper representative of him, for he was longer than a rail and thinner. Nothing would ever fetch him but a line shot, and then as like as not he would split the bullet—the worst material for duelling purposes that could be imagined. I began on the rail. I couldn't hit the rail; then I tried the barn door; but I couldn't hit the barn door. There was nobody in danger except stragglers around on the flanks of that mark. I was thoroughly discouraged, and I didn't cheer up any when we presently heard pistol-shots over in the next little ravine. I knew what that was—that was Laird's gang out practising him. They would hear my shots, and of course they would come up over the ridge to see what kind of a record I was making—see what their chances were against me. Well, I hadn't any record; and I knew that if Laird came over that ridge and saw my barn door without a scratch on it, he would be as anxious to fight as I was—or as I had been at midnight, before that disastrous acceptance came.

Now just at this moment, a little bird, no bigger than a sparrow, flew along by and lit on a sage-bush about thirty yards away. Steve whipped out his revolver and shot its head off. Oh, he was a marksman—much better than I was. We ran down there to pick up the bird, and just then, sure enough, Mr. Laird and his people came over the ridge, and they joined us. And when Laird's second saw that bird, with its head shot off, he lost color, he faded, and you could see that he was interested. He said:

" Who did that?"

Before I could answer, Steve spoke up and said quite calmly, and in a matter-of-fact way,

" Clemens did it."

The second said, " Why, that is wonderful. How far off was that bird ?"

Steve said, " Oh, not far—about thirty yards."

The second said, " Well, that is astonishing shooting. How often can he do that?"

Steve said languidly, " Oh, about four times out of five."

I knew the little rascal was lying, but I didn't say anything. The second said, "Why, that is *amazing* shooting; I supposed he couldn't hit a church."

He was supposing very sagaciously, but I didn't say anything. Well, they said good morning. The second took Mr. Laird home, a little tottery on his legs, and Laird sent back a note in his own hand declining to fight a duel with me on any terms whatever.

Well, my life was saved—saved by that accident. I don't know what the bird thought about that interposition of Providence, but I felt very, very comfortable over it—satisfied and content. Now, we found out, later, that Laird had *hit* his mark four times out of six, right along. If the duel had come off, he would have so filled my skin with bullet-holes that it wouldn't have held my principles.

By breakfast-time the news was all over town that I had sent a challenge and Steve Gillis had carried it. Now that would entitle us to two years apiece in the penitentiary, according to the brand-new law. Judge North sent us no message as coming from himself, but a message *came* from a close friend of his. He said it would be a good idea for us to leave the territory by the first stage-coach. This would sail next morning, at four o'clock—and in the meantime we would be searched for, but not with avidity; and if we were in the Territory after that stage-coach left, we would be the first victims of the new law. Judge North was anxious to have some object-lessons for that law, and he would absolutely keep us in the prison the full two years.

Well, it seemed to me that our society was no longer desirable in Nevada; so we stayed in our quarters and observed proper caution all day—except that once Steve went over to the hotel to attend to another customer of mine. That was a Mr. Cutler. You see Laird was not the only person whom I had tried to reform during my occupancy of the editorial chair. I had looked around and selected several other people, and delivered a new zest of life into them through warm criticism and disapproval

—so that when I laid down my editorial pen I had four horse-whippings and two duels owing to me. We didn't care for the horse-whippings; there was no glory in them; they were not worth the trouble of collecting. But honor required that some notice should be taken of that other duel. Mr. Cutler had come up from Carson City, and had sent a man over with a challenge from the hotel. Steve went over to pacify him. Steve weighed only ninety-five pounds, but it was well known throughout the territory that with his fists he could whip anybody that walked on two legs, let his weight and science be what they might. Steve was a Gillis, and when a Gillis confronted a man and had a proposition to make, the proposition always contained business. When Cutler found that Steve was my second he cooled down; he became calm and rational, and was ready to listen. Steve gave him fifteen minutes to get out of the hotel, and half an hour to get out of town or there would be results. So *that* duel went off successfully, because Mr. Cutler immediately left for Carson a convinced and reformed man.

I have never had anything to do with duels since. I thoroughly disapprove of duels. I consider them unwise, and I know they are dangerous. Also, sinful. If a man should challenge me now, I would go to that man and take him kindly and forgivingly by the hand and lead him to a quiet retired spot, and *kill* him.

MARK TWAIN.

*(To be Continued.)*

# Chapter XI

## January 4, 1907. Pages 1–14.

PREFATORY NOTE.—Mr. Clemens began to write his autobiography many years ago, and he continues to add to it day by day. It was his original intention to permit no publication of his memoirs until after his death; but, after leaving " Pier No. 70," he concluded that a considerable portion might now suitably be given to the public. It is that portion, garnered from the quarter-million of words already written, which will appear in this REVIEW during the coming year. No part of the autobiography will be published in book form during the lifetime of the author.—EDITOR N. A. R.

[*Dictated December 13, 1906.*] As regards the coming American monarchy. It was before the Secretary of State had been heard from that the chairman of the banquet said:

" In this time of unrest it is of great satisfaction that such a man as you, Mr. Root, is chief adviser of the President."

Mr. Root then got up and in the most quiet and orderly manner touched off the successor to the San Francisco earthquake. As a result, the several State governments were well shaken up and considerably weakened. Mr. Root was prophesying. He was prophesying, and it seems to me that no shrewder and surer forecasting has been done in this country for a good many years.

He did not say, in so many words, that we are proceeding, in a steady march, toward eventual and unavoidable replacement of the republic by monarchy; but I suppose he was aware that that is the case. He notes the several steps, the customary steps, which in all the ages have led to the consolidation of loose and scattered governmental forces into formidable centralizations of authority; but he stops there, and doesn't add up the sum. He is not unaware that heretofore the sum has been ultimate monarchy, and that the same figures can fairly be depended upon to furnish the same sum whenever and wherever they can be produced, so long as human nature shall remain as it is; but it was not needful that he do the adding, since any one can do it; neither would it have been gracious in him to do it.

In observing the changed conditions which in the course of time have made certain and sure the eventual seizure by the Washington government of a number of State duties and prerogatives which have been betrayed and neglected by the several States, he does not attribute those changes and the vast results which are to flow from them to any thought-out policy of any party or of any body of dreamers or schemers, but properly and rightly attributes them to that stupendous power—*Circumstance*—which moves by laws of its own, regardless of parties and policies, and whose decrees are final, and must be obeyed by all—and will be. The railway is a Circumstance, the steamship is a Circumstance, the telegraph is a Circumstance. They were mere happenings; and to the whole world, the wise and the foolish alike, they were entirely trivial, wholly inconsequential; indeed silly, comical, grotesque. No man, and no party, and no thought-out policy said, "Behold, we will build railways and steamships and telegraphs, and presently you will see the condition and way of life of every man and woman and child in the nation totally changed; unimaginable changes of law and custom will follow, in spite of anything that anybody can do to prevent it."

The changed conditions have come, and Circumstance knows what is following, and will follow. So does Mr. Root. His language is not unclear, it is crystal:

" Our whole life has swung away from the old State centres, and is crystallizing about national centres."

" . . . . The old barriers which kept the States as separate communities are completely lost from sight."

" . . . . That [State] power of regulation and control is gradually passing into the hands of the national government."

"Sometimes by an assertion of the inter-State commerce power, sometimes by an assertion of the taxing power, the national government is taking up the performance of duties which under the changed conditions the separate States are no longer capable of adequately performing."

"We are urging forward in a development of business and social life which tends more and more to the obliteration of State lines and the decrease of State power as compared with national power."

"It is useless for the advocates of State rights to inveigh against . . . the extension of national authority in the fields of necessary control where the States themselves fail in the performance of their duty."

He is not announcing a policy; he is not forecasting what a party of planners will bring about; he is merely telling what the people will require and compel. And he could have added—which would be perfectly true—that the people will not be moved to it by speculation and cogitation and planning, but by *Circumstance* —that power which arbitrarily compels all their actions, and over which they have not the slightest control.

"*The end is not yet.*"

It is a true word. We are on the march, but at present we are only just getting started.

If the States continue to fail to do their duty as required by the people—

"*. . . constructions of the Constitution will be found* to vest the power where it will be exercised—in the national government."

I do not know whether that has a sinister meaning or not, and so I will not enlarge upon it lest I should chance to be in the wrong. It sounds like ship-money come again, but it may not be so intended.

Human nature being what it is, I suppose we must expect to drift into monarchy by and by. It is a saddening thought, but we cannot change our nature: we are all alike, we human beings; and in our blood and bone, and ineradicable, we carry the seeds out of which monarchies and aristocracies are grown: worship of gauds, titles, distinctions, power. We have to worship these things and their possessors, we are all born so, and we cannot help it. We have to be despised by somebody whom we regard as above us, or we are not happy; we have to have somebody to worship and envy, or we cannot be content. In America we manifest this in all the ancient and customary ways. In public we scoff at titles and hereditary privilege, but privately we hanker after them, and when we get a chance we buy them for cash and a daughter. Sometimes we get a good man and worth the price, but we are ready to take him anyway, whether he be ripe or rotten, whether he be clean and decent, or merely a basket of noble and sacred and long-descended offal. And when we get him the whole nation publicly chaffs and scoffs—and privately envies; and also is proud of the honor which has been conferred upon us. We run over our list of titled purchases every now and then, in the newspapers, and discuss them and caress them, and are thankful and happy.

Like all the other nations, we worship money and the possessors of it—they being our aristocracy, and we have to have one. We like to read about rich people in the papers; the papers know it, and they do their best to keep this appetite liberally fed. They even leave out a football bull-fight now and then to get room for all the particulars of how—according to the display heading— "Rich Woman Fell Down Cellar—Not Hurt." The falling down the cellar is of no interest to us when the woman is not rich, but no rich woman can fall down cellar and we not yearn to know all about it and wish it was us.

In a monarchy the people willingly and rejoicingly revere and take pride in their nobilities, and are not humiliated by the reflection that this humble and hearty homage gets no return but contempt. Contempt does not shame them, they are used to it, and they recognize that it is their proper due. We are all made like that. In Europe we easily and quickly learn to take that attitude toward the sovereigns and the aristocracies; moreover, it has been observed that when we get the attitude we go on and exaggerate it, presently becoming more servile than the natives, and vainer of it. The next step is to rail and scoff at republics and democracies. All of which is natural, for we have not ceased to be human beings by becoming Americans, and the human race was always intended to be governed by kingship, not by popular vote.

I suppose we must expect that unavoidable and irresistible Circumstances will gradually take away the powers of the States and concentrate them in the central government, and that the republic will then repeat the history of all time and become a monarchy;

but I believe that if we obstruct these encroachments and steadily resist them the monarchy can be postponed for a good while yet.

[*Dictated December 1, 1906.*] An exciting event in our village (Hannibal) was the arrival of the mesmerizer. I think the year was 1850. As to that I am not sure, but I know the month—it was May; that detail has survived the wear of fifty-five years. A pair of connected little incidents of that month have served to keep the memory of it green for me all this time; incidents of no consequence, and not worth embalming, yet my memory has preserved them carefully and flung away things of real value to give them space and make them comfortable. The truth is, a person's memory has no more sense than his conscience, and no appreciation whatever of values and proportions. However, never mind those trifling incidents; my subject is the mesmerizer, now.

(1849-'51.)

He advertised his show, and promised marvels. Admission as usual: 25 cents, children and negroes half price. The village had heard of mesmerism, in a general way, but had not encountered it yet. Not many people attended, the first night, but next day they had so many wonders to tell that everybody's curiosity was fired, and after that for a fortnight the magician had prosperous times. I was fourteen or fifteen years old—the age at which a boy is willing to endure all things, suffer all things, short of death by fire, if thereby he may be conspicuous and show off before the public; and so, when I saw the " subjects " perform their foolish antics on the platform and make the people laugh and shout and admire, I had a burning desire to be a subject myself. Every night, for three nights, I sat in the row of candidates on the platform, and held the magic disk in the palm of my hand, and gazed at it and tried to get sleepy, but it was a failure; I remained wide awake, and had to retire defeated, like the majority. Also, I had to sit there and be gnawed with envy of Hicks, our journeyman; I had to sit there and see him scamper and jump when Simmons the enchanter exclaimed, " See the snake! see the snake!" and hear him say, " My, how beautiful!" in response to the suggestion that he was observing a splendid sunset; and so on—the whole insane business. I couldn't laugh, I couldn't applaud; it filled me with bitterness to have others do it, and to have people make a hero of Hicks, and crowd around him when the show was over, and ask him for more and more particulars of the wonders he had seen in his visions, and manifest in many ways that they were proud to be acquainted with him. Hicks—the idea! I couldn't stand it; I was getting boiled to death in my own bile.

On the fourth night temptation came, and I was not strong enough to resist. When I had gazed at the disk awhile I pretended to be sleepy, and began to nod. Straightway came the professor and made passes over my head and down my body and legs and arms, finishing each pass with a snap of his fingers in the air, to discharge the surplus electricity; then he began to " draw " me with the disk, holding it in his fingers and telling me I could not take my eyes off it, try as I might; so I rose slowly, bent and gazing, and followed that disk all over the place, just as I had seen the others do. Then I was put through the other paces. Upon suggestion I fled from snakes; passed buckets at a fire; became excited over hot steamboat-races; made love to imaginary girls and kissed them; fished from the platform and landed mud-cats that outweighed me—and so on, all the customary marvels. But not in the customary way. I was cautious at first, and watchful, being afraid the professor would discover that I was an impostor and drive me from the platform in disgrace; but as soon as I realized that I was not in danger, I set myself the task of terminating Hicks's usefulness as a subject, and of usurping his place.

It was a sufficiently easy task. Hicks was born honest; I, without that incumbrance—so some people said. Hicks saw what he saw, and reported accordingly; I saw more than was visible, and added to it such details as could help. Hicks had no imagination, I had a double supply. He was born calm, I was born excited. No vision could start a rapture in him, and he was constipated as to language, anyway; but if I saw a vision I emptied the dictionary onto it and lost the remnant of my mind into the bargain.

At the end of my first half-hour Hicks was a thing of the past, a fallen hero, a broken idol, and I knew it and was glad, and said in my heart, Success to crime! Hicks could never have been mesmerized to the point where he could kiss an imaginary girl in public, or a real one either, but I was competent. Whatever Hicks had failed in, I made it a point to succeed in, let the cost be what it might, physically or morally. He had shown several bad defects, and I had made a note of them. For instance, if the magician asked, "What do you see?" and left him to invent a vision for himself, Hicks was dumb and blind, he couldn't see a thing nor say a word, whereas the magician soon found that when it came to seeing visions of a stunning and marketable sort I could get along better without his help than with it. Then there was another thing: Hicks wasn't worth a tallow dip on mute mental suggestion. Whenever Simmons stood behind him and gazed at the back of his skull and tried to drive a mental suggestion into it, Hicks sat with vacant face, and never suspected. If he had been noticing, he could have seen by the rapt faces of the audience that something was going on behind his back that required a response. Inasmuch as I was an impostor I dreaded to have this test put upon me, for I knew the professor would be "willing" me to do something, and as I couldn't know what it was, I should be exposed and denounced. However, when my time came, I took my chance. I perceived by the tense and expectant faces of the people that Simmons was behind me willing me with all his might. I tried my best to imagine what he wanted, but nothing suggested itself. I felt ashamed and miserable, then. I believed that the hour of my disgrace was come, and that in another moment I should go out of that place disgraced. I ought to be ashamed to confess it, but my next thought was, not how I could win the compassion of kindly hearts by going out humbly and in sorrow for my misdoings, but how I could go out most sensationally and spectacularly.

There was a rusty and empty old revolver lying on the table, among the "properties" employed in the performances. On May-day, two or three weeks before, there had been a celebration by the schools, and I had had a quarrel with a big boy who was the school-bully, and I had not come out of it with credit. That boy was now seated in the middle of the house, half-way down the main aisle. I crept stealthily and impressively toward the table, with a dark and murderous scowl on my face, copied from a popular romance, seized the revolver suddenly, flourished it, shouted the bully's name, jumped off the platform, and made a rush for him and chased him out of the house before the paralyzed people could interfere to save him. There was a storm of applause, and the magician, addressing the house, said, most impressively—

"That you may know how really remarkable this is, and how wonderfully developed a subject we have in this boy, I assure you that without a single spoken word to guide him he has carried out what I mentally commanded him to do, to the minutest detail. I could have stopped him at a moment in his vengeful career by a mere exertion of my will, therefore the poor fellow who has escaped was at no time in danger."

So I was not in disgrace. I returned to the platform a hero, and happier than I have ever been in this world since. As regards mental suggestion, my fears of it were gone. I judged that in case I failed to guess what the professor might be willing me to do, I could count on putting up something that would answer just as well. I was right, and exhibitions of unspoken suggestion became a favorite with the public. Whenever I perceived that I was being willed to do something I got up and did something—anything that occurred to me—and the magician, not being a fool, always ratified it. When people asked me, "How *can* you tell what he is willing you to do?" I said, "It's just as easy," and they always said, admiringly, "Well it beats *me* how you can do it."

Hicks was weak in another detail. When the professor made passes over him and said "his whole body is without sensation now—come forward and test him, ladies and gentlemen," the ladies and gentlemen always complied eagerly, and stuck pins into Hicks, and if they went deep Hicks was sure to wince, then that poor professor would have to explain that Hicks "wasn't sufficiently under the influence." But I didn't wince; I only suffered, and shed tears on the inside. The miseries that a conceited boy will endure to keep up his "reputation"! And so will a conceited man; I know it in my own person, and have seen it in a hundred thousand others. That professor ought to have protected me, and I often hoped he would, when the tests were unusually severe, but he didn't. It may be that he was deceived as well as the others, though I did not believe it nor think it possible. Those were dear good people, but they must have carried simplicity and credulity to the limit. They would stick a pin in my arm and bear on it until they drove it a third of its length in, and then be lost in wonder that by a mere exercise

of will-power the professor could turn my arm to iron and make
it insensible to pain. Whereas it was not insensible at all; I was
suffering agonies of pain.

After that fourth night, that proud night, that triumphant
night, I was the only subject. Simmons invited no more candidates to the platform. I performed alone, every night, the rest
of the fortnight. In the beginning of the second week I conquered the last doubters. Up to that time a dozen wise old
heads, the intellectual aristocracy of the town, had held out, as
implacable unbelievers. I was as hurt by this as if I were engaged in some honest occupation. There is nothing surprising
about this. Human beings feel dishonor the most, sometimes,
when they most deserve it. That handful of overwise old gentlemen kept on shaking their heads all the first week, and saying
they had seen no marvels there that could not have been produced by collusion; and they were pretty vain of their unbelief,
too, and liked to show it and air it, and be superior to the ignorant and the gullible. Particularly old Dr. Peake, who was the
ringleader of the irreconcilables, and very formidable; for he
was an F.F.V., he was learned, white-haired and venerable, nobly
and richly clad in the fashions of an earlier and a courtlier day,
he was large and stately, and he not only seemed wise, but was
what he seemed, in that regard. He had great influence, and his
opinion upon any matter was worth much more than that of any
other person in the community. When I conquered him, at
last, I knew I was undisputed master of the field; and now,
after more than fifty years, I acknowledge, with a few dry old
tears, that I rejoiced without shame.

[*Dictated December 2, 1906.*] In 1847 we were living in a
large white house on the corner of Hill and Main Streets—a
house that still stands, but isn't large now, although it
**(1847.)** hasn't lost a plank; I saw it a year ago and noticed that
shrinkage. My father died in it in March of the year mentioned,
but our family did not move out of it until some months afterward. Ours was not the only family in the house, there was
another—Dr. Grant's. One day Dr. Grant and Dr. Reyburn
argued a matter on the street with sword-canes, and Grant was
brought home multifariously punctured. Old Dr. Peake calked
the leaks, and came every day for a while, to look after him.

The Grants were Virginians, like Peake, and one day when Grant was getting well enough to be on his feet and sit around in the parlor and talk, the conversation fell upon Virginia and old times. I was present, but the group were probably quite unconscious of me, I being only a lad and a negligible quantity. Two of the group—Dr. Peake and Mrs. Crawford, Mrs. Grant's mother—had been of the audience when the Richmond theatre burned down, thirty-six years before, and they talked over the frightful details of that memorable tragedy. These were eyewitnesses, and with their eyes I saw it all with an intolerable vividness: I saw the black smoke rolling and tumbling toward the sky, I saw the flames burst through it and turn red, I heard the shrieks of the despairing, I glimpsed their faces at the windows, caught fitfully through the veiling smoke, I saw them jump to their death, or to mutilation worse than death. The picture is before me yet, and can never fade.

In due course they talked of the colonial mansion of the Peakes, with its stately columns and its spacious grounds, and by odds and ends I picked up a clearly defined idea of the place. I was strongly interested, for I had not before heard of such palatial things from the lips of people who had seen them with their own eyes. One detail, casually dropped, hit my imagination hard. In the wall, by the great front door, there was a round hole as big as a saucer—a British cannon-ball had made it, in the war of the Revolution. It was breath-taking; it made history real; history had never been real to me before.

Very well, three or four years later, as already mentioned, I was king-bee and sole " subject " in the mesmeric show; it was the beginning of the second week; the performance was half over; just then the majestic Dr. Peake, with his ruffled bosom and wristbands and his gold-headed cane, entered, and a deferential citizen vacated his seat beside the Grants and made the great chief take it. This happened while I was trying to invent something fresh in the way of a vision, in response to the professor's remark—

" Concentrate your powers. Look—look attentively. There—don't you see something? Concentrate—concentrate. Now then —describe it."

Without suspecting it, Dr. Peake, by entering the place, had reminded me of the talk of three years before. He had also furnished me capital and was become my confederate, an accomplice in my frauds. I began on a vision, a vague and dim one (that was part of the game at the beginning of a vision; it isn't best to see it too clearly at first, it might look as if you had come loaded with it). The vision developed, by degrees, and gathered swing, momentum, energy. It was the Richmond fire. Dr. Peake was cold, at first, and his fine face had a trace of polite scorn in it; but when he began to recognize that fire, that expression changed, and his eyes began to light up. As soon as I saw that, I threw the valves wide open and turned on all the steam, and gave those people a supper of fire and horrors that was calculated to last them one while! They couldn't gasp, when I got through—they were petrified. Dr. Peake had risen, and was standing,—and breathing hard. He said, in a great voice—

"My doubts are ended. No collusion could produce that miracle. It was totally impossible for him to know those details, yet he has described them with the clarity of an eyewitness—and with what unassailable truthfulness God knows I know!"

I saved the colonial mansion for the last night, and solidified and perpetuated Dr. Peake's conversion with the cannon-ball hole. He explained to the house that I could never have heard of that small detail, which differentiated this mansion from all other Virginian mansions and perfectly identified it, therefore the fact stood proven that I had *seen* it in my vision. Lawks!

It is curious. When the magician's engagement closed there was but one person in the village who did not believe in mesmerism, and I was the one. All the others were converted, but I was to remain an implacable and unpersuadable disbeliever in mesmerism and hypnotism for close upon fifty years. This was because I never would examine them, in after life. I couldn't. The subject revolted me. Perhaps because it brought back to me a passage in my life which for pride's sake I wished to forget; though I thought—or persuaded myself I thought— I should never come across a "proof" which wasn't thin and cheap, and probably had a fraud like me behind it.

The truth is, I did not have to wait long to get tired of my triumphs. Not thirty days, I think. The glory which is built upon a lie soon becomes a most unpleasant incumbrance. No

doubt for a while I enjoyed having my exploits told and re-
told and told again in my presence and wondered over and
exclaimed about, but I quite distinctly remember that there
presently came a time when the subject was wearisome and
odious to me and I could not endure the disgusting discomfort of
it. I am well aware that the world-glorified doer of a deed of
great and real splendor has just my experience; I know that he
deliciously enjoys hearing about it for three or four weeks, and
that pretty soon after that he begins to dread the mention of it,
and by and by wishes he had been with the damned before he
ever thought of doing that deed; I remember how General
Sherman used to rage and swear over " When we were Marching through Georgia," which was played at him and sung at him
everywhere he went; still, I think I suffered a shade more than
the legitimate hero does, he being privileged to soften his misery
with the reflection that his glory was at any rate golden and
reproachless in its origin, whereas I had no such privilege, there
being no possible way to make mine respectable.

How easy it is to make people believe a lie, and how hard it
is to undo that work again! Thirty-five years after those evil
exploits of mine I visited my old mother, whom I had not seen
for ten years; and being moved by what seemed to me a rather
noble and perhaps heroic impulse, I thought I would humble
myelf and confess my ancient fault. It cost me a great effort to
make up my mind; I dreaded the sorrow that would rise in her
face, and the shame that would look out of her eyes; but after
long and troubled reflection, the sacrifice seemed due and right,
and I gathered my resolution together and made the confession.

To my astonishment there were no sentimentalities, no dra-
matics, no George Washington effects; she was not moved in the
least degree; she simply did not believe me, and said so! I
was not merely disappointed, I was nettled, to have my costly
truthfulness flung out of the market in this placid and confident
way when I was expecting to get a profit out of it. I asserted, and
reasserted, with rising heat, my statement that every single thing
I had done on those long-vanished nights was a lie and a swindle;
and when she shook her head tranquilly and said she knew
better, I put up my hand and *swore* to it—adding a triumphant
" *Now* what do you say?"

It did not affect her at all; it did not budge her the fraction of an inch from her position. If this was hard for me to endure, it did not begin with the blister she put upon the raw when she began to put my sworn oath out of court with *arguments* to prove that I was under a delusion and did not know what I was talking about. Arguments! Arguments to show that a person on a man's outside can know better what is on his inside than he does himself! I had cherished some contempt for arguments before, I have not enlarged my respect for them since. She refused to believe that I had invented my visions myself; she said it was folly: that I was only a child at the time and could not have done it. She cited the Richmond fire and the colonial mansion and said they were quite beyond my capacities. Then I saw my chance! I said she was right—I didn't invent those, I got them from Dr. Peake. Even this great shot did no damage. She said Dr. Peake's evidence was better than mine, and he had said in plain words that it was impossible for me to have heard about those things. Dear, dear, what a grotesque and unthinkable situation: a confessed swindler convicted of honesty and condemned to acquittal by circumstantial evidence furnished by the swindled!

I realized, with shame and with impotent vexation, that I was defeated all along the line. I had but one card left, but it was a formidable one. I played it—and stood from under. It seemed ignoble to demolish her fortress, after she had defended it so valiantly; but the defeated know not mercy. I played that master card. It was the pin-sticking. I said, solemnly—

"I give you my honor, a pin was never stuck into me without causing me cruel pain."

She only said—

"It is thirty-five years. I believe you do think that, *now,* but I was there, and I know better. You never winced."

She was so calm! and I was so far from it, so nearly frantic.

"Oh, my goodness!" I said, "let me *show* you that I am speaking the truth. Here is my arm; drive a pin into it—drive it to the head—I shall not wince."

She only shook her gray head and said, with simplicity and conviction—

"You are a man, now, and could dissemble the hurt; but you were only a child then, and could not have done it."

And so the lie which I played upon her in my youth remained with her as an unchallengeable truth to the day of her death. Carlyle said " a lie cannot live." It shows that he did not know how to tell them. If I had taken out a life policy on this one the premiums would have bankrupted me ages ago.

MARK TWAIN.

*(To be Continued.)*

# Chapter X

January 18, 1907. Pages 113–19.

PREFATORY NOTE.—Mr. Clemens began to write his autobiography many years ago, and he continues to add to it day by day. It was his original intention to permit no publication of his memoirs until after his death; but, after leaving "Pier No. 70," he concluded that a considerable portion might now suitably be given to the public. It is that portion, garnered from the quarter-million of words already written, which will appear in this REVIEW during the coming year. No part of the autobiography will be published in book form during the lifetime of the author.—EDITOR N. A. R.

[*Dictated March 28, 1906.*] Orion Clemens was born in Jamestown, Fentress County, Tennessee, in 1825. He was the family's
(1825.) first-born, and antedated me ten years. Between him and me came a sister, Margaret, who died, aged ten, in 1837, in that village of Florida, Missouri, where I was born; and Pamela, mother of Samuel E. Moffett, who was an invalid all
(1837.) her life and died in the neighborhood of New York a year ago, aged about seventy-five. Her character was without blemish, and she was of a most kindly and gentle dis-

99

position.  Also there was a brother, Benjamin, who died in 1848
(1843.) aged ten or twelve.

Orion's boyhood was spent in that wee little log hamlet
of Jamestown up there among the " knobs "—so called—of East
Tennessee.  The family migrated to Florida, Missouri, then
moved to Hannibal, Missouri, when Orion was twelve and a half
years old.  When he was fifteen or sixteen he was sent to St.
Louis and there he learned the printer's trade.  One of his char-
acteristics was eagerness.  He woke with an eagerness about some
matter or other every morning; it consumed him all day; it
perished in the night and he was on fire with a fresh new interest next morning before he could get his clothes on.  He
exploited in this way three hundred and sixty-five red-hot new
eagernesses every year of his life.  But I am forgetting another
characteristic, a very pronounced one.  That was his deep glooms,
his despondencies, his despairs; these had their place in each and
every day along with the eagernesses.  Thus his day was divided
—no, not divided, mottled—from sunrise to midnight with alter-
nating brilliant sunshine and black cloud.  Every day he was
the most joyous and hopeful man that ever was, I think, and
also every day he was the most miserable man that ever was.

While he was in his apprenticeship in St. Louis, he got well
acquainted with Edward Bates, who was afterwards in Mr. Lincoln's first cabinet.  Bates was a very fine man, an honorable and
upright man, and a distinguished lawyer.  He patiently allowed
Orion to bring to him each new project; he discussed it with
him and extinguished it by argument and irresistible logic—at
first.  But after a few weeks he found that this labor was not
necessary; that he could leave the new project alone and it
would extinguish itself the same night.  Orion thought he would
like to become a lawyer.  Mr. Bates encouraged him, and he
studied law nearly a week, then of course laid it aside to try
something new.  He wanted to become an orator.  Mr. Bates
gave him lessons.  Mr. Bates walked the floor reading from an
English book aloud and rapidly turning the English into French,
and he recommended this exercise to Orion.  But as Orion knew
no French, he took up that study and wrought at it like a vol-
cano for two or three days; then gave it up.  During his apprenticeship in St. Louis he joined a number of churches, one
after another, and taught in their Sunday-schools—changing his

Sunday-school every time he changed his religion. He was correspondingly erratic in his politics—Whig to-day, Democrat next week, and anything fresh that he could find in the political market the week after. I may remark here that throughout his long life he was always trading religions and enjoying the change of scenery. I will also remark that his sincerity was never doubted; his truthfulness was never doubted; and in matters of business and money his honesty was never questioned. Notwithstanding his forever-recurring caprices and changes, his principles were high, always high, and absolutely unshakable. He was the strangest compound that ever got mixed in a human mould. Such a person as that is given to acting upon impulse and without reflection; that was Orion's way. Everything he did he did with conviction and enthusiasm and with a vainglorious pride in the thing he was doing—and no matter what that thing was, whether good, bad or indifferent, he repented of it every time in sackcloth and ashes before twenty-four hours had sped. Pessimists are born, not made. Optimists are born, not made. But I think he was the only person I have ever known in whom pessimism and optimism were lodged in exactly equal proportions. Except in the matter of grounded principle, he was as unstable as water. You could dash his spirits with a single word; you could raise them into the sky again with another one. You could break his heart with a word of disapproval; you could make him as happy as an angel with a word of approval. And there was no occasion to put any sense or any vestige of mentality of any kind into these miracles; anything you might say would answer.

He had another conspicuous characteristic, and it was the father of those which I have just spoken of. This was an intense lust for approval. He was so eager to be approved, so girlishly anxious to be approved by anybody and everybody, without discrimination, that he was commonly ready to forsake his notions, opinions and convictions at a moment's notice in order to get the approval of any person who disagreed with them. I wish to be understood as reserving his fundamental principles all the time. He never forsook those to please anybody. Born and reared among slaves and slaveholders, he was yet an abolitionist from his boyhood to his death. He was always truthful; he was always sincere; he was always honest and honorable. But in light matters—matters of small consequence, like religion and politics and such things—he never acquired a conviction that could survive a disapproving remark from a cat.

He was always dreaming; he was a dreamer from birth, and this characteristic got him into trouble now and then.

Once when he was twenty-three or twenty-four years old, and was become a journeyman, he conceived the romantic idea of coming to Hannibal without giving us notice, in order that he might furnish to the family a pleasant surprise. If he had given notice, he would have been informed that we had changed our residence and that that gruff old bass-voiced sailorman, Dr. G., our family physician, was living in the house which we had formerly occupied and that Orion's former room in that house was now occupied by Dr. G.'s two middle-aged maiden sisters. Orion arrived at Hannibal per steamboat in the middle of the night, and started with his customary eagerness on his excursion, his mind all on fire with his romantic project and building and enjoying his surprise in advance. He was always enjoying things in advance; it was the make of him. He never could wait for the event, but must build it out of dream-stuff and enjoy it beforehand—consequently sometimes when the event happened he saw that it was not as good as the one he had invented in his imagination, and so he had lost profit by not keeping the imaginary one and letting the reality go.

When he arrived at the house he went around to the back door and slipped off his boots and crept up-stairs and arrived at the room of those elderly ladies without having wakened any sleepers. He undressed in the dark and got into bed and snuggled up against somebody. He was a little surprised, but not much—for he thought it was our brother Ben. It was winter, and the bed was comfortable, and the supposed Ben added to the comfort—and so he was dropping off to sleep very well satisfied with his progress so far and full of happy dreams of what was going to happen in the morning. But something else was going to happen sooner than that, and it happened now. The maid that was being crowded fumed and fretted and struggled and presently came to a half-waking condition and protested against the crowding. That voice paralyzed Orion. He couldn't move a limb; he couldn't get his breath; and the crowded one discovered his new whiskers and began to scream. This removed the paralysis, and Orion was out of bed and clawing round in the dark for his clothes in a fraction of a second. Both maids began to scream, then, so Orion did not wait to get his whole wardrobe. He started with such parts of it as he could grab. He flew to the head of the stairs and started down, and was paralyzed again at that point, because he saw the faint yellow flame of a candle soaring up the stairs from below and he judged that Dr. G. was behind it, and he was. He had no clothes on to speak of, but no matter, he was well enough fixed for an occasion like this, because he had a butcher-knife in his hand. Orion shouted to him, and this saved his life, for the Doctor recognized his voice. Then in those deep-sea-going bass tones of his that I used to admire so much when I was a little boy, he explained to Orion the change that had been made, told him where to find the Clemens family, and closed with some quite unnecessary advice about posting himself before he undertook another adventure like that —advice which Orion probably never needed again as long as he lived.

One bitter December night, Orion sat up reading until three o'clock in the morning and then, without looking at a clock, sallied forth to call on a young lady. He hammered and hammered at the door; couldn't get any response; didn't understand it. Anybody else would have regarded that as an indication of some kind or other and would have drawn inferences and gone home. But Orion didn't draw inferences, he merely hammered and hammered, and finally the father of the girl appeared at the door in a dressing-gown. He had a candle in his hand and the dressing-gown was all the clothing he had on—except an expression of unwelcome which was so thick and so large that it extended all down his front to his instep and nearly obliterated the dressing-gown. But Orion didn't notice that this was an unpleasant expression. He merely walked in. The old gentleman took him into the parlor, set the candle on a table, and stood Orion made the usual remarks about the weather, and sat down —sat down and talked and talked and went on talking—that old man looking at him vindictively and waiting for his chance —waiting treacherously and malignantly for his chance. Orion had not asked for the young lady. It was not customary. It was understood that a young fellow came to see the girl of the house, not the founder of it. At last Orion got up and made some remark to the effect that probably the young lady was busy and he would go now and call again. That was the old man's chance, and he said with fervency " Why good land, aren't you going to stop to breakfast?"

Orion did not come to Hannibal until two or three years after my father's death. Meantime he remained in St. Louis. He was a journeyman printer and earning wages. Out of his wage he supported my mother and my brother Henry, who was two years younger than I. My sister Pamela helped in this support by taking piano pupils. Thus we got along, but it was pretty hard sledding. I was not one of the burdens, because I was taken from school at once, upon my father's death, and placed in the office of the Hannibal " Courier," as printer's apprentice, and Mr. S., the editor and proprietor of the paper, allowed me the usual emolument of the office of apprentice— that is to say board and clothes, but no money. The clothes consisted of two suits a year, but one of the suits always failed to materialize and the other suit was not purchased so long as Mr. S.'s old clothes held out. I was only about half as big as Mr. S., consequently his shirts gave me the uncomfortable sense of living in a circus tent, and I had to turn up his pants to my ears to make them short enough.

There were two other apprentices. One was Steve Wilkins, seventeen or eighteen years old and a giant. When he was in Mr. S.'s clothes they fitted him as the candle-mould fits the candle—thus he was generally in a suffocated condition, particularly in the summer-time. He was a reckless, hilarious, admirable creature; he had no principles, and was delightful company. At first we three apprentices had to feed in the kitchen with the old slave cook and her very handsome and bright and well-behaved young mulatto daughter. For his own amusement —for he was not generally laboring for other people's amusement—Steve was constantly and persistently and loudly and elaborately making love to that mulatto girl and distressing the life out of her and worrying the old mother to death. She would say, " Now, Marse Steve, Marse Steve, can't you behave yourself?" With encouragement like that, Steve would naturally renew his attentions and emphasize them. It was killingly funny to Ralph and me. And, to speak truly, the old mother's distress about it was merely a pretence. She quite well understood that by the customs of slaveholding communities it was Steve's right to make love to that girl if he wanted to. But the girl's distress was very real. She had a refined nature, and she took all Steve's extravagant love-making in resentful earnest.

We got but little variety in the way of food at that kitchen table, and there wasn't enough of it anyway. So we apprentices used to keep alive by arts of our own—that is to say, we crept into the cellar nearly every night, by a private entrance which we had discovered, and we robbed the cellar of potatoes and onions and such things, and carried them down-town to the printing-office, where we slept on pallets on the floor, and cooked them at the stove and had very good times.

As I have indicated, Mr. S.'s economies were of a pretty close and rigid kind. By and by, when we apprentices were promoted from the basement to the ground floor and allowed to sit at the family table, along with the one journeyman, Harry H., the economies continued. Mrs. S. was a bride. She had attained to that distinction very recently, after waiting a good part of a lifetime for it, and she was the right woman in the right place, according to the economics of the place, for she did not trust the sugar-bowl to us, but sweetened our coffee herself. That is, she went through the motions. She didn't really sweeten it. She seemed to put one heaping teaspoonful of brown sugar into each cup, but, according to Steve, that was a deceit. He said she dipped the spoon in the coffee first to make the sugar stick, and then scooped the sugar out of the bowl with the spoon upside down, so that the effect to the eye was a heaped-up spoon, whereas the sugar on it was nothing but a layer. This all seems perfectly true to me, and yet that thing would be so difficult to perform that I suppose it really didn't happen, but was one of Steve's lies.

MARK TWAIN.

*(To be Continued.)*

# Chapter XI

February 1, 1907. Pages 225–32.

PREFATORY NOTE.—Mr. Clemens began to write his autobiography many years ago, and he continues to add to it day by day. It was his original intention to permit no publication of his memoirs until after is death; but, after leaving "Pier No. 70," he concluded that a considerable portion might now suitably be given to the public. It is that portion, garnered from the quarter-million of words already written, which will appear in this REVIEW during the coming year. No part of the autobiography will be published in book form during the lifetime of the author.—EDITOR N. A. R.

[*Dictated March 28th, 1906.*] About 1849 or 1850 Orion severed his connection with the printing-house in St. Louis and came up to Hannibal, and bought a weekly paper **(1850.)** called the Hannibal "Journal," together with its plant and its good-will, for the sum of five hundred dollars cash. He borrowed the cash at ten per cent. interest, from an old farmer named Johnson who lived five miles out of town. Then he reduced the subscription price of the paper from two dollars to one dollar. He reduced the rates for advertising in about the same proportion, and thus he created one absolute and unassailable certainty—to wit: that the business would never pay him a single cent of profit. He took me out of the " Courier " office and engaged my services in his own at three dollars and a half a week, which was an extravagant wage, but Orion was always generous, always liberal with everybody except himself. It cost him nothing in my case, for he never was able to pay me a penny as long as I was with him. By the end of the first year he found he must make some economies. The office rent was cheap, but it was not cheap enough. He could not afford to pay rent of any kind, so he moved the whole plant into the house we lived in, and it cramped the dwelling-place cruelly. He kept that paper alive during four years, but I have at this time no idea how he accomplished it. Toward the end of each year he had to turn out and scrape and scratch for the fifty dollars of interest due Mr. Johnson, and that fifty dollars was about the only cash he ever received or paid out, I suppose, while he was proprietor of that newspaper, except for ink and printing-paper. The paper was a dead failure. It had to be that from the start. Finally he handed it over to Mr. Johnson, and went up to Muscatine, Iowa, and acquired a small interest in a weekly newspaper there. It was not a sort of property to marry on—but no matter. He came across a winning and pretty girl who lived in Quincy, Illinois, a few miles below Keokuk, and they became engaged. He was always falling in love wiť girls, but by some accident or other he had never gone so far as engagement before. And now he achieved nothing but misfortune by it, because he straightway fell in love with a Keokuk girl. He married the Keokuk girl and they began a struggle for life which turned out to be a difficult enterprise, and very unpromising.

To gain a living in Muscatine was plainly impossible, so Orion and his new wife went to Keokuk to live, for she wanted to be near her relatives. He bought a little bit of a job-printing plant—on credit, of course—and at once put prices down to where not even the apprentices could get a living out of it, and this sort of thing went on.

I had not joined the Muscatine migration. Just before that **(1853.)** happened (which I think was in 1853) I disappeared one night and fled to St. Louis. There I worked in the composing-room of the "Evening News" for a time, and then started on my travels to see the world. The world was New York City, and there was a little World's Fair there. It had just been opened where the great reservoir afterward was, and where the sumptuous public library is now being built—Fifth Avenue and Forty-second Street. I arrived in New York with two or three dollars in pocket change and a ten-dollar bank-bill concealed in the lining of my coat. I got work at villainous wages in the establishment of John A. Gray and Green in Cliff Street, and I found board in a sufficiently villainous mechanics' boarding-house in Duane Street. The firm paid my wages in wildcat money at its face value, and my week's wage merely sufficed to pay board and lodging. By and by I went to Philadelphia and worked there some months as a "sub" on the "Inquirer" and the "Public Ledger." Finally I made a flying trip to Wash-

(1854.) ington to see the sights there, and in 1854 I went back to the Mississippi Valley, sitting upright in the smoking-car two or three days and nights. When I reached St. Louis I was exhausted. I went to bed on board a steamboat that was bound for Muscatine. I fell asleep at once, with my clothes on, and didn't wake again for thirty-six hours.

. . . I worked in that little job-office in Keokuk as much as two years, I should say, without ever collecting a cent of wages, for Orion was never able to pay anything—but Dick Higham and I had good times. I don't know what Dick got, but it was proba-bly only uncashable promises.

One day in the midwinter of 1856 or 1857—I think it was 1856—I was coming along the main street of Keokuk in the

(1856.) middle of the forenoon. It was bitter weather — so bitter that that street was deserted, almost. A light dry snow was blowing here and there on the ground and on the pave-ment, swirling this way and that way and making all sorts of beautiful figures, but very chilly to look at. The wind blew a piece of paper past me and it lodged against a wall of a house. Something about the look of it attracted my attention and I gathered it in. It was a fifty-dollar bill, the only one I had ever seen, and the largest assemblage of money I had ever encountered in one spot. I advertised it in the papers and suffered more than a thousand dollars' worth of solicitude and fear and distress dur-ing the next few days lest the owner should see the advertisement and come and take my fortune away. As many as four days went by without an applicant; then I could endure this kind of misery no longer. I felt sure that another four could not go by in this safe and secure way. I felt that I must take that money out of danger. So I bought a ticket for Cincinnati and went to that city. I worked there several months in the printing-office of Wrightson and Company. I had been reading Lieutenant Herndon's account of his explorations of the Amazon and had been mightily attracted by what he said of coca. I made up my mind that I would go to the head waters of the Amazon and collect coca and trade in it and make a fortune. I left for New Orleans in the steamer " Paul Jones " with this great idea filling my mind. One of the pilots of that boat was Horace Bixby. Little by little I got acquainted with him, and pretty soon I was doing a lot of steering for him in his daylight watches. When I got to New Orleans I inquired about ships leaving for Pará and discovered that there weren't any, and learned that there probably wouldn't be any during that century. It had not occurred to me to inquire about these particulars before leaving Cincinnati, so there I was. I couldn't get to the Amazon. I had no friends in New Orleans and no money to speak of. I went to Horace Bixby and asked him to make a pilot out of me. He said he would do it for a hundred dollars cash in advance. So I steered for him up to St. Louis, borrowed the money from my brother-in-law and closed the bargain. I had acquired this brother-in-law several years before. This was Mr. William A. Moffett, a merchant, a Virginian—a fine man in every way. He had married my sister Pamela, and the Samuel E. Moffett of whom I have been speaking was their son. Within eighteen months I became a competent pilot, and I served that office until the Mississippi River traffic was brought to a standstill by the breaking out of the civil war.

. . . Meantime Orion had gone down the river and established his little job-printing-office in Keokuk. On account of charging next to nothing for the work done in his job-office, he had almost nothing to do there. He was never able to comprehend that work done on a profitless basis deteriorates and is presently not worth anything, and that customers are then obliged to go where they can get better work, even if they must pay better prices for it. He had plenty of time, and he took up Blackstone again.

He also put up a sign which offered his services to the public as a lawyer. He never got a case, in those days, nor even an applicant, although he was quite willing to transact law business for nothing and furnish the stationery himself. He was always liberal that way.

Presently he moved to a wee little hamlet called Alexandria, two or three miles down the river, and he put up that sign there. He got no custom. He was by this time very hard aground. But by this time I was beginning to earn a wage of two hundred and fifty dollars a month as pilot, and so I supported him **(1861.)** thenceforth until 1861, when his ancient friend, Edward Bates, then a member of Mr. Lincoln's first cabinet, got him the place of Secretary of the new Territory of Nevada, and Orion and I cleared for that country in the overland stage-coach, I paying the fares, which were pretty heavy, and carrying with me what money I had been able to save—this was eight hundred dollars, I should say—and it was all in silver coin and a good deal of a nuisance because of its weight. And we had another nuisance, which was an Unabridged Dictionary. It weighed about a thousand pounds, and was a ruinous expense, because the stage-coach Company charged for extra baggage by the ounce. We could have kept a family for a time on what that dictionary cost in the way of extra freight—and it wasn't a good dictionary anyway—didn't have any modern words in it—only had obsolete ones that they used to use when Noah Webster was a child.

The Government of the new Territory of Nevada was an interesting menagerie. Governor Nye was an old and seasoned politician from New York—politician, not statesman. He had white hair; he was in fine physical condition; he had a winningly friendly face and deep lustrous brown eyes that could talk as a native language the tongue of every feeling, every passion, every emotion. His eyes could outtalk his tongue, and this is saying a good deal, for he was a very remarkable talker, both in private and on the stump. He was a shrewd man; he generally saw through surfaces and perceived what was going on inside without being suspected of having an eye on the matter.

When grown-up persons indulge in practical jokes, the fact gauges them. They have lived narrow, obscure, and ignorant lives, and at full manhood they still retain and cherish a job-lot of left-over standards and ideals that would have been discarded with their boyhood if they had then moved out into the world and a broader life. There were many practical jokers in the new Territory. I do not take pleasure in exposing this fact, for I liked those people; but what I am saying is true. I wish I could say a kindlier thing about them instead — that they were burglars, or hat - rack thieves, or something like that, that wouldn't be utterly uncomplimentary. I would prefer it, but I can't say those things, they would not be true. These people were practical jokers, and I will not try to disguise it. In other respects they were plenty good-enough people; honest people; reputable and likable. They played practical jokes upon each other with success, and got the admiration and applause and also the envy of the rest of the community. Naturally they were eager to try their arts on big game, and that was what the Governor was. But they were not able to score. They made several efforts, but the Governor defeated these efforts without any trouble and went on smiling his pleasant smile as if nothing had happened. Finally the joker chiefs of Carson City and Virginia City conspired together to see if their combined talent couldn't win a victory, for the jokers were getting into a very uncomfortable place: the people were laughing at them, instead of at their proposed victim. They banded themselves together to the number of ten and invited the Governor to what was a most extraordinary attention in those days—pickled oyster stew and champagne—luxuries very seldom seen in that region, and existing rather as fabrics of the imagination than as facts.

The Governor took me with him. He said disparagingly,

"It's a poor invention. It doesn't deceive. Their idea is to get me drunk and leave me under the table, and from their standpoint this will be very funny. But they don't know me. I am familiar with champagne and have no prejudices against it."

The fate of the joke was not decided until two o'clock in the morning. At that hour the Governor was serene, genial, comfortable, contented, happy and sober, although he was so full that he couldn't laugh without shedding champagne tears. Also, at that hour the last joker joined his comrades under the table, drunk to the last perfection. The Governor remarked,

"This is a dry place, Sam, let's go and get something to drink and go to bed."

The Governor's official menagerie had been drawn from the

humblest ranks of his constituents at home—harmless good fellows who had helped in his campaigns, and now they had their reward in petty salaries payable in greenbacks that were worth next to nothing. Those boys had a hard time to make both ends meet. Orion's salary was eighteen hundred dollars a year, and he couldn't even support his dictionary on it. But the Irishwoman who had come out on the Governor's staff charged the menagerie only ten dollars a week apiece for board and lodging. Orion and I were of her boarders and lodgers; and so, on these cheap terms the silver I had brought from home held out very well.

At first I roamed about the country seeking silver, but at the end of '62 or the beginning of '63 when I came up from Aurora ('62 or '63.) to begin a journalistic life on the Virginia City "Enterprise," I was presently sent down to Carson City to report the legislative session. Orion was soon very popular with the members of the legislature, because they found that whereas they couldn't usually trust each other, nor anybody else, they could trust him. He easily held the belt for honesty in that country, but it didn't do him any good in a pecuniary way, because he had no talent for either persuading or scaring legislators. But I was differently situated. I was there every day in the legislature to distribute compliment and censure with evenly balanced justice and spread the same over half a page of the "Enterprise" every morning, consequently I was an influence. I got the legislature to pass a wise and very necessary law requiring every corporation doing business in the Territory to record its charter in full, without skipping a word, in a record to be kept by the Secretary of the Territory—my brother. All the charters were framed in exactly the same words. For this record-service he was authorized to charge forty cents a folio of one hundred words for making the record; also five dollars for furnishing a certificate of each record, and so on. Everybody had a toll-road franchise but no toll-road. But the franchise had to be recorded and paid for. Everybody was a mining corporation, and had to have himself recorded and pay for it. Very well, we prospered. The record-service paid an average of a thousand dollars a month, in gold.

Governor Nye was often absent from the Territory. He liked to run down to San Francisco every little while and enjoy a rest from Territorial civilization. Nobody complained, for he was prodigiously popular. He had been a stage-driver in his early days in New York or New England, and had acquired the habit of remembering names and faces, and of making himself agreeable to his passengers. As a politician this had been valuable to him, and he kept his arts in good condition by practice. By the time he had been Governor a year, he had shaken hands with every human being in the Territory of Nevada, and after that he always knew these people instantly at sight and could call them by name. The whole population, of 20,000 persons, were his personal friends, and he could do anything he chose to do and count upon their being contented with it. Whenever he was absent from the Territory—which was generally—Orion served his office in his place, as Acting Governor, a title which was soon and easily shortened to " Governor." He recklessly built and furnished a house at a cost of twelve thousand dollars, and there was no other house in the sage-brush capital that could approach this property for style and cost.

When Governor Nye's four-year term was drawing to a close, the mystery of why he had ever consented to leave the great State of New York and help inhabit that jack-rabbit desert was solved: he had gone out there in order to become a United States Senator. All that was now necessary was to turn the Territory into a State. He did it without any difficulty. That undeveloped country and that sparse population were not well fitted for the heavy burden of a State Government, but no matter, the people were willing to have the change, and so the Governor's game was made.

Orion's game was made too, apparently, for he was as popular because of his honesty as the Governor was for more substantial reasons; but at the critical moment the inborn capriciousness of his character rose up without warning, and disaster followed.

MARK TWAIN.

*(To be Continued.)*

# Chapter XII

## February 15, 1907. Pages 337–46.

PREFATORY NOTE.—Mr. Clemens began to write his autobiography many years ago, and he continues to add to it day by day. It was his original intention to permit no publication of his memoirs until after his death; but, after leaving " Pier No. 70," he concluded that a considerable portion might now suitably be given to the public. It is that portion, garnered from the quarter-million of words already written, which will appear in this REVIEW during the coming year. No part of the autobiography will be published in book form during the lifetime of the author.—EDITOR N. A. R.

*Orion Clemens—resumed.*

[*Dictated April 5, 1906.*] There were several candidates for all the offices in the gift of the new State of Nevada save two— (1864-5.) United States Senator, and Secretary of State. Nye was certain to get a Senatorship, and Orion was so sure to get the Secretaryship that no one but him was named for that office. But he was hit with one of his spasms of virtue on the very day that the Republican party was to make its nominations in the Convention, and refused to go near the Convention. He was urged, but all persuasions failed. He said his presence there would be an unfair and improper influence and that if he was to be nominated the compliment must come to him as a free and unspotted gift. This attitude would have settled his case for him without further effort, but he had another attack of virtue on the same day, that made it absolutely sure. It had been his habit for a great many years to change his religion with his shirt, and his ideas about temperance at the same time. He would be a teetotaler for a while and the champion of the cause; then he would change to the other side for a time. On nomination day he suddenly changed from a friendly attitude toward whiskey—which was the popular attitude—to uncompromising teetotalism, and went absolutely dry. His friends besought and implored, but all in vain. He could not be persuaded to cross the threshold of a saloon. The paper next morning contained the list of chosen nominees. His name was not in it. He had not received a vote.

His rich income ceased when the State government came into power. He was without an occupation. Something had to be done. He put up his sign as attorney-at-law, but he got no clients. It was strange. It was difficult to account for. I cannot account for it—but if I were going to guess at a solution I should guess that by the make of him he would examine both sides of a case so diligently and so conscientiously that when he got through with his argument neither he nor a jury would know which side he was on. I think that his client would find out his make in laying his case before him, and would take warning and withdraw it in time to save himself from probable disaster.

I had taken up my residence in San Francisco about a year before the time I have just been speaking of. One day I got a tip from Mr. Camp, a bold man who was always making big fortunes in ingenious speculations and losing them again in the course of six months by other speculative ingenuities. Camp told me to buy some shares in the Hale and Norcross. I bought fifty shares at three hundred dollars a share. I bought on a margin, and put up twenty per cent. It exhausted my funds. I wrote Orion and offered him half, and asked him to send his share of the money. I waited and waited. He wrote and said he was going to attend to it. The stock went along up pretty briskly. It went higher and higher. It reached a thousand dollars a share. It climbed to two thousand, then to three thousand; then to twice that figure. The money did not come, but I was not disturbed. By and by that stock took a turn and began to gallop down. Then I wrote urgently. Orion answered that he had sent the money long ago—said he had sent it to the Occidental Hotel. I inquired for it. They said it was not there. To cut a long story short, that stock went on down until it fell below the price I had paid for it. Then it began to eat up the margin, and when at last I got out I was very badly crippled.

When it was too late, I found out what had become of Orion's money. Any other human being would have sent a check, but he sent gold. The hotel clerk put it in the safe and went on vacation, and there it had reposed all this time enjoying its fatal work, no doubt. Another man might have thought to tell me that the money was not in a letter, but was in an express package, but it never occurred to Orion to do that.

Later, Mr. Camp gave me another chance. He agreed to buy our Tennessee land for two hundred thousand dollars, pay a part of the amount in cash and give long notes for the rest. His scheme was to import foreigners from grape-growing and wine-making districts in Europe, settle them on the land, and turn it into a wine-growing country. He knew what Mr. Longworth thought of those Tennessee grapes, and was satisfied. I sent the contracts and things to Orion for his signature, he being one of the three heirs. But they arrived at a bad time—in a doubly bad time, in fact. The temperance virtue was temporarily upon him in strong force, and he wrote and said that he would not be a party to debauching the country with wine. Also he said how could he know whether Mr. Camp was going to deal fairly and honestly with those poor people from Europe or not?—and so, without waiting to find out, he quashed the whole trade, and there it fell, never to be brought to life again. The land, from being suddenly worth two hundred thousand dollars, became as suddenly worth what it was before—nothing, and taxes to pay. I had paid the taxes and the other expenses for some years, but I dropped the Tennessee land there, and have never taken any interest in it since, pecuniarily or otherwise, until yesterday.

I had supposed, until yesterday, that Orion had frittered away the last acre, and indeed that was his own impression. But a gentleman arrived yesterday from Tennessee and brought a map showing that by a correction of the ancient surveys we still own a thousand acres, in a coal district, out of the hundred thousand acres which my father left us when he died in 1847. The gen-

tleman brought a proposition; also he brought a reputable and
well-to-do citizen of New York. The proposition was that the
Tennesseean gentleman should sell that land; that the New York
gentleman should pay all the expenses and fight all the law-
suits, in case any should turn up, and that of such profit as might
eventuate the Tennesseean gentleman should take a third, the
New-Yorker a third, and Sam Moffett and his sister and I—
who are surviving heirs—the remaining third.

This time I hope we shall get rid of the Tennessee land for
good and all and never hear of it again.

I came East in January, 1867. Orion remained in Carson City
perhaps a year longer. Then he sold his twelve-thousand-dollar
house and its furniture for thirty-five hundred in green-
**(1867.)** backs at about sixty per cent. discount. He and his wife
took passage in the steamer for home in Keokuk. About 1871
or '72 they came to New York. Orion had been trying to make
**(1871.)** a living in the law ever since he had arrived from the
Pacific Coast, but he had secured only two cases. Those
he was to try free of charge—but the possible result will never
be known, because the parties settled the cases out of court without his help.

Orion got a job as proof-reader on the New York " Evening
Post " at ten dollars a week. By and by he came to Hartford
and wanted me to get him a place as reporter on a Hartford
paper. Here was a chance to try my scheme again, and I did it.
I made him go to the Hartford " Evening Post," without any
letter of introduction, and propose to scrub and sweep and do
all sorts of things for nothing, on the plea that he didn't need
money but only needed work, and that that was what he was
pining for. Within six weeks he was on the editorial staff of
that paper at twenty dollars a week, and he was worth the money.
He was presently called for by some other paper at better wages,
but I made him go to the " Post " people and tell them about it.
They stood the raise and kept him. It was the pleasantest berth
he had ever had in his life. It was an easy berth. He was in
every way comfortable. But ill-luck came. It was bound to
come.

A new Republican daily was to be started in a New England
city by a stock company of well-to-do politicians, and they offered
him the chief editorship at three thousand a year. He was eager

to accept.  My beseechings and reasonings went for nothing.  I said,

"You are as weak as water.  Those people will find it out right away.' They will easily see that you have no backbone; that they can deal with you as they would deal with a slave.  You may last six months, but not longer.  Then they will not dismiss you as they would dismiss a gentleman: they will fling you out as they would fling out an intruding tramp."

It happened just so.  Then he and his wife migrated to Keokuk once more.  Orion wrote from there that he was not resuming the law; that he thought that what his health needed was the open air, in some sort of outdoor occupation; that his father-in-law had a strip of ground on the river border a mile above Keokuk with some sort of a house on it, and his idea was to buy that place and start a chicken-farm and provide Keokuk with chickens and eggs, and perhaps butter—but I don't know whether you can raise butter on a chicken-farm or not.  He said the place could be had for three thousand dollars cash, and I sent the money.  He began to raise chickens, and he made a detailed monthly report to me, whereby it appeared that he was able to work off his chickens on the Keokuk people at a dollar and a quarter a pair.  But it also appeared that it cost a dollar and sixty cents to raise the pair.  This did not seem to discourage Orion, and so I let it go.  Meantime he was borrowing a hundred dollars per month of me regularly, month by month.  Now to show Orion's stern and rigid business ways—and he really prided himself on his large business capacities—the moment he received the advance of a hundred dollars at the beginning of each month, he always sent me his note for the amount, and with it he sent, *out of that money, three months' interest* on the hundred dollars at six per cent. per annum, these notes being always for three months.

As I say, he always sent a detailed statement of the month's profit and loss on the chickens—at least the month's loss on the chickens—and this detailed statement included the various items of expense—corn for the chickens, boots for himself, and so on; even car fares, and the weekly contribution of ten cents to help out the missionaries who were trying to damn the Chinese after a plan not satisfactory to those people.

I think the poultry experiment lasted about a year, possibly two years.  It had then cost me six thousand dollars.

Orion returned to the law business, and I suppose he remained in that harness off and on for the succeeding quarter of a century, but so far as my knowledge goes he was only a lawyer in name, and had no clients.

My mother died, in her eighty-eighth year, in the summer of 1890. She had saved some money, and she left it to me, **(1890.)** because it had come from me. I gave it to Orion and he said, with thanks, that I had supported him long enough and now he was going to relieve me of that burden, and would also hope to pay back some of that expense, and maybe the whole of it. Accordingly, he proceeded to use up that money in building a considerable addition to the house, with the idea of taking boarders and getting rich. We need not dwell upon this venture. It was another of his failures. His wife tried hard to make the scheme succeed, and if anybody could have made it succeed she would have done it. She was a good woman, and was greatly liked. She had a practical side, and she would have made that boarding-house lucrative if circumstances had not been against her.

Orion had other projects for recouping me, but as they always required capital I stayed out of them, and they did not materialize. Once he wanted to start a newspaper. It was a ghastly idea, and I squelched it with a promptness that was almost rude. Then he invented a wood-sawing machine and patched it together himself, and he really sawed wood with it. It was ingenious; it was capable; and it would have made a comfortable little fortune for him; but just at the wrong time Providence interfered again. Orion applied for a patent and found that the same machine had already been patented and had gone into business and was thriving.

Presently the State of New York offered a fifty-thousand-dollar prize for a practical method of navigating the Erie Canal with steam canal-boats. Orion worked at that thing for two or three years, invented and completed a method, and was once more ready to reach out and seize upon imminent wealth when somebody pointed out a defect: his steam canal-boat could not be used in the winter-time; and in the summer-time the commotion its wheels would make in the water would wash away the State of New York on both sides.

Innumerable were Orion's projects for acquiring the means to pay off the debt to me. These projects extended straight through the succeeding thirty years, but in every case they failed. During all those thirty years his well-established honesty kept him in offices of trust where other people's money had to be taken care of, but where no salary was paid. He was treasurer of all the benevolent institutions; he took care of the money and other property of widows and orphans; he never lost a cent for anybody, and never made one for himself. Every time he changed his religion the church of his new faith was glad to get him; made him treasurer at once, and at once he stopped the graft and the leaks in that church. He exhibited a facility in changing his political complexion that was a marvel to the whole community. Once the following curious thing happened, and he wrote me all about it himself.

One morning he was a Republican, and upon invitation he agreed to make a campaign speech at the Republican mass-meeting that night. He prepared the speech. After luncheon he became a Democrat and agreed to write a score of exciting mottoes to be painted upon the transparencies which the Democrats would carry in their torchlight procession that night. He wrote these shouting Democratic mottoes during the afternoon, and they occupied so much of his time that it was night before he had a chance to change his politics again; so he actually made a rousing Republican campaign speech in the open air while his Democratic transparencies passed by in front of him, to the joy of every witness present.

He was a most strange creature—but in spite of his eccentricities he was beloved, all his life, in whatsoever community he lived. And he was also held in high esteem, for at bottom he was a sterling man.

About twenty-five years ago—along there somewhere—I suggested to Orion that he write an autobiography. I asked him to try to tell the straight truth in it; to refrain from exhibiting himself in creditable attitudes exclusively, and to honorably set down all the incidents of his life which he had found interesting to him, including those which were burned into his memory because he was ashamed of them. I said that this had never been done, and that if he could do it his autobiography would be a most valuable piece of literature. I said I was offering him a job which I could not duplicate in my own case, but I would cherish the hope that he might succeed with it. I recognize now that I was trying to saddle upon him an impossibility. I have been dictating this autobiography of mine daily for three months; I have thought of fifteen hundred or two thousand incidents in my life which I am ashamed of, but I have not gotten one of them to consent to go on paper yet. I think that that stock will still be complete and unimpaired when I finish these memoirs, if I ever finish them. I believe that if I should put in all or any of those incidents I should be sure to strike them out when I came to revise this book.

Orion wrote his autobiography and sent it to me. But great was my disappointment; and my vexation, too. In it he was constantly making a hero of himself, exactly as I should have done and am doing now, and he was constantly forgetting to put in the episodes which placed him in an unheroic light. I knew several incidents of his life which were distinctly and painfully unheroic, but when I came across them in his autobiography they had changed color. They had turned themselves inside out, and were things to be intemperately proud of. In my dissatisfaction I destroyed a considerable part of that autobiography. But in what remains there are passages which are interesting, and I shall quote from them here and there and now and then, as I go along.

While we were living in Vienna in 1898 a cablegram came from Keokuk announcing Orion's death. He was seventy-two **(1898.)** years old. He had gone down to the kitchen in the early hours of a bitter December morning; he had built the fire, and had then sat down at a table to write something; and there he died, with the pencil in his hand and resting against the paper in the middle of an unfinished word—an indication that his release from the captivity of a long and troubled and pathetic and unprofitable life was mercifully swift and painless.

[*Dictated in 1904.*] A quarter of a century ago I was visiting John Hay at Whitelaw Reid's house in New York, which Hay was occupying for a few months while Reid was absent on a holiday in Europe. Temporarily also, Hay was editing Reid's paper, the New York " Tribune." I remember two incidents of that Sunday visit particularly well. I had known John Hay a good many years, I had known him when he was an obscure young editorial writer on the " Tribune " in Horace Greeley's time, earning three or four times the salary he got, considering the high character of the work which came from his pen. In those earlier days he was a picture to look at, for beauty of feature, perfection of form and grace of carriage and movement. He had a charm about him of a sort quite unusual to my Western ignorance and inexperience—a charm of manner, intonation, apparently native and unstudied elocution, and all that—the groundwork of it native, the ease of it, the polish of it, the winning naturalness of it, acquired in Europe where he had been Chargé d'Affaires some time at the Court of Vienna. He was joyous and cordial, a most pleasant comrade. One of the two incidents above referred to as marking that visit was this:

In trading remarks concerning our ages I confessed to forty-two and Hay to forty. Then he asked if I had begun to write my autobiography, and I said I hadn't. He said that I ought to begin at once, and that I had already lost two years. Then he said in substance this:

" At forty a man reaches the top of the hill of life and starts down on the sunset side. The ordinary man, the average man, not to particularize too closely and say the commonplace man, has at that age succeeded or failed; in either case he has lived all of his life that is likely to be worth recording; also in either case the life lived is worth setting down, and cannot fail to be interesting if he comes as near to telling the truth about himself as he can. And he *will* tell the truth in spite of himself, for his facts and his fictions will work loyally together for the protection of the reader; each fact and each fiction will be a dab of paint, each will fall in its right place, and together they will paint his portrait; not the portrait *he* thinks they are painting, but his real portrait, the inside of him, the soul of him, his character. Without intending to lie he will lie all the time; not bluntly, consciously, not dully unconsciously, but half-consciously—consciousness in twilight; a soft and gentle and merciful twilight which makes his general form comely, with his virtuous prominences and projections discernible and his ungracious ones in shadow. His truths will be recognizable as truths, his modifications of facts which would tell against him will go for nothing, the reader will see the fact through the film and know his man.

" There is a subtle devilish something or other about autobiographical composition that defeats all the writer's attempts to paint his portrait *his* way."

Hay meant that he and I were ordinary average commonplace people, and I did not resent my share of the verdict, but nursed my wound in silence. His idea that we had finished our work in life, passed the summit and were westward bound down-hill, with me two years ahead of him and neither of us with anything further to do as benefactors to mankind, was all a mistake. I had written four books then, possibly five. I have been drowning the world in literary wisdom ever since, volume after volume; since that day's sun went down he has been the historian of Mr. Lincoln, and his book will never perish; he has been ambassador, brilliant orator, competent and admirable Secretary of State.

MARK TWAIN.

*(To be Continued.)*

# Chapter XIII

## March 1, 1907. Pages 449–63.

PREFATORY NOTE.—Mr. Clemens began to write his autobiography many years ago, and he continues to add to it day by day. It was his original intention to permit no publication of his memoirs until after his death; but, after leaving "Pier No. 70," he concluded that a considerable portion might now suitably be given to the public. It is that portion, garnered from the quarter-million of words already written, which will appear in this REVIEW during the coming year. No part of the autobiography will be published in book form during the lifetime of the author.—EDITOR N. A. R.

. . . As I have said, that vast plot of Tennessee land† was held by my father twenty years—intact. When he died in 1847, **(1847.)** we began to manage it ourselves. Forty years afterward, we had managed it all away except 10,000 acres, and gotten nothing to remember the sales by. About 1887—possibly it was earlier—the 10,000 went. My brother found a chance to trade it for a house and lot in the town of Corry, in the oil regions of Pennsylvania. About 1894 he sold this property for $250. That ended the Tennessee Land.

If any penny of cash ever came out of my father's wise investment but that, I have no recollection of it. No, I am overlooking

† 100,000 acres.

a detail. It furnished me a field for Sellers and a book. Out of
my half of the book I got $15,000 or $20,000; out of the play I
got $75,000 or $80,000—just about a dollar an acre. It is curious: I was not alive when my father made the investment, therefore he was not intending any partiality; yet I was the only
member of the family that ever profited by it. I shall have occasion to mention this land again, now and then, as I go along,
for it influenced our life in one way or another during more than
a generation. Whenever things grew dark it rose and put out its
hopeful Sellers hand and cheered us up, and said " Do not be
afraid—trust in me—wait." It kept us hoping and hoping, during forty years, and forsook us at last. It put our energies to
sleep and made visionaries of us—dreamers and indolent. We
were always going to be rich next year—no occasion to work. It
is good to begin life poor; it is good to begin life rich—these are
wholesome; but to begin it *prospectively* rich! The man who has
not experienced it cannot imagine the curse of it.

My parents removed to Missouri in the early thirties; I do not
remember just when, for I was not born then, and cared nothing
for such things. It was a long journey in those days, and must
have been a rough and tiresome one. The home was made in the
wee village of Florida, in Monroe county, and I was born there
in 1835. The village contained a hundred people and I increased
the population by one per cent. It is more than the best man in
history ever did for any other town. It may not be modest in me
to refer to this, but it is true. There is no record of a person
doing as much—not even Shakespeare. But I did it for Florida,
and it shows that I could have done it for any place—even London, I suppose.

Recently some one in Missouri has sent me a picture of the
house I was born in. Heretofore I have always stated that it was
a palace, but I shall be more guarded, now.

I remember only one circumstance connected with my life in it.
I remember it very well, though I was but two and a half years
old at the time. The family packed up everything and started in
wagons for Hannibal, on the Mississippi, thirty miles away.
Toward night, when they camped and counted up the children,
one was missing. I was the one. I had been left behind. Parents
ought always to count the children before they start. I was having a good enough time playing by myself until I found that the

doors were fastened and that there was a grisly deep silence brooding over the place. I knew, then, that the family were gone, and that they had forgotten me. I was well frightened, and I made all the noise I could, but no one was near and it did no good. I spent the afternoon in captivity and was not rescued until the gloaming had fallen and the place was alive with ghosts.

My brother Henry was six months old at that time. I used to remember his walking into a fire outdoors when he was a week old. It was remarkable in me to remember a thing like that, which occurred when I was so young. And it was still more remarkable that I should cling to the delusion, for thirty years, that I *did* remember it — for of course it never happened; he would not have been able to walk at that age. If I had stopped to reflect, I should not have burdened my memory with that impossible rubbish so long. It is believed by many people that an impression deposited in a child's memory within the first two years of its life cannot remain there five years, but that is an error. The incident of Benvenuto Cellini and the salamander must be accepted as authentic and trustworthy; and then that remarkable and indisputable instance in the experience of Helen Keller—however, I will speak of that at another time. For many years I believed that I remembered helping my grandfather drink his whiskey toddy when I was six weeks old, but I do not tell about that any more, now; I am grown old, and my memory is not as active as it used to be. When I was younger I could remember anything, whether it had happened or not; but my faculties are decaying, now, and soon I shall be so I cannot remember any but the things that happened. It is sad to go to pieces like this, but we all have to do it.

My uncle, John A. Quarles, was a farmer, and his place was in the country four miles from Florida. He had eight children, and fifteen or twenty negroes, and was also fortunate in other ways. Particularly in his character. I have not come across a better man than he was. I was his guest for two or three months every year, from the fourth year after we removed to Hannibal till I was eleven or twelve years old. I have never consciously used him or his wife in a book, but his farm has come very handy to me in literature, once or twice. In " Huck Finn " and in " Tom Sawyer Detective " I moved it down to Arkansas. It was all of six hundred miles, but it was no trouble, it was not a very large farm; five hundred acres, perhaps, but I could have done it if it had been twice as large. And as for the morality of it, I cared nothing for that; I would move a State if the exigencies of literature required it.

It was a heavenly place for a boy, that farm of my uncle John's. The house was a double log one, with a spacious floor (roofed in) connecting it with the kitchen. In the summer the table was set in the middle of that shady and breezy floor, and the sumptuous meals—well, it makes me cry to think of them. Fried chicken, roast pig, wild and tame turkeys, ducks and geese; venison just killed; squirrels, rabbits, pheasants, partridges, prairie-chickens; biscuits, hot batter cakes, hot buckwheat cakes, hot " wheat bread," hot rolls, hot corn pone; fresh corn boiled on the ear, succotash, butter-beans, string-beans, tomatoes, pease, Irish potatoes, sweet-potatoes; buttermilk, sweet milk, " clabber "; watermelons, musk-melons, cantaloups—all fresh from the garden—apple pie, peach pie, pumpkin pie, apple dumplings, peach cobbler—I can't re-member the rest. The way that the things were cooked was per-haps the main splendor—particularly a certain few of the dishes. For instance, the corn bread, the hot biscuits and wheat bread, and the fried chicken. These things have never been properly cooked in the North—in fact, no one there is able to learn the art, so far as my experience goes. The North thinks it knows how to make corn bread, but this is gross superstition. Perhaps no bread in the world is quite as good as Southern corn bread, and perhaps no bread in the world is quite so bad as the Northern imitation of it. The North seldom tries to fry chicken, and this is well; the art cannot be learned north of the line of Mason and Dixon, nor anywhere in Europe. This is not hearsay; it is experience that is speaking. In Europe it is imagined that the custom of serving various kinds of bread blazing hot is "American," but that is too broad a spread; it is custom in the South, but is much less than that in the North. In the North and in Europe hot bread is considered unhealthy. This is probably another fussy superstition, like the European superstition that ice-water is unhealthy. Europe does not need ice-water, and does not drink it; and yet, notwithstanding this, its word for it is better than ours, because it describes it, whereas ours doesn't. Europe calls it " iced " water. Our word describes water made from melted ice—a drink which we have but little acquaintance with.

It seems a pity that the world should throw away so many good things merely because they are unwholesome. I doubt if God has given us any refreshment which, taken in moderation, is unwholesome, except microbes. Yet there are people who strictly deprive themselves of each and every eatable, drinkable and smokable which has in any way acquired a shady reputation. They pay this price for health. And health is all they get for it. How strange it is; it is like paying out your whole fortune for a cow that has gone dry.

The farmhouse stood in the middle of a very large yard, and the yard was fenced on three sides with rails and on the rear side with high palings; against these stood the smokehouse; beyond the palings was the orchard; beyond the orchard were the negro quarter and the tobacco-fields. The front yard was entered over a stile, made of sawed-off logs of graduated heights; I do not remember any gate. In a corner of the front yard were a dozen lofty hickory-trees and a dozen black-walnuts, and in the nutting season riches were to be gathered there.

Down a piece, abreast the house, stood a little log cabin against the rail fence; and there the woody hill fell sharply away, past the barns, the corn-crib, the stables and the tobacco-curing house, to a limpid brook which sang along over its gravelly bed and curved and frisked in and out and here and there and yonder in the deep shade of overhanging foliage and vines—a divine place for wading, and it had swimming-pools, too, which were forbidden to us and therefore much frequented by us. For we were little Christian children, and had early been taught the value of forbidden fruit.

In the little log cabin lived a bedridden white-headed slave woman whom we visited daily, and looked upon with awe, for we believed she was upwards of a thousand years old and had talked with Moses. The younger negroes credited these statistics, and had furnished them to us in good faith. We accommodated all the details which came to us about her; and so we believed that she had lost her health in the long desert trip coming out of Egypt, and had never been able to get it back again. She had a round bald place on the crown of her head, and we used to creep around and gaze at it in reverent silence, and reflect that it was caused by fright through seeing Pharaoh drowned. We called her "Aunt" Hannah, Southern fashion.

She was superstitious like the other negroes; also, like them, she was deeply religious. Like them, she had great faith in prayer, and employed it in all ordinary exigencies, but not in cases where a dead certainty of result was urgent. Whenever witches were around she tied up the remnant of her wool in little tufts, with white thread, and this promptly made the witches impotent.

All the negroes were friends of ours, and with those of our own age we were in effect comrades. I say in effect, using the phrase as a modification. We were comrades, and yet not comrades; color and condition interposed a subtle line which both parties were conscious of, and which rendered complete fusion impossible. We had a faithful and affectionate good friend, ally and adviser in " Uncle Dan'l," a middle-aged slave whose head was the best one in the negro quarter, whose sympathies were wide and warm, and whose heart was honest and simple and knew no guile. He has served me well, these many, many years. I have not seen him for more than half a century, and yet spiritually I have had his welcome company a good part of that time, and have staged him in books under his own name and as " Jim," and carted him all around—to Hannibal, down the Mississippi on a raft, and even across the Desert of Sahara in a balloon— and he has endured it all with the patience and friendliness and loyalty which were his birthright. It was on the farm that I got my strong liking for his race and my appreciation of certain of its fine qualities. This feeling and this estimate have stood the test of sixty years and more and have suffered no impairment. The black face is as welcome to me now as it was then.

In my schoolboy days I had no aversion to slavery. I was not aware that there was anything wrong about it. No one arraigned it in my hearing; the local papers said nothing against it; the local pulpit taught us that God approved it, that it was a holy thing, and that the doubter need only look in the Bible if he wished to settle his mind—and then the texts were read aloud to us to make the matter sure; if the slaves themselves had an aversion to slavery they were wise and said nothing. In Hannibal we seldom saw a slave misused; on the farm, never.

There was, however, one small incident of my boyhood days which touched this matter, and it must have meant a good deal to me or-it would not have stayed in my memory, clear and sharp, vivid and shadowless, all these slow-drifting years. We had a little slave boy whom we had hired from some one, there in Hannibal. He was from the Eastern Shore of Maryland, and had been brought away from his family and his friends, half - way across the American continent, and sold. He was a cheery spirit, innocent and gentle, and the noisiest creature that ever was, perhaps. All day long he was singing, whistling, yelling, whooping, laughing—it was maddening, devastating, unendurable. At last, one day, I lost all my temper, and went raging to my mother, and said Sandy had been singing for an hour without a single break, and I couldn't stand it, and *wouldn't* she please shut him up. The tears came into her eyes, and her lip trembled, and she said something like this—

" Poor thing, when he sings, it shows that he is not remembering, and that comforts me; but when he is still, I am afraid he is thinking, and I cannot bear it. He will never see his mother again; if he can sing, I must not hinder it, but be thankful for it. If you were older, you would understand me; then that friendless child's noise would make you glad."

It was a simple speech, and made up of small words, but it went home, and Sandy's noise was not a trouble to me any more. She never used large words, but she had a natural gift for making small ones do effective work. She lived to reach the neighborhood of ninety years, and was capable with her tongue to the last—especially when a meanness or an injustice roused her spirit. She has come handy to me several times in my books, where she figures as Tom Sawyer's " Aunt Polly." I fitted her out with a dialect, and tried to think up other improvements for her, but did not find any. I used Sandy once, also; it was in " Tom Sawyer "; I tried to get him to whitewash the fence, but it did not work. I do not remember what name I called him by in the book.

I can see the farm yet, with perfect clearness. I can see all its belongings, all its details; the family room of the house, with a " trundle " bed in one corner and a spinning - wheel in another—a wheel whose rising and falling wail, heard from a distance, was the mournfulest of all sounds to me, and made me homesick and low-spirited, and filled my atmosphere with the wandering spirits of the dead; the vast fireplace, piled high, on winter nights, with flaming hickory logs from whose ends a sugary sap bubbled out but did not go to waste, for we scraped it off and ate it; the lazy cat spread out on the rough hearthstones, the drowsy dogs braced against the jambs and blinking; my aunt in one chimney-corner knitting, my uncle in the other smoking his corn-cob pipe; the slick and carpetless oak floor faintly mirroring the dancing flame-tongues and freckled with black indentations where fire-coals had popped out and died a leisurely death; half a dozen children romping in the background twilight; "split"-bottomed chairs here and there, some with rockers; a cradle—out of service, but waiting, with confidence; in the early cold mornings a snuggle of children, in shirts and chemises, occupying the hearthstone and procrastinating — they could not bear to leave that comfortable place and go out on the wind-swept floor-space between the house and kitchen where the general tin basin stood, and wash.

Along outside of the front fence ran the country road; dusty in the summer-time, and a good place for snakes—they liked to lie in it and sun themselves; when they were rattlesnakes or puff adders, we killed them: when they were black snakes, or racers, or belonged to the fabled "hoop" breed, we fled, without shame; when they were "house snakes" or "garters" we carried them home and put them in Aunt Patsy's work-basket for a surprise; for she was prejudiced against snakes, and always when she took the basket in her lap and they began to climb out of it it disordered her mind. She never could seem to get used to them; her opportunities went for nothing. And she was always cold toward bats, too, and could not bear them; and yet I think a bat is as friendly a bird as there is. My mother was Aunt Patsy's sister, and had the same wild superstitions. A bat is beautifully soft and silky; I do not know any creature that is pleasanter to the touch, or is more grateful for caressings, if offered in the right spirit. I know all about these coleoptera, because our great cave, three miles below Hannibal, was multitudinously stocked with them, and often I brought them home to amuse my mother with. It was easy to manage if it was a school day, because then I had ostensibly been to school and hadn't any bats. She was not a suspicious person, but full of trust and confidence; and when I said "There's something in my coat pocket for you," she would put her hand in. But she always took it out again, herself; I didn't have to tell her. It was remarkable, the way she couldn't learn to like private bats.

I think she was never in the cave in her life; but everybody else went there. Many excursion parties came from considerable distances up and down the river to visit the cave. It was miles in extent, and was a tangled wilderness of narrow and lofty clefts and passages. It was an easy place to get lost in; anybody could do it—including the bats. I got lost in it myself, along with a lady, and our last candle burned down to almost nothing before we glimpsed the search-party's lights winding about in the distance.

"Injun Joe" the half-breed got lost in there once, and would have starved to death if the bats had run short. But there was no chance of that; there were myriads of them. He told me all his story. In the book called "Tom Sawyer" I starved him entirely to death in the cave, but that was in the interest of art; it never happened. "General" Gaines, who was our first town drunkard before Jimmy Finn got the place, was lost in there for the space of a week, and finally pushed his handkerchief out of a hole in a hilltop near Saverton, several miles down the river from the cave's mouth, and somebody saw it and dug him out. There is nothing the matter with his statistics except the handkerchief. I knew him for years, and he hadn't any. But it could have been his nose. That would attract attention.

Beyond the road where the snakes sunned themselves was a dense young thicket, and through it a dim-lighted path led a quarter of a mile; then out of the dimness one emerged abruptly upon a level great prairie which was covered with wild strawberry-plants, vividly starred with prairie pinks, and walled in on all sides by forests. The strawberries were fragrant and fine, and in the season we were generally there in the crisp freshness of the early morning, while the dew-beads still sparkled upon the grass and the woods were ringing with the first songs of the birds.

Down the forest slopes to the left were the swings. They were made of bark stripped from hickory saplings. When they became dry they were dangerous. They usually broke when a child was forty feet in the air, and this was why so many bones had to be mended every year. I had no ill-luck myself, but none of my cousins escaped. There were eight of them, and at one time and another they broke fourteen arms among them. But it cost next to nothing, for the doctor worked by the year—$25 for the whole family. I remember two of the Florida doctors, Chowning and Meredith. They not only tended an entire family for $25 a year, but furnished the medicines themselves. Good measure, too. Only the largest persons could hold a whole dose. Castor-oil was the principal beverage. The dose was half a dipperful, with half a dipperful of New Orleans molasses added to help it down and make it taste good, which it never did. The next standby was calomel; the next, rhubarb; and the next, jalap. Then they bled the patient, and put mustard-plasters on him. It was a dreadful system, and yet the death-rate was not heavy. The calomel was nearly sure to salivate the patient and cost him some of his teeth. There were no dentists. When teeth became touched with decay or were otherwise ailing, the doctor knew of but one thing to do: he fetched his tongs and dragged them out. If the jaw remained, it was not his fault.

Doctors were not called, in cases of ordinary illness; the family's grandmother attended to those. Every old woman was a doctor, and gathered her own medicines in the woods, and knew how to compound doses that would stir the vitals of a cast-iron dog. And then there was the " Indian doctor "; a grave savage, remnant of his tribe, deeply read in the mysteries of nature and the secret properties of herbs; and most backwoodsmen had high faith in his powers and could tell of wonderful cures achieved by him. In Mauritius, away off yonder in the solitudes of the Indian Ocean, there is a person who answers to our Indian doctor of the old times. He is a negro, and has had no teaching as a doctor, yet there is one disease which he is master of and can cure, and the doctors can't. They send for him when they have a case. It is a child's disease of a strange and deadly sort, and the negro cures it with a herb medicine which he makes, himself, from a prescription which has come down to him from his father and grandfather. He will not let any one see it. He keeps the secret of its components to himself, and it is feared that he will die without divulging it; then there will be consternation in Mauritius. I was told these things by the people there, in 1896.

We had the " faith doctor," too, in those early days—a woman. Her specialty was toothache. She was a farmer's old wife, and lived five miles from Hannibal. She would lay her hand on the patient's jaw and say " Believe!" and the cure was prompt. Mrs. Utterback. I remember her very well. Twice I rode out there behind my mother, horseback, and saw the cure performed. My mother was the patient.

Dr. Meredith removed to Hannibal, by and by, and was our family physician there, and saved my life several times. Still, he was a good man and meant well. Let it go.

I was always told that I was a sickly and precarious and tiresome and uncertain child, and lived mainly on allopathic medicines during the first seven years of my life. I asked my mother about this, in her old age—she was in her 88th year—and said:

"I suppose that during all that time you were uneasy about me?"

"Yes, the whole time."

"Afraid I wouldn't live?"

After a reflective pause—ostensibly to think out the facts—

"No—afraid you would."

It sounds like a plagiarism, but it probably wasn't. The country schoolhouse was three miles from my uncle's farm. It stood in a clearing in the woods, and would hold about twenty-five boys and girls. We attended the school with more or less regularity once or twice a week, in summer, walking to it in the cool of the morning by the forest paths, and back in the gloaming at the end of the day. All the pupils brought their dinners in baskets — corn-dodger, buttermilk and other good things — and sat in the shade of the trees at noon and ate them. It is the part of my education which I look back upon with the most satisfaction. My first visit to the school was when I was seven. A strapping girl of fifteen, in the customary sunbonnet and calico dress, asked me if I "used tobacco"—meaning did I chew it. I said, no. It roused her scorn. She reported me to all the crowd, and said—

"Here is a boy seven years old who can't chaw tobacco."

By the looks and comments which this produced, I realized that I was a degraded object; I was cruelly ashamed of myself. I determined to reform. But I only made myself sick; I was not able to learn to chew tobacco. I learned to smoke fairly well, but that did not conciliate anybody, and I remained a poor thing, and characterless. I longed to be respected, but I never was able to rise. Children have but little charity for each other's defects.

As I have said, I spent some part of every year at the farm until I was twelve or thirteen years old. The life which I led there with my cousins was full of charm, and so is the memory of it yet. I can call back the solemn twilight and mystery of the deep woods, the earthy smells, the faint odors of the wild flowers, the sheen of rain-washed foliage, the rattling clatter of drops when the wind shook the trees, the far-off hammering of woodpeckers and the muffled drumming of wood-pheasants in the remoteness of the forest, the snap-shot glimpses of disturbed wild creatures skurrying through the grass,—I can call it all back and make it as real as it ever was, and as blessed. I can call back the prairie, and its loneliness and peace, and a vast hawk hanging motionless in the sky, with his wings spread wide and the blue of the vault showing through the fringe of their end-feathers. I can see the woods in their autumn dress, the oaks purple, the hickories washed with gold, the maples and the sumacs luminous with crimson fires, and I can hear the rustle made by the fallen leaves as we ploughed through them. I can see the blue clusters of wild grapes hanging amongst the foliage of the saplings, and I remember the taste of them and the smell. I know how the wild blackberries looked, and how they tasted; and the same with the pawpaws, the hazelnuts and the persimmons; and I can feel the thumping rain, upon my head, of hickory-nuts and walnuts when we were out in the frosty dawn to scramble for them with the pigs, and the gusts of wind loosed them and sent them down. I know the stain of blackberries, and how pretty it is; and I know the stain of walnut hulls, and how little it minds soap and water; also what grudged experience it had of either of them. I know the taste of maple sap, and when to gather it, and how to arrange the troughs and the delivery tubes, and how to boil down the juice, and how to hook the sugar after it is made; also how much better hooked sugar tastes than any that is honestly come by, let bigots say what they will. I know how a prize watermelon looks when it is sunning its fat rotundity among pumpkin-vines and " simblins "; I know how to tell when it is ripe without " plugging " it; I know how inviting it looks when it is cooling itself in a tub of water under the bed, waiting; I know how it looks when it lies on the table in the sheltered great floor-space between house and kitchen, and the children gathered for the sacrifice and their mouths watering; I know the crackling sound it makes when the carving-knife enters its end, and I can see the split fly along in front of the blade as the knife cleaves its way to the other end; I can see its halves fall apart and display the rich red meat and the black seeds, and the heart standing up, a luxury fit for the elect; I know how a boy looks, behind a yard-long slice of that melon, and I know how he feels; for I have been there. I know the taste of the watermelon which has been honestly come by, and I know the taste of the watermelon which has been acquired by art. Both taste good, but the experienced know which tastes best. I know the look of green apples and peaches and pears on the trees, and I know how entertaining they are when they are inside of a person. I know how ripe ones look when they are piled in pyramids under the trees, and how pretty they are and how vivid their colors. I know how a frozen apple looks, in a barrel down cellar in the winter-time, and how hard it is to bite, and how the frost makes the teeth ache, and yet how good it is, notwithstanding. I know the disposition of elderly people to select the specked apples for the children, and I once knew ways to beat the game. I know the look of an apple that is roasting and sizzling on a hearth on a winter's evening, and I know the comfort that comes of eating it hot, along with some sugar and a drench of cream. I know the delicate art and mystery of so cracking hickory-nuts and walnuts on a flatiron with a hammer that the kernels will be delivered whole, and I know how the nuts, taken in conjunction with winter apples, cider and doughnuts, make old people's tales and old jokes sound fresh and crisp and enchanting, and juggle an evening away before you know what went with the time. I know the look of Uncle Dan'l's kitchen as it was on privileged nights when I was a child, and I can see the white and black children grouped on the hearth, with the firelight playing on their faces and the shadows flickering upon the walls, clear back toward the cavernous gloom of the rear, and I can hear Uncle Dan'l telling the immortal tales which Uncle Remus Harris was to gather into his books and charm the world with, by and by; and I can feel again the creepy joy which quivered through me when the time for the ghost-story of the " Golden Arm " was reached—and the sense of regret, too, which came over me, for it was always the last story of the evening, and there was nothing between it and the unwelcome bed.

I can remember the bare wooden stairway in my uncle's house, and the turn to the left above the landing, and the rafters and the slanting roof over my bed, and the squares of moonlight on the floor, and the white cold world of snow outside, seen through the curtainless window. I can remember the howling of the wind and the quaking of the house on stormy nights, and how snug and cozy one felt, under the blankets, listening, and how the powdery snow used to sift in, around the sashes, and lie in little ridges on the floor, and make the place look chilly in the morning, and curb the wild desire to get up—in case there was any. I can remember how very dark that room was, in the dark of the moon, and how packed it was with ghostly stillness when one woke up by accident away in the night, and forgotten sins came flocking out of the secret chambers of the memory and wanted a hearing; and how ill chosen the time seemed for this kind of business; and how dismal was the hoo-hooing of the owl and the wailing of the wolf, sent mourning by on the night wind.

I remember the raging of the rain on that roof, summer nights, and how pleasant it was to lie and listen to it, and enjoy the white splendor of the lightning and the majestic booming and crashing of the thunder. It was a very satisfactory room; and there was a lightning-rod which was reachable from the window, an adorable and skittish thing to climb up and down, summer nights, when there were duties on hand of a sort to make privacy desirable.

I remember the 'coon and 'possum hunts, nights, with the negroes, and the long marches through the black gloom of the woods, and the excitement which fired everybody when the distant bay of an experienced dog announced that the game was treed; then the wild scramblings and stumblings through briars and bushes and over roots to get to the spot; then the lighting of a fire and the felling of the tree, the joyful frenzy of the dogs and the negroes, and the weird picture it all made in the red glare—I remember it all well, and the delight that every one got out of it, except the 'coon.

I remember the pigeon seasons, when the birds would come in millions, and cover the trees, and by their weight break down the branches. They were clubbed to death with sticks; guns were not necessary, and were not used. I remember the squirrel hunts, and the prairie-chicken hunts, and the wild-turkey hunts, and all that; and how we turned out, mornings, while it was still dark, to go on these expeditions, and how chilly and dismal it was, and how often I regretted that I was well enough to go. A toot on a tin horn brought twice as many dogs as were needed, and in their happiness they raced and scampered about, and knocked small people down, and made no end of unnecessary noise. At the word, they vanished away toward the woods, and we drifted silently after them in the melancholy gloom. But presently the gray dawn stole over the world, the birds piped up, then the sun rose and poured light and comfort all around, everything was fresh and dewy and fragrant, and life was a boon again. After three hours of tramping we arrived back wholesomely tired, overladen with game, very hungry, and just in time for breakfast.

MARK TWAIN.

*(To be Continued.)*

# Chapter XIV

## March 15, 1907. Pages 561–71.

PREFATORY NOTE.—Mr. Clemens began to write his autobiography many years ago, and he continues to add to it day by day. It was his original intention to permit no publication of his memoirs until after his death; but, after leaving "Pier No. 70," he concluded that a considerable portion might now suitably be given to the public. It is that portion, garnered from the quarter-million of words already written, which will appear in this REVIEW during the coming year. No part of the autobiography will be published in book form during the lifetime of the author.—EDITOR N. A. R.

*[Dictated Thursday, December 6, 1906.]*

### From Susy's Biography of Me.

*Feb. 27, Sunday.*

Clara's reputation as a baby was always a fine one, mine exactly the contrary. One often related story concerning her braveness as a baby and her own opinion of this quality of hers is this. Clara and I often got slivers in our hands and when mama took them out with a much dreaded needle, Clara was always very brave, and I very cowardly. One day Clara got one of these slivers in her hand, a very bad one, and while mama was taking it out, Clara stood perfectly still without even wincing; I saw how brave she was and turning to mamma said "Mamma isn't

she a brave little thing! presently mamma had to give the little hand
quite a dig with the needle and noticing how perfectly quiet Clara was
about it she exclaimed, Why Clara! you *are* a brave little thing! Clara
responded " No bodys braver but God!"—

Clara's pious remark is the main detail, and Susy has accurate-
ly remembered its phrasing.  The three-year-older's wound was of
a formidable sort, and not one which the mother's surgery would
have been equal to.  The flesh of the finger had been burst
by a cruel accident.  It was the doctor that sewed it up, and to
all appearances it was he, and the other independent witnesses,
that did the main part of the suffering; each stitch that he took
made Clara wince slightly, but it shrivelled the others.

I take pride in Clara's remark, because it shows that although
she was only three years old, her fireside teachings were already
making her a thinker—a thinker and also an observer of proportions.  I am not claiming any credit for this.  I furnished to
the children worldly knowledge and wisdom, but was not competent to go higher, and so I left their spiritual education in the
hands of the mother..  A result of this modesty of mine was
made manifest to me in a very striking way, some years afterward,
when Jean was nine years old.  We had recently arrived in Berlin, at the time, and had begun housekeeping in a furnished
apartment.  One morning at breakfast a vast card arrived—an invitation.  To be precise, it was a command from the Emperor
of Germany to come to dinner.  During several months I had encountered socially, on the Continent, men bearing lofty titles;
and all this while Jean was becoming more and more impressed,
and awed, and subdued, by these imposing events, for she had
not been abroad before, and they were new to her—wonders out
of dreamland turned into realities.  The imperial card was passed from hand to hand, around the table, and examined with interest; when it reached Jean she exhibited excitement and emotion, but for a time was quite speechless; then she said,

" Why, papa, if it keeps going on like this, pretty soon there
won't be anybody left for you to get acquainted with but God."

It was not complimentary to think I was not acquainted in
that quarter, but she was young, and the young jump to con-
clusions without reflection.

Necessarily, I did myself the honor to obey the command of
the Emperor Wilhelm II.  Prince Heinrich, and six or eight

other guests were present. The Emperor did most of the talking, and he talked well, and in faultless English. In both of these conspicuousnesses I was gratified to recognize a resemblance to myself—a very exact resemblance; no, almost exact, but not quite that—a modified exactness, with the advantage in favor of the Emperor. My English, like his, is nearly faultless; like him I talk well; and when I have guests at dinner I prefer to do all the talking myself. It is the best way, and the pleasantest. Also the most profitable for the others.

I was greatly pleased to perceive that his Majesty was familiar with my books, and that his attitude toward them was not uncomplimentary. In the course of his talk he said that my best and most valuable book was " Old Times on the Mississippi." I will refer to that remark again, presently.

An official who was well up in the Foreign Office at that time, and had served under Bismarck for fourteen years, was still occupying his old place under Chancellor Caprivi. Smith, I will call him of whom I am speaking, though that is not his name. He was a special friend of mine, and I greatly enjoyed his society, although in order to have it it was necessary for me to seek it as late as midnight, and not earlier. This was because Government officials of his rank had to work all day, after nine in the morning, and then attend official banquets in the evening; wherefore they were usually unable to get life - restoring fresh air and exercise for their jaded minds and bodies earlier than midnight; then they turned out, in groups of two or three, and gratefully and violently tramped the deserted streets until two in the morning. Smith had been in the Government service, at home and abroad, for more than thirty years, and he was now sixty years old, or close upon it. He could not remember a year in which he had had a vacation of more than a fortnight's length; he was weary all through to the bones and the marrow, now, and was yearning for a holiday of a whole three months— yearning so longingly and so poignantly that he had at last made up his mind to make a desperate cast for it and stand the consequences, whatever they might be. It was against all rules to *ask* for a vacation—quite against all etiquette; the shock of it would paralyze the Chancellery; stern etiquette and usage required another form: the applicant was not privileged to ask for a vacation, he must send in his *resignation*. The chancellor would know that the applicant was not really trying to resign, and didn't want to resign, but was merely trying in this left-handed way to get a vacation.

The night before the Emperor's dinner I helped Smith take his exercise, after midnight, and he was full of his project. He had sent in his resignation that day, and was trembling for the result; and naturally, because it might possibly be that the chancellor would be happy to fill his place with somebody else, in which case he could accept the resignation without comment and without offence. Smith was in a very anxious frame of mind; not that he feared that Caprivi was dissatisfied with him, for he had no such fear; it was the Emperor that he was afraid of; he did not know how he stood with the Emperor. He said that while apparently it was Caprivi who would decide his case, it was in reality the Emperor who would perform that service; that the Emperor kept personal watch upon everything, and that no official sparrow could fall to the ground without his privity and consent; that the resignation would be laid before his Majesty, who would accept it or decline to accept it, according to his pleasure, and that then his pleasure in the matter would be communicated by Caprivi. Smith said he would know his fate the next evening, after the imperial dinner; that when I should escort his Majesty into the large salon contiguous to the dining-room, I would find there about thirty men—Cabinet ministers, admirals, generals and other great officials of the Empire—and that these men would be standing talking together in little separate groups of two or three persons; that the Emperor would move from group to group and say a word to each, sometimes two words, sometimes ten words; and that the length of h's speech, whether brief or not so brief, would indicate the exact standing in the Emperor's regard, of the man accosted; and that by observing this thermometer an expert could tell, to half a degree, the state of the imperial weather in each case; that in Berlin, as in the imperial days of Rome, the Emperor was the sun, and that his smile or his frown meant good fortune or disaster to the man upon whom it should fall. Smith suggested that I watch the thermometer while the Emperor went his rounds of the groups; and added that if his Majesty talked four minutes with any person there present, it meant high favor, and that the sun was in the zenith, and cloudless, for that man.

I mentally recorded that four-minute altitude, and resolved to see if any man there on that night stood in sufficient favor to achieve it.

Very well. After the dinner I watched the Emperor while he passed from group to group, and privately I timed him with a watch. Two or three times he came near to reaching the four-minute altitude, but always he fell short a little. The last man he came to was Smith. He put his hand on Smith's shoulder and began to talk to him; and when he finished, the thermometer had scored seven minutes! The company then moved toward the smoking-room, where cigars, beer and anecdotes would be in brisk service until midnight, and as Smith passed me he whispered,

" That settles it. The chancellor will ask me how much of a vacation I want, and I sha'n't be afraid to raise the limit. I shall call for six months."

Smith's dream had been to spend his three months' vacation— in case he got a vacation instead of the other thing—in one of the great capitals of the Continent—a capital whose name I shall suppress, at present. The next day the chancellor asked him how much of a vacation he wanted, and where he desired to spend it. Smith told him. His prayer was granted, and rather more than granted. The chancellor augmented his salary and attached him to the German Embassy of that selected capital, giving him a place of high dignity bearing an imposing title, and with nothing to do except attend banquets of an extraordinary character at the Embassy, once or twice a year. The term of his vacation was not specified; he was to continue it until requested to come back to his work in the Foreign Office. This **(1891.)** was in 1891. Eight years later Smith was passing through Vienna, and he called upon me. There had been no interruption of his vacation, as yet, and there was no **(1899.)** likelihood that an interruption of it would occur while he should still be among the living.

[*Dictated Monday, December 17, 1906.*] As I have already remarked, " Old Times on the Mississippi " got the Kaiser's best praise. It was after midnight when I reached home; I was usually out until toward midnight, and the pleasure of being out late was poisoned, every night, by the dread of what I must meet at my front door—an indignant face, a resentful face, the face of the *portier*. The *portier* was a tow-headed young German, twenty-two or three years old; and it had been for some time apparent to me that he did not enjoy being hammered out of his sleep, nights, to let me in. He never had a kind word for me, nor a pleasant look. I couldn't under-stand it, since it was his business to be on watch and let the occupants of the several flats in at any and all hours of the night. I could not see why he so distinctly failed to get reconciled to it.

The fact is, I was ignorantly violating, every night, a custom in which he was commercially interested. I did not suspect this. No one had told me of the custom, and if I had been left to guess it, it would have taken me a very long time to make a suc-cess of it. It was a custom which was so well established and so universally recognized, that it had all the force and dignity of law. By authority of this custom, whosoever entered a Berlin house after ten at night must pay a trifling toll to the *portier* for breaking his sleep to let him in. This tax was either two and a half cents or five cents, I don't remember which; but I had never paid it, and didn't know I owed it, and as I had been residing in Berlin several weeks, I was so far in arrears that my presence in the German capital was getting to be a serious dis-aster to that young fellow.

I arrived from the imperial dinner sorrowful and anxious, made my presence known and prepared myself to wait in patience the tedious minute or two which the *portier* usually allowed him-self to keep me tarrying—as a punishment. But this time there was no stage-wait; the door was instantly unlocked, un-bolted, unchained and flung wide; and in it appeared the strange and welcome apparition of the *portier's* round face all sunshine and smiles and welcome, in place of the black frowns and hostility that I was expecting. Plainly he had not come out of his bed: he had been waiting for me, watching for me. He began to pour out upon me in the most enthusiastic and energetic way a generous stream of German welcome and homage, meanwhile dragging me excitedly to his small bedroom beside the front door; there he made me bend down over a row of German translations of my books and said,

"There—you wrote them! I have found it out! By God, I did not know it before, and I ask a million pardons! That one

there, the ' Old Times on the Mississippi,' is the best book you
ever wrote !"

The usual number of those curious accidents which we call
coincidences have fallen to my share in this life, but for picturesqueness this one puts all the others in the shade: that a
crowned head and a *portier,* the very top of an empire and the
very bottom of it, should pass the very same criticism and deliver the very same verdict upon a book of mine—and almost
in the same hour and the same breath—is a coincidence which out-
coincidences any coincidence which I could have imagined with
such powers of imagination as I have been favored with; and I
have not been accustomed to regard them as being small or of
an inferior quality. It is always a satisfaction to me to remember
that whereas I do not know, for sure, what any other nation
thinks of any one of my twenty-three volumes, I do at least
know for a certainty what one nation of fifty millions thinks
of one of them, at any rate; for if the mutual verdict of the top
of an empire and the bottom of it does not establish for good and
all the judgment of the entire nation concerning that book,
then the axiom that we can get a sure estimate of a thing by
arriving at a general average of all the opinions involved, is a
fallacy.

[*Dictated Monday, February 10, 1907.*] Two months ago
(December 6) I was dictating a brief account of a private dinner
in Berlin, where the Emperor of Germany was host and I the
chief guest. Something happened day before yesterday which
moves me to take up that matter again.

At the dinner his Majesty chatted briskly and entertainingly
along in easy and flowing English, and now and then he interrupted himself to address a remark to me, or to some other individual of the guests. When the reply had been delivered, he
resumed his talk. I noticed that the table etiquette tallied with
that which was the law of my house at home when we had
guests: that is to say, the guests answered when the host favored
them with a remark, and then quieted down and behaved themselves until they got another chance. If I had been in the Emperor's chair and he in mine, I should have felt infinitely comfortable and at home, and should have done a world of talking,
and done it well; but I was guest now, and consequently I felt
less at home. From old experience, I was familiar with the

rules of the game, and familiar with their exercise from the
high place of host; but I was not familiar with the trammelled
and less satisfactory position of guest, therefore I felt a little
strange and out of place.  But there was no animosity—no, the
Emperor was host, therefore according to my own rule he had
a right to do the talking, and it was my honorable duty to in-
trude no interruptions or other improvements, except upon invitation; and of course it could be *my* turn some day: some day,
on some friendly visit of inspection to America, it might be my
pleasure and distinction to have him as guest at my table; then
I would give him a rest, and a remarkably quiet time.

In one way there was a difference between his table and mine
—for instance, atmosphere; the guests stood in awe of him, and
naturally they conferred that feeling upon me, for, after all,
I am only human, although I regret it.  When a guest answered a
question he did it with deferential voice and manner; he did
not put any emotion into it, and he did not spin it out, but
got it out of his system as quickly as he could, and then looked
relieved.  The Emperor was used to this atmosphere, and it did
not chill his blood; maybe it was an inspiration to him, for he
was alert, brilliant and full of animation; also he was most
gracefully and felicitously complimentary to my books,—and I
will remark here that the happy phrasing of a compliment is one
of the rarest of human gifts, and the happy delivery of it another.  In that other chapter I mentioned the high compliment
which he paid to the book, " Old Times on the Mississippi," but
there were others; among them some gratifying praise of my
description in " A Tramp Abroad " of certain striking phases
of German student life.  I mention these things here because I
shall have occasion to hark back to them presently.

[*Dictated Tuesday, February 12, 1907.*]

*      *      *      *      *      *      *      *      *

Those stars indicate the long chapter which I dictated yesterday,
a chapter which is much too long for magazine purposes, and therefore must wait until this Autobiography shall appear in book form,
five years hence, when I am dead: five years according to my calculation, twenty-seven years according to the prediction furnished me
a week ago by the latest and most confident of all the palmists who
have ever read my future in my hand.  The Emperor's dinner,
and its beer-and-anecdote appendix, covered six hours of diligent

industry, and this accounts for the extraordinary length of that chapter.

A couple of days ago a gentleman called upon me with a message. He had just arrived from Berlin, where he had been acting for our Government in a matter concerning tariff revision, he being a member of the commission appointed by our Government to conduct our share of the affair. Upon the completion of the commission's labors, the Emperor invited the members of it to an audience, and in the course of the conversation he made a reference to me; continuing, he spoke of my chapter on the German language in " A Tramp Abroad," and characterized it by an adjective which is too complimentary for me to repeat here without bringing my modesty under suspicion. Then he paid some compliments to " The Innocents Abroad," and followed these with the remark that my account in one of my books of certain striking phases of German student life was the best and truest that had ever been written. By this I perceive that he remembers that dinner of sixteen years ago, for he said the same thing to me about the student-chapter at that time. Next he said he wished this gentleman to convey two messages to America from him and deliver them—one to the President, the other to me. The wording of the message to me was:

" Convey to Mr. Clemens my kindest regards. Ask him if he remembers that dinner, and ask him why he didn't do any talking."

Why, how could I talk when he was talking? He " held the age," as the poker-clergy say, and two can't talk at the same time with good effect. It reminds me of the man who was reproached by a friend, who said,

" I think it a shame that you have not spoken to your wife for fifteen years. How do you explain it? How do you justify it?"

That poor man said,

" I didn't want to interrupt her."

If the Emperor had been at my table, he would not have suffered from my silence, he would only have suffered from the sorrows of his own solitude. If I were not too old to travel I would go to Berlin and introduce the etiquette of my own table, which tallies with the etiquette observable at other royal tables. I would say, " Invite me again, your Majesty, and give me a chance "; then I would courteously waive rank and do all the talking myself. I thank his Majesty for his kind message, and am proud to have it and glad to express my sincere reciprocation of its sentiments.

[*Dictated January 17, 1906.*] . . . Rev. Joseph T. Harris and I have been visiting General Sickles. Once, twenty or twenty-five years ago, just as Harris was coming out of his gate Sunday morning to walk to his church and preach, a telegram was put into his hand. He read it immediately, and then, in a manner, collapsed. It said: " General Sickles died last night at midnight." [He had been a chaplain under Sickles through the war.]

It wasn't so. But no matter — it was so to Harris at the time. He walked along—walked to the church—but his mind **(1880.)** was far away. All his affection and homage and worship of his General had come to the fore. His heart was full of these emotions. He hardly knew where he was. In his pulpit, he stood up and began the service, but with a voice over which he had almost no command. The congregation had never seen him thus moved, before, in his pulpit. They sat there and gazed at him and wondered what was the matter; because he was now reading, in this broken voice and with occasional tears trickling down his face, what to them seemed a quite unemotional chapter—that one about Moses begat Aaron, and Aaron begat Deuteronomy, and Deuteronomy begat St. Peter, and St. Peter begat Cain, and Cain begat Abel—and he was going along with this, and half crying—his voice continually breaking. The congregation left the church that morning without being able to account for this most extraordinary thing—as it seemed to them. That a man who had been a soldier for more than four years, and who had preached in that pulpit so many, many times on really moving subjects, without even the quiver of a lip, should break all down over the Begats, they couldn't understand. But there it is—any one can see how such a mystery as that would arouse the curiosity of those people to the boiling-point.

Harris has had many adventures. He has more adventures in a year than anybody else has in five. One Saturday night he noticed a bottle on his uncle's dressing-bureau. He thought the label said " Hair Restorer," and he took it in his room and gave his head a good drenching and sousing with it and carried it back and thought no more about it. Next morning when he got up his head was a bright green! He sent around everywhere and couldn't get a substitute preacher, so he had to go to his church himself and preach—and he did it. He hadn't a sermon in his barrel—as it happened—of any lightsome character, so he had to preach a very grave one—a very serious one—and it made the matter worse. The gravity of the sermon did not harmonize with the gayety of his head, and the people sat all through it with handkerchiefs stuffed in their mouths to try to keep down their joy. And Harris told me that he was sure he never had seen his congregation—the whole body of his congregation—the *entire* body of his congregation—absorbed in interest in his sermon, from beginning to end, before. Always there had been an aspect of indifference, here and there, or wandering, somewhere; but this time there was nothing of the kind. Those people sat there as if they thought, "Good for this day and train only: we must have all there is of this show, not waste any of it." And he said that when he came down out of the pulpit more people waited to shake him by the hand and tell him what a good sermon it was, than ever before. And it seemed a pity that these people should do these fictions in such a place—right in the church—when it was quite plain they were not interested in the sermon at all; they only wanted to get a near view of his head.

Well, Harris said—no, Harris didn't say, I say, that as the days went on and Sunday followed Sunday, the interest in Harris's hair grew and grew; because it didn't stay merely and monotonously green, it took on deeper and deeper shades of green; and then it would change and become reddish, and would go from that to some other color—purplish, yellowish, bluish, and so on—but it was never a solid color. It was always mottled. And each Sunday it was a little more interesting than it was the Sunday before—and Harris's head became famous, and people came from New York, and Boston, and South Carolina, and Japan, and so on, to look. There wasn't seating-capacity for all the people that came while his head was undergoing these various and fascinating mottlings. And it was a good thing in several ways, because the business had been languishing a little, and now a lot of people joined the church so that they could have the show, and it was the beginning of a prosperity for that church which has never diminished in all these years.

MARK TWAIN.

*(To be Continued.)*

# Chapter XV

April 5, 1907. Pages 673–82.

PREFATORY NOTE.—Mr. Clemens began to write his autobiography many years ago, and he continues to add to it day by day. It was his original intention to permit no publication of his memoirs until after his death; but, after leaving "Pier No. 70," he concluded that a considerable portion might now suitably be given to the public. It is that portion, garnered from the quarter-million of words already written, which will appear in this REVIEW during the coming year. No part of the autobiography will be published in book form during the lifetime of the author.—EDITOR N. A. R.

[*Dictated October 8, 1906.*]

*From Susy's Biography of Me.*

**Papa says that if the collera comes here he will take Sour Mash to the mountains.**

This remark about the cat is followed by various entries, covering a month, in which Jean, General Grant, the sculptor Gerhardt, Mrs. Candace Wheeler, Miss Dora Wheeler, Mr. Frank Stockton, Mrs. Mary Mapes Dodge, and the widow of General Custer appear and drift in procession across the page, then vanish forever from the Biography; then Susy drops this remark in the wake of the vanished procession:

**(1885.)**

Sour Mash is a constant source of anxiety, care, and pleasure to papa.

I did, in truth, think a great deal of that old tortoise-shell harlot; but I haven't a doubt that in order to impress Susy I was pretending agonies of solicitude which I didn't honestly feel. Sour Mash never gave me any real anxiety; she was always able to take care of herself, and she was ostentatiously vain of the fact; vain of it to a degree which often made me ashamed of her, much as I esteemed her.

Many persons would like to have the society of cats during the summer vacation in the country, but they deny themselves this pleasure because they think they must either take the cats along when they return to the city, where they would be a trouble and an encumbrance, or leave them in the country, houseless and homeless. These people have no ingenuity, no invention, no wisdom; or it would occur to them to do as I do: rent cats by the month for the summer and return them to their good homes at the end of it. Early last May I rented a kitten of a farmer's wife, by the month; then I got a discount by taking three. They have been good company for about five months now, and are still kittens—at least they have not grown much, and to all intents and purposes are still kittens, and as full of romping energy and enthusiasm as they were in the beginning. This is remarkable. I am an expert in cats, but I have not seen a kitten keep its kittenhood nearly so long before.

These are beautiful creatures—these triplets. Two of them wear the blackest and shiniest and thickest of sealskin vestments all over their bodies except the lower half of their faces and the terminations of their paws. The black masks reach down below the eyes, therefore when the eyes are closed they are not visible; the rest of the face, and the gloves and stockings, are snow white. These markings are just the same on both cats—so exactly the same that when you call one the other is likely to answer, because they cannot tell each other apart. Since the cats are precisely alike, and can't be told apart by any of us, they do not need two names, so they have but one between them. We call both of them Sackcloth, and we call the gray one Ashes. I believe I have never seen such intelligent cats as these before. They are full of the nicest discriminations. When I read German aloud they weep; you can see the tears run down. It shows what pathos there is in the German tongue. I had not noticed before

that all German is pathetic, no matter what the subject is nor
how it is treated. It was these humble observers that brought
the knowledge to me. I have tried all kinds of German on
these cats; romance, poetry, philosophy, theology, market reports;
and the result has always been the same—the cats sob, and let
the tears run down, which shows that all German is pathetic.
French is not a familiar tongue to me, and the pronunciation is
difficult, and comes out of me encumbered with a Missouri accent;
but the cats like it, and when I make impassioned speeches in
that language they sit in a row and put up their paws, palm to
palm, and frantically give thanks. Hardly any cats are affected
by music, but these are; when I sing they go reverently away,
showing how deeply they feel it. Sour Mash never cared for
these things. She had many noble qualities, but at bottom she was
not refined, and cared little or nothing for theology and the arts.

It is a pity to say it, but these cats are not above the grade of
human beings, for I know by certain signs that they are not
sincere in their exhibitions of emotion, but exhibit them merely
to show off and attract attention—conduct which is distinctly
human, yet with a difference: they do not know enough to conceal
their desire to show off, but the grown human being does. What
is ambition? It is only the desire to be conspicuous. The desire
for fame is only the desire to be continuously conspicuous and
attract attention and be talked about.

These cats are like human beings in another way: when Ashes
began to work his fictitious emotions, and show off, the other
members of the firm followed suit, in order to be in the fashion.
That is the way with human beings; they are afraid to be outside;
whatever the fashion happens to be, they conform to it, whether
it be a pleasant fashion or the reverse, they lacking the courage
to ignore it and go their own way. All human beings would
like to dress in loose and comfortable and highly colored and
showy garments, and they had their desire until a century ago,
when a king, or some other influential ass, introduced sombre
hues and discomfort and ugly designs into masculine clothing.
The meek public surrendered to the outrage, and by consequence
we are in that odious captivity to-day, and are likely to remain in
it for a long time to come.

Fortunately the women were not included in the disaster, and
so their graces and their beauty still have the enhancing help

of delicate fabrics and varied and beautiful colors. Their clothing makes a great opera audience an enchanting spectacle, a delight to the eye and the spirit, a Garden of Eden for charm and color. The men, clothed in dismal black, are scattered here and there and everywhere over the Garden, like so many charred stumps, and they damage the effect, but cannot annihilate it.

In summer we poor creatures have a respite, and may clothe ourselves in white garments; loose, soft, and in some degree shapely; but in the winter—the sombre winter, the depressing winter, the cheerless winter, when white clothes and bright colors are especially needed to brighten our spirits and lift them up—we all conform to the prevailing insanity, and go about in dreary black, each man doing it because the others do it, and not because he wants to. They are really no sincerer than Sackcloth and Ashes. At bottom the Sackcloths do not care to exhibit their emotions when I am performing before them, they only do it because Ashes started it.

I would like to dress in a loose and flowing costume made all of silks and velvets, resplendent with all the stunning dyes of the rainbow, and so would every sane man I have ever known; but none of us dares to venture it. There is such a thing as carrying conspicuousness to the point of discomfort; and if I should appear on Fifth Avenue on a Sunday morning, at church-time, clothed as I would like to be clothed, the churches would be vacant, and I should have all the congregations tagging after me, to look, and secretly envy, and publicly scoff. It is the way human beings are made; they are always keeping their real feelings shut up inside, and publicly exploiting their fictitious ones.

Next after fine colors, I like plain white. One of my sorrows, when the summer ends, is that I must put off my cheery and comfortable white clothes and enter for the winter into the depressing captivity of the shapeless and degrading black ones. It is mid-October now, and the weather is growing cold up here in the New Hampshire hills, but it will not succeed in freezing me out of these white garments, for here the neighbors are few, and it is only of crowds that I am afraid. I made a brave experiment, the other night, to see how it would feel to shock a crowd with these unseasonable clothes, and also to see how long it might take the crowd to reconcile itself to them and stop looking astonished and outraged. On a stormy evening I made a talk before a full house, in the village, clothed like a ghost, and looking as conspicuously, all solitary and alone on that platform, as any ghost could have looked; and I found, to my gratification, that it took the house less than ten minutes to forget about the ghost and give its attention to the tidings I had brought.

I am nearly seventy-one, and I recognize that my age has given me a good many privileges; valuable privileges; privileges which are not granted to younger persons. Little by little I hope to get together courage enough to wear white clothes all through the winter, in New York. It will be a great satisfaction to me to show off in this way; and perhaps the largest of all the satisfactions will be the knowledge that every scoffer, of my sex, will secretly envy me and wish he dared to follow my lead.

That mention that I have acquired new and great privileges by grace of my age, is not an uncalculated remark. When I passed the seventieth mile-stone, ten months ago, I instantly realized that I had entered a new country and a new atmosphere. To all the public I was become recognizably old, undeniably old; and from that moment everybody assumed a new attitude toward me— the reverent attitude granted by custom to age—and straightway the stream of generous new privileges began to flow in upon me and refresh my life. Since then, I have lived an ideal existence; and I now believe what Choate said last March, and which at the time I didn't credit: that the best of life begins at seventy; for then your work is done; you know that you have done your best, let the quality of the work be what it may; that you have earned your holiday—a holiday of peace and contentment—and that thenceforth, to the setting of your sun, nothing will break it, nothing interrupt it.

[*Dictated January 22, 1907.*] In an earlier chapter I inserted some verses beginning " Love Came at Dawn " which had been found among Susy's papers after her death. I was not able to say that they were hers, but I judged that they might be, for the reason that she had not enclosed them in quotation marks according to her habit when storing up treasures gathered from other people. Stedman was not able to determine the authorship for me, as the verses were new to him, but the authorship has now been traced. The verses were written by William Wilfred Campbell, a Canadian poet, and they form a part of the contents of his book called " Beyond the Hills of Dream."

The authorship of the beautiful lines which my wife and I inscribed upon Susy's gravestone was untraceable for a time. We had found them in a book in India, but had lost the book and with it the author's name. But in time an application to the editor of " Notes and Queries " furnished me the author's name,* and it has been added to the verses upon the gravestone.

Last night, at a dinner-party where I was present, Mr. Peter Dunne Dooley handed to the host several dollars, in satisfaction of a lost bet. I seemed to see an opportunity to better my condition, and I invited Dooley, apparently disinterestedly, to come to my house Friday and play billiards. He accepted, and I judge that there is going to be a deficit in the Dooley treasury as a result. In great qualities of the heart and brain, Dooley is gifted beyond all propriety. He is brilliant; he is an expert with his pen, and he easily stands at the head of all the satirists of this generation—but he is going to walk in darkness Friday afternoon. It will be a fraternal kindness to teach him that with all his light and culture, he does not know all the valuable things; and it will also be a fraternal kindness to him to complete his education for him—and I shall do this on Friday, and send him home in that perfected condition.

I possess a billiard secret which can be valuable to the Dooley sept, after I shall have conferred it upon Dooley—for a consideration. It is a discovery which I made by accident, thirty-eight years ago, in my father-in-law's house in Elmira. There was a scarred and battered and ancient billiard-table in the garret, and along with it a peck of checked and chipped balls, and a rackful of crooked and headless cues. I played solitaire up there every day with that difficult outfit. The table was not level, but slanted sharply to the southeast; there wasn't a ball that was round, or would complete the journey you started it on, but would always get tired and stop half-way and settle, with a jolty wabble, to a standstill on its chipped side. I tried making counts with four balls, but found it difficult and discouraging, so I added a fifth ball, then a sixth, then a seventh, and kept on adding until at last I had twelve balls on the table and a thirteenth to play with. My game was caroms—caroms solely—caroms plain, or caroms with cushion to help—anything that could furnish a count. In the course of time I found to my astonishment that I was never

* Robert Richardson, deceased, of Australia.

able to run fifteen, under any circumstances.  By huddling the
balls advantageously in the beginning, I could now and then
coax fourteen out of them, but I couldn't reach fifteen by either
luck or skill.  Sometimes the balls would get scattered into difficult positions and defeat me in that way; sometimes if I managed to keep them together, I would freeze; and always when I
froze, and had to play away from the contact, there was sure to be
nothing to play at but a wide and uninhabited vacancy.

One day Mr. Dalton called on my brother-in-law, on a matter
of business, and I was asked if I could entertain him awhile, until my brother-in-law should finish an engagement with another
gentleman.  I said I could, and took him up to the billiard-table.
I had played with him many times at the club, and knew that
he could play billiards tolerably well—only tolerably well—but
not any better than I could.  He and I were just a match.  He
didn't know our table; he didn't know those balls; he didn't
know those warped and headless cues; he didn't know the south-
eastern slant of the table, and how to allow for it.  I judged it
would be safe and profitable to offer him a bet on my scheme.  I
emptied the avalanche of thirteen balls on the table and said:

" Take a ball and begin, Mr. Dalton.  How many can you run
with an outlay like that?"

He said, with the half-affronted air of a mathematician who
has been asked how much of the multiplication table he can
recite without a break:

" I suppose a million—eight hundred thousand, anyway."

I said " You shall have the privilege of placing the balls to
suit yourself, and I want to bet you a dollar that you can't run
fifteen."

I will not dwell upon the sequel.  At the end of an hour his
face was red, and wet with perspiration; his outer garments lay
scattered here and there over the place; he was the angriest man
in the State, and there wasn't a rag or remnant of an injurious
adjective left in him anywhere—and I had all his small change.

When the summer was over, we went home to Hartford, and one
day Mr. George Robertson arrived from Boston with two or three
hours to spare between then and the return train, and as he
was a young gentleman to whom we were in debt for much
social pleasure, it was my duty, and a welcome duty, to make his
two or three hours interesting for him.  So I took him up-stairs

and set up my billiard scheme for his comfort. Mine was a good table, in perfect repair; the cues were in perfect condition; the balls were ivory, and flawless—but I knew that Mr. Robertson was my prey, just the same, for by exhaustive tests with this outfit I had found that my limit was thirty-one. I had proved to my satisfaction that whereas I could not fairly expect to get more than six or eight or a dozen caroms out of a run, I could now and then reach twenty and twenty-five, and after a long procession of failures finally achieve a run of thirty-one; but in no case had I ever got beyond thirty-one. Robertson's game, as I knew, was a little better than mine, so I resolved to require him to make thirty-two. I believed it would entertain him. He was one of these brisk and hearty and cheery and self-satisfied young fellows who are brimful of confidence, and who plunge with grateful eagerness into any enterprise that offers a showy test of their abilities. I emptied the balls on the table and said,

"Take a cue and a ball, George, and begin. How many caroms do you think you can make out of that layout?"

He laughed the laugh of the gay and the care-free, as became his youth and inexperience, and said,

"I can punch caroms out of that bunch a week without a break."

I said "Place the balls to suit yourself, and begin."

Confidence is a necessary thing in billiards, but overconfidence is bad. George went at his task with much too much lightsomeness of spirit and disrespect for the situation. On his first shot he scored three caroms; on his second shot he scored four caroms; and on his third shot he missed as simple a carom as could be devised. He was very much astonished, and said he would not have supposed that careful play could be needed with an acre of bunched balls in front of a person.

He began again, and played more carefully, but still with too much lightsomeness; he couldn't seem to learn to take the situation seriously. He made about a dozen caroms and broke down. He was irritated with himself now, and he thought he caught me laughing. He didn't. I do not laugh publicly at my client when this game is going on; I only do it inside—or save it for after the exhibition is over. But he thought he had caught me laughing, and it increased his irritation. Of course I knew he thought I was laughing privately—for I was experienced; they all think that, and it has a good effect; it sharpens their annoyance and debilitates their play.

He made another trial and failed. Once more he was astonished; once more he was humiliated—and as for his anger, it rose to summer-heat. He arranged the balls again, grouping them carefully, and said he would win this time, or die. When a client reaches this condition, it is a good time to damage his nerve further, and this can always be done by saying some little mocking thing or other that has the outside appearance of a friendly remark—so I employed this art. I suggested that a bet might tauten his nerves, and that I would offer one, but that as I did not want it to be an expense to him, but only a help, I would make it small—a cigar, if he were willing—a cigar that he would fail again; not an expensive one, but a cheap native one, of the Crown Jewel breed, such as is manufactured in Hartford for the clergy. It set him afire all over! I could see the blue flame issue from his eyes. He said,

"Make it a hundred!—and no Connecticut cabbage-leaf product, but Havana, $25 the box!"

I took him up, but said I was sorry to see him do this, because it did not seem to me right or fair for me to rob him under our own roof, when he had been so kind to us. He said, with energy and acrimony:

"You take care of your own pocket, if you'll be so good, and leave me to take care of mine."

And he plunged at the congress of balls with a vindictiveness which was infinitely contenting to me. He scored a failure—and began to undress. I knew it would come to that, for he was in the condition now that Mr. Dooley will be in at about that stage of the contest on Friday afternoon. A clothes-rack will be provided for Mr. Dooley to hang his things on as fast as he shall from time to time shed them. George raised his voice four degrees and flung out the challenge—

"Double or quits!"

"Done," I responded, in the gentle and compassionate voice of one who is apparently getting sorrier and sorrier.

There was an hour and a half of straight disaster after that, and if it was a sin to enjoy it, it is no matter—I did enjoy it. It is half a lifetime ago, but I enjoy it yet, every time I think of it. George made failure after failure. His fury increased with each failure as he scored it. With each defeat he flung off one or another rag of his raiment, and every time he started on a fresh inning he made it "double or quits" once more. Twice he reached thirty and broke down; once he reached thirty-one and broke down. These "nears" made him frantic, and I believe I was never so happy in my life, except the time, a few years later, when the Rev. J. H. Twichell and I walked to Boston and he had the celebrated conversation with the hostler at the Inn at Ashford, Connecticut.

At last, when we were notified that Patrick was at the door to drive him to his train, George owed me five thousand cigars at twenty-five cents apiece, and I was so sorry I could have hugged him. But he shouted,

"Give me ten minutes more!" and added stormily, "it's double or quits again, and I'll win out free of debt or owe you ten thousand cigars, and you'll pay the funeral expenses."

He began on his final effort, and I believe that in all my experience among both amateurs and experts, I have never seen a cue so carefully handled in my lifetime as George handled his upon this intensely interesting occasion. He got safely up to twenty-five, and then ceased to breathe. So did I. He labored along, and added a point, another point, still another point, and finally reached thirty-one. He stopped there, and we took a breath. By this time the balls were scattered all down the cushions, about a foot or two apart, and there wasn't a shot in sight anywhere that any man might hope to make. In a burst of anger and confessed defeat, he sent his ball flying around the table at random, and it crotched a ball that was packed against the cushion and sprang across to a ball against the bank on the opposite side, and counted!

His luck had set him free, and he didn't owe me anything. He had used up all his spare time, but we carried his clothes to the carriage, and he dressed on his way to the station, greatly wondered at and admired by the ladies, as he drove along—but he got his train.

I am very fond of Mr. Dooley, and shall await his coming with affectionate and pecuniary interest.

*P.S. Saturday.* He has been here. Let us not talk about it.

MARK TWAIN.

*(To be Continued.)*

# Chapter XVI

## April 19, 1907. Pages 785–93.

PREFATORY NOTE.—Mr. Clemens began to write his autobiography many years ago, and he continues to add to it day by day. It was his original intention to permit no publication of his memoirs until after his death; but, after leaving "Pier No. 70," he concluded that a considerable portion might now suitably be given to the public. It is that portion, garnered from the quarter-million of words already written, which will appear in this REVIEW during the coming year. No part of the autobiography will be published in book form during the lifetime of the author.—EDITOR N. A. R.

[*Dictated January 12th, 1905.*] . . . But I am used to having my statements discounted. My mother began it before I was seven years old. Yet all through my life my facts have had a substratum of truth, and therefore they were not without preciousness. Any person who is familiar with me knows how to strike my average, and therefore knows how to get at the jewel of any fact of mine and dig it out of its blue-clay matrix. My mother knew that art. When I was seven or eight, or ten, or twelve years old—along there—a neighbor said to her,

"Do you ever believe anything that that boy says?"

My mother said,

" He is the well-spring of truth, but you can't bring up the whole well with one bucket "—and she added, " I know his average, therefore he never deceives me. I discount him thirty per cent. for embroidery, and what is left is perfect and priceless truth, without a flaw in it anywhere."

Now to make a jump of forty years, without breaking the connection: that word " embroidery " was used again in my presence and concerning me, when I was fifty years old, one night at Rev. Frank Goodwin's house in Hartford, at a meeting of the Monday Evening Club. The Monday Evening Club still exists. It was founded about forty-five years ago by that theological giant, Rev. Dr. Bushnell, and some comrades of his, men of large intellectual calibre and more or less distinction, local or national. I was admitted to membership in it in the fall of 1871 and was an active member thenceforth until I left Hartford in the summer of 1891. The membership was restricted, in those days, to eighteen—possibly twenty. The meetings began about the 1st of October and were held in the private houses of the members every fortnight thereafter throughout the cold months until the 1st of May. Usually there were a dozen members present—sometimes as many as fifteen. There was an essay and a discussion. The essayists followed each other in alphabetical order through the season. The essayist could choose his own subject and talk twenty minutes on it, from MS. or orally, according to his preference. Then the discussion followed, and each member present was allowed ten minutes in which to express his views. The wives of these people were always present. It was their privilege. It was also their privilege to keep still; they were not allowed to throw any light upon the discussion. After the discussion there was a supper, and talk, and cigars. This supper began at ten o'clock promptly, and the company broke up and went away at midnight. At least they did except upon one occasion. In my recent Birthday speech I remarked upon the fact that I have always bought cheap cigars, and that is true. I have never bought costly ones.

Well, that night at the Club meeting—as I was saying—George, our colored butler, came to me when the supper was nearly over, and I noticed that he was pale. Normally his complexion was a clear black, and very handsome, but now it had modified to old amber. He said:

" Mr. Clemens, what are we going to do?  There is not a cigar in the house but those old Wheeling long nines.  Can't nobody smoke them but you.  They kill at thirty yards.  It is too late to telephone—we couldn't get any cigars out from town —what can we do?  Ain't it best to say nothing, and let on that we didn't think?"

" No," I said, " that would not be honest.  Fetch out the long nines "—which he did.

I had just come across those " long nines " a few days or a week before.  I hadn't seen a long nine for years.  When I was a cub pilot on the Mississippi in the late '50's, I had had a great affection for them, because they were not only—to my mind— perfect, but you could get a basketful of them for a cent—or a dime, they didn't use cents out there in those days.  So when I saw them advertised in Hartford I sent for a thousand at once. They came out to me in badly battered and disreputable-looking old square pasteboard boxes, two hundred in a box.  George brought a box, which was caved in on all sides, looking the worst it could, and began to pass them around.  The conversation had been brilliantly animated up to that moment—but now a frost fell upon the company.  That is to say, not all of a sudden, but the frost fell upon each man as he took up a cigar and held it poised in the air—and there, in the middle, his sentence broke off.  That kind of thing went on all around the table, until when George had completed his crime the whole place was full of a thick solemnity and silence.

Those men began to light the cigars.  Rev. Dr. Parker was the first man to light.  He took three or four heroic whiffs—then gave it up.  He got up with the remark that he had to go to the bedside of a sick parishioner.  He started out.  Rev. Dr. Burton was the next man.  He took only one whiff, and followed Parker.  He furnished a pretext, and you could see by the sound of his voice that he didn't think much of the pretext, and was vexed with Parker for getting in ahead with a fictitious ailing client.  Rev. Mr. Twichell followed, and said he had to go now because he must take the midnight train for Boston.  Boston was the first place that occurred to him, I suppose.

It was only a quarter to eleven when they began to distribute pretexts.  At ten minutes to eleven all those people were out of the house.  When nobody was left but George and me I was cheerful—I had no compunctions of conscience, no griefs of any kind. But George was beyond speech, because he held the honor and credit of the family above his own, and he was ashamed that this smirch had been put upon it. I told him to go to bed and try to sleep it off. I went to bed myself. At breakfast in the morning when George was passing a cup of coffee, I saw it tremble in his hand. I knew by that sign that there was something on his mind. He brought the cup to me and asked impressively,

" Mr. Clemens, how far is it from the front door to the upper gate?"

I said, " It is a hundred and twenty-five steps."

He said, " Mr. Clemens, you can start at the front door and you can go plumb to the upper gate and tread on one of them cigars every time."

It wasn't true in detail, but in essentials it was.

The subject under discussion on the night in question was Dreams. The talk passed from mouth to mouth in the usual serene way.

I do not now remember what form my views concerning dreams took at the time. I don't remember now what my notion about dreams was then, but I do remember telling a dream by way of illustrating some detail of my speech, and I also remember that when I had finished it Rev. Dr. Burton made that doubting remark which contained that word I have already spoken of as having been uttered by my mother, in some such connection, forty or fifty years before. I was probably engaged in trying to make those people believe that now and then, by some accident, or otherwise, a dream which was prophetic turned up in the dreamer's mind. The date of my memorable dream was about the beginning of May, 1858. It was a remarkable dream, and I had been telling it several times every year for more than fifteen years— and now I was telling it again, here in the club.

In 1858 I was a steersman on board the swift and popular New Orleans and St. Louis packet, " Pennsylvania," Captain Kleinfelter. I had been lent to Mr. Brown, one of the pilots of the " Pennsylvania," by my owner, Mr. Horace E. Bixby, and I had been steering for Brown about eighteen months, I think. Then in the early days of May, 1858, came a tragic trip—the last trip of that fleet and famous steamboat. I have told all about it in one of my books called " Old Times on the Mississippi."

But it is not likely that I told the dream in that book. It is impossible that I can ever have published it, I think, because I never wanted my mother to know about the dream, and she lived several years after I published that volume.

I had found a place on the "Pennsylvania" for my brother Henry, who was two years my junior. It was not a place of profit, it was only a place of promise. He was "mud" clerk. Mud clerks received no salary, but they were in the line of promotion. They could become, presently, third clerk and second clerk, then chief clerk—that is to say, purser. The dream begins when Henry had been mud clerk about three months. We were lying in port at St. Louis. Pilots and steersmen had nothing to do during the three days that the boat lay in port in St. Louis and New Orleans, but the mud clerk had to begin his labors at dawn and continue them into the night, by the light of pine-knot torches. Henry and I, moneyless and unsalaried, had billeted ourselves upon our brother-in-law, Mr. Moffet, as night lodgers while in port. We took our meals on board the boat. No, I mean *I* lodged at the house, not Henry. He spent the *evenings* at the house, from nine until eleven, then went to the boat to be ready for his early duties. On the night of the dream he started away at eleven, shaking hands with the family, and said good-by according to custom. I may mention that hand-shaking as a good-by was not merely the custom of that family, but the custom of the region—the custom of Missouri, I may say. In all my life, up to that time, I had never seen one member of the Clemens family kiss another one—except once. When my father lay dying in our home in Hannibal— the 24th of March, 1847—he put his arm around my sister's neck and drew her down and kissed her, saying "Let me die." I remember that, and I remember the death rattle which swiftly followed those words, which were his last. These good-bys of Henry's were always executed in the family sitting-room on the second floor, and Henry went from that room and down-stairs without further ceremony. But this time my mother went with him to the head of the stairs and said good-by *again*. As I remember it she was moved to this by something in Henry's manner, and she remained at the head of the stairs while he descended. When he reached the door he hesitated, and climbed the stairs and shook hands good-by once more.

In the morning, when I awoke I had been dreaming, and the dream was so vivid, so like reality, that it deceived me, and I thought it *was* real. In the dream I had seen Henry a corpse. He lay in a metallic burial - case. He was dressed in a suit of my clothing, and on his breast lay a great bouquet of flowers, mainly white roses, with a red rose in the centre. The casket stood upon a couple of chairs. I dressed, and moved toward that door, thinking I would go in there and look at it, but I changed my mind. I thought I could not yet bear to meet my mother. I thought I would wait awhile and make some preparation for that ordeal. The house was in Locust Street, a little above 13th, and I walked to 14th, and to the middle of the block beyond, before it suddenly flashed upon me that there was nothing real about this—it was only a dream. I can still feel something of the grateful upheaval of joy of that moment, and I can also still feel the remnant of doubt, the suspicion that maybe it *was* real, after all. I returned to the house almost on a run, flew up the stairs two or three steps at a jump, and rushed into that sitting-room—and was made glad again, for there was no casket there.

We made the usual eventless trip to New Orleans—no, it was not eventless, for it was on the way down that I had the fight with Mr. Brown* which resulted in his requiring that I be left ashore at New Orleans. In New Orleans I always had a job. It was my privilege to watch the freight-piles from seven in the evening until seven in the morning, and get three dollars for it. It was a three-night job and occurred every thirty-five days. Henry always joined my watch about nine in the evening, when his own duties were ended, and we often walked my rounds and chatted together until midnight. This time we were to part, and so the night before the boat sailed I gave Henry some advice. I said, " In case of disaster to the boat, don't lose your head—leave that unwisdom to the passengers—they are competent—they'll attend to it. But you rush for the hurricane-deck, and astern to one of the life-boats lashed aft the wheel-house, and obey the mate's orders—thus you will be useful. When the boat is launch-ed, give such help as you can in getting the women and children into it, and be sure you don't try to get into it yourself. It is summer weather, the river is only a mile wide, as a rule, and

* See " Old Times on the Mississippi."

you can swim that without any trouble." Two or three days afterward the boat's boilers exploded at Ship Island, below Memphis,
early one morning—and what happened afterward I have already
told in "Old Times on the Mississippi." As related there, I
followed the "Pennsylvania" about a day later, on another boat,
and we began to get news of the disaster at every port we touched
at, and so by the time we reached Memphis we knew all about it.

I found Henry stretched upon a mattress on the floor of a
great building, along with thirty or forty other scalded and
wounded persons, and was promptly informed, by some indis-
creet person, that he had inhaled steam; that his body was badly
scalded, and that he would live but a little while; also, I was
told that the physicians and nurses were giving their whole attention to persons who had a chance of being saved. They were
short-handed in the matter of physicians and nurses; and Henry
and such others as were considered to be fatally hurt were re-
ceiving only such attention as could be spared, from time to
time, from the more urgent cases. But Dr. Peyton, a fine and
large-hearted old physician of great reputation in the community,
gave me his sympathy and took vigorous hold of the case, and in
about a week he had brought Henry around. Dr. Peyton never
committed himself with prognostications which might not materialize, but at eleven o'clock one night he told me that Henry
was out of danger, and would get well. Then he said, "At
midnight these poor fellows lying here and there all over this
place will begin to mourn and mutter and lament and make out-
cries, and if this commotion should disturb Henry it will be bad
for him; therefore ask the physician on watch to give him an
eighth of a grain of morphine, but this is not to be done unless
Henry shall show signs that he is being disturbed."

Oh well, never mind the rest of it. The physicians on watch
were young fellows hardly out of the medical college, and they
made a mistake—they had no way of measuring the eighth of a
grain of morphine, so they guessed at it and gave him a vast
quantity heaped on the end of a knife-blade, and the fatal effects
were soon apparent. I think he died about dawn, I don't remember as to that. He was carried to the dead-room and I
went away for a while to a citizen's house and slept off some of
my accumulated fatigue—and meantime something was happening. The coffins provided for the dead were of unpainted white

pine, but in this instance some of the ladies of Memphis had made up a fund of sixty dollars and bought a metallic case, and when I came back and entered the dead-room Henry lay in that open case, and he was dressed in a suit of my clothing. He had borrowed it without my knowledge during our last sojourn in St. Louis; and I recognized instantly that my dream of several weeks before was here exactly reproduced, so far as these details went—and I think I missed one detail; but that one was immediately supplied, for just then an elderly lady entered the place with a large bouquet consisting mainly of white roses, and in the centre of it was a red rose, and she laid it on his breast.

I told the dream there in the Club that night just as I have told it here.

Rev. Dr. Burton swung his leonine head around, focussed me with his eye, and said:

" When was it that this happened ?"

" In June, '58."

" It is a good many years ago. Have you told it several times since ?"

" Yes, I have, a good many times."

" How many ?"

" Why, I don't know how many."

" Well, strike an average. How many times a year do you think you have told it ?"

" Well, I have told it as many as six times a year, possibly oftener."

" Very well, then you've told it, we'll say, seventy or eighty times since it happened ?"

" Yes," I said, " that's a conservative estimate."

" Now then, Mark, a very extraordinary thing happened to me a great many years ago, and I used to tell it a number of times—a good many times—every year, for it was so wonderful that it always astonished the hearer, and that astonishment gave me a distinct pleasure every time. I never suspected that that tale was acquiring any auxiliary advantages through repetition until one day after I had been telling it ten or fifteen years it struck me that either I was getting old, and slow in delivery, or that the tale was longer than it was when it was born. Mark, I diligently and prayerfully examined that tale with this result: that I found that its proportions were now, as nearly as I could make out, one part fact, straight fact, fact pure and undiluted, golden fact, and twenty-four parts embroidery. I never told that tale afterwards—I was never able to tell it again, for I had lost confidence in it, and so the pleasure of telling it was gone, and gone permanently. How much of this tale of yours is embroidery?"

"Well," I said, "I don't know. I don't think any of it is embroidery. I think it is all just as I have stated it, detail by detail."

"Very well," he said, "then it is all right, but I wouldn't tell it any more; because if you keep on, it will begin to collect embroidery sure. The safest thing is to stop now."

That was a great many years ago. And to-day is the first time that I have told that dream since Dr. Burton scared me into fatal doubts about it. No, I don't believe I can say that. I don't believe that I ever really had any doubts whatever concerning the salient points of the dream, for those points are of such a nature that they are *pictures,* and pictures can be remembered, when they are vivid, much better than one can remember remarks and unconcreted facts. Although it has been so many years since I have told that dream, I can see those pictures now just as clearly defined as if they were before me in this room. I have not told the entire dream. There was a good deal more of it. I mean I have not told all that happened in the dream's fulfilment. After the incident in the death-room I may mention one detail, and that is this. When I arrived in St. Louis with the casket it was about eight o'clock in the morning, and I ran to my brother-in-law's place of business, hoping to find him there, but I missed him, for while I was on the way to his office he was on his way from the house to the boat. When I got back to the boat the casket was gone. He had conveyed it out to his house. I hastened thither, and when I arrived the men were just removing the casket from the vehicle to carry it up-stairs. I stopped that procedure, for I did not want my mother to see the dead face, because one side of it was drawn and distorted by the effects of the opium. When I went up-stairs, there stood the two chairs—placed to receive the coffin—just as I had seen them in my dream; and if I had arrived two or three minutes later, the casket would have been resting upon them, precisely as in my dream of several weeks before.                                    MARK TWAIN.

*(To be Continued.)*

# Chapter XVII

May 3, 1907. Pages 1–12.

PREFATORY NOTE.—Mr. Clemens began to write his autobiography many years ago, and he continues to add to it day by day. It was his original intention to permit no publication of his memoirs until after his death; but, after leaving "Pier No. 70," he concluded that a considerable portion might now suitably be given to the public. It is that portion, garnered from the quarter-million of words already written, which will appear in this REVIEW during the coming year. No part of the autobiography will be published in book form during the lifetime of the author.—EDITOR N. A. R.

*From Susy's Biography of Me.*

*Sept. 9, '85.*—Mamma is teaching Jean a little natural history and is making a little collection of insects for her. But mamma does not allow Jean to kill any insects she only collects those insects that are found dead. Mamma has told us all, perticularly Jean, to bring her all the little dead insects that she finds. The other day as we were all sitting at supper Jean broke into the room and ran triumfantly up to Mamma and presented her with a plate full of dead flies. Mamma thanked Jean very enthusiastically although she with difficulty concealed her amusement. Just then Sour Mash entered the room and Jean believing her hungry asked Mamma for permission to give her the flies. Mamma laughingly consented and the flies almost immediately dissapeared.

[*Monday, October 15, 1906.*] Sour Mash's presence indicates that this adventure occurred at Quarry Farm. Susy's Biography interests itself pretty exclusively with historical facts; where they happen is not a matter of much concern to her. When other historians refer to the Bunker Hill Monument they know it is not necessary to mention that that monument is in Boston. Susy recognizes that when she mentions Sour Mash it is not necessary to localize her. To Susy, Sour Mash is the Bunker Hill Monument of Quarry Farm.

Ordinary cats have some partiality for living flies, but none for dead ones; but Susy does not trouble herself to apologize for Sour Mash's eccentricities of taste. This Biography was for *us*, and Susy knew that nothing that Sour Mash might do could startle us or need explanation, we being aware that she was not an ordinary cat, but moving upon a plane far above the prejudices and superstitions which are law to common catdom.

Once in Hartford the flies were so numerous for a time, and so troublesome, that Mrs. Clemens conceived the idea of paying George* a bounty on all the flies he might kill. The children saw an opportunity here for the acquisition of sudden wealth. They supposed that their mother merely wanted to accumulate dead flies, for some æsthetic or scientific reason or other, and they judged that the more flies she could get the happier she would be; so they went into business with George on a commission. Straightway the dead flies began to arrive in such quantities that Mrs. Clemens was pleased beyond words with the success of her idea. Next, she was astonished that one house could furnish so many. She was paying an extravagantly high bounty, and it presently began to look as if by this addition to our expenses we were now probably living beyond our income. After a few days there was peace and comfort; not a fly was discoverable in the house; there wasn't a straggler left. Still, to Mrs. Clemens's surprise, the dead flies continued to arrive by the plateful, and the bounty expense was as crushing as ever. Then she made inquiry, and found that our innocent little rascals had established a Fly Trust, and had hired all the children in the neighborhood to collect flies on a cheap and unburdensome commission.

Mrs. Clemens's experience in this matter was a new one for

* The colored butler.

her, but the governments of the world had tried it, and wept over it, and discarded it, every half-century since man was created. Any Government could have told her that the best way to increase wolves in America, rabbits in Australia, and snakes in India, is to pay a bounty on their scalps. Then every patriot goes to raising them.

*From Susy's Biography of Me.*

*Sept. 10, '85.*—The other evening Clara and I brought down our new soap bubble water and we all blew soap bubles. Papa blew his soap bubles and filled them with tobacco smoke and as the light shone on them they took very beautiful opaline colors. Papa would hold them and then let us catch them in our hand and they felt delightful to the touch the mixture of the smoke and water had a singularly pleasant effect.

It is human life. We are blown upon the world; we float buoyantly upon the summer air a little while, complacently showing off our grace of form and our dainty iridescent colors; then we vanish with a little puff, leaving nothing behind but a memory—and sometimes not even that. I suppose that at those solemn times when we wake in the deeps of the night and reflect, there is not one of us who is not willing to confess that he is really only a soap-bubble, and as little worth the making.

I remember those days of twenty-one years ago, and a certain pathos clings about them. Susy, with her manifold young charms and her iridescent mind, was as lovely a bubble as any we made that day—and as transitory. She passed, as they passed, in her youth and beauty, and nothing of her is left but a heartbreak and a memory. That long-vanished day came vividly back to me a few weeks ago when, for the first time in twenty-one years, I found myself again amusing a child with smoke-charged soap-bubbles.

Susy's next date is November 29th, 1885, the eve of my fiftieth birthday. It seems a good while ago. I must have been rather **(1885.)** young for my age then, for I was trying to tame an old-fashioned bicycle nine feet high. It is to me almost unbelievable, at my present stage of life, that there have really been people willing to trust themselves upon a dizzy and un-stable altitude like that, and that I was one of them. Twichell and I took lessons every day. He succeeded, and became a master of the art of riding that wild vehicle, but I had no gift in that direction and was never able to stay on mine long enough to get any satisfactory view of the planet.  Every time I tried to steal a look at a pretty girl, or any other kind of scenery, that single moment of inattention gave the bicycle the chance it had been waiting for, and I went over the front of it and struck the ground on my head or my back before I had time to realize that something was happening.  I didn't always go over the front way; I had other ways, and practised them all; but no matter which way was chosen for me there was always one monotonous result —the bicycle skinned my leg and leaped up into the air and came down on top of me.  Sometimes its wires were so sprung by this violent performance that it had the collapsed look of an umbrella that had had a misunderstanding with a cyclone.  After each day's practice I arrived at home with my skin hanging in ribbons, from my knees down.  I plastered the ribbons on where they belonged, and bound them there with handkerchiefs steeped in Pond's Extract, and was ready for more adventures next day. It was always a surprise to me that I had so much skin, and that it held out so well.  There was always plenty, and I soon came to understand that the supply was going to remain sufficient for all my needs.  It turned out that I had nine skins, in layers, one on top of the other like the leaves of a book, and some of the doctors said it was quite remarkable.

I was full of enthusiasm over this insane amusement.  My teacher was a young German from the bicycle factory, a gentle, kindly, patient creature, with a pathetically grave face.  He never smiled; he never made a remark; he always gathered me tenderly up when I plunged off, and helped me on again without a word. When he had been teaching me twice a day for three weeks I introduced a new gymnastic—one that he had never seen before— and so at last a compliment was wrung from him, a thing which I had been risking my life for days to achieve.  He gathered me up and said mournfully: " Mr. Clemens, you can fall off a bicycle in more different ways than any person I ever saw before."

A boy's life is not all comedy; much of the tragic enters into it.  The drunken tramp — mentioned in " Tom Sawyer " or " Huck Finn "—who was burned up in the village jail, **(1849.)** lay upon my conscience a hundred nights afterward and filled them with hideous dreams—dreams in which I saw his appealing face as I had seen it in the pathetic reality, pressed against the window-bars, with the red hell glowing behind him

—a face which seemed to say to me, " If you had not give me the matches, this would not have happened; you are responsible for my death." I was *not* responsible for it, for I had meant him no harm, but only good, when I let him have the matches; but no matter, mine was a trained Presbyterian conscience, and knew but the one duty—to hunt and harry its slave upon all pretexts and on all occasions; particularly when there was no sense or reason in it. The tramp—who was to blame—suffered ten minutes; I, who was not to blame, suffered three months.

The shooting down of poor old Smarr in the main street* at noonday supplied me with some more dreams; and in them I always saw again the grotesque closing picture—the great family Bible spread open on the profane old man's breast by some thoughtful idiot, and rising and sinking to the labored breathings, and adding the torture of its leaden weight to the dying struggles. We are curiously made. In all the throng of gaping and sympathetic onlookers there was not one with common sense enough to perceive that an anvil would have been in better taste there than the Bible, less open to sarcastic criticism, and swifter in its atrocious work. In my nightmares I gasped and struggled for breath under the crush of that vast book for many a night.

All within the space of a couple of years we had two or three other tragedies, and I had the ill-luck to be too near by on each occasion. There was the slave man who was struck down with a chunk of slag for some small offence; I saw him die. And the young California emigrant who was stabbed with a bowie knife by a drunken comrade: I saw the red life gush from his breast. And the case of the rowdy young Hyde brothers and their harmless old uncle: one of them held the old man down with his knees on his breast while the other one tried repeatedly to kill him with an Allen revolver which wouldn't go off. I happened along just then, of course.

Then there was the case of the young California emigrant who got drunk and proposed to raid the " Welshman's house " all alone one dark and threatening night.† This house stood halfway up Holliday's Hill (" Cardiff " Hill), and its sole occupants were a poor but quite respectable widow and her young and blameless daughter. The invading ruffian woke the whole village with

---

* See " Adventures of Huckleberry Finn." † Used in " Huck Finn," I think.

his ribald yells and coarse challenges and obscenities. I went
up there with a comrade—John Briggs, I think—to look and
listen. The figure of the man was dimly visible; the women were
on their porch, but not visible in the deep shadow of its roof,
but we heard the elder woman's voice. She had loaded an old
musket with slugs, and she warned the man that if he stayed
where he was while she counted ten it would cost him his life.
She began to count, slowly: he began to laugh. He stopped
laughing at " six "; then through the deep stillness, in a steady
voice, followed the rest of the tale: " seven . . . eight . . .
nine "—a long pause, we holding our breath—" ten !" A red
spout of flame gushed out into the night, and the man dropped,
with his breast riddled to rags. Then the rain and the thunder
burst loose and the waiting town swarmed up the hill in the glare
of the lightning like an invasion of ants. Those people saw the
rest; I had had my share and was satisfied. I went home to
dream, and was not disappointed.

My teaching and training enabled me to see deeper into these
tragedies than an ignorant person could have done. I knew what
they were for. I tried to disguise it from myself, but down in
the secret deeps of my heart I knew—and I *knew* that I knew.
They were inventions of Providence to beguile me to a better life.
It sounds curiously innocent and conceited, now, but to me there
was nothing strange about it; it was quite in accordance with the
thoughtful and judicious ways of Providence as I understood
them. It would not have surprised me, nor even over-flattered
me, if Providence had killed off that whole community in trying
to save an asset like me. Educated as I had been, it would have
seemed just the thing, and well worth the expense. *Why* Providence should take such an anxious interest in such a property—
that idea never entered my head, and there was no one in that
simple hamlet who would have dreamed of putting it there. For
one thing, no one was equipped with it.

It is quite true I took all the tragedies to myself; and tallied
them off, in turn as they happened, saying to myself in each
case, with a sigh, " Another one gone—and on my account; this
ought to bring me to repentance; His patience will not always
endure." And yet privately I believed it would. That is, I
believed it in the daytime; but not in the night. With the going
down of the sun my faith failed, and the clammy fears gathered

about my heart. It was then that I repented. Those were awful nights, nights of despair, nights charged with the bitterness of death. After each tragedy I recognized the warning and repented; repented and begged; begged like a coward, begged like a dog; and not in the interest of those poor people who had been extinguished for my sake, but only in my own interest. It seems selfish, when I look back on it now.

My repentances were very real, very earnest; and after each tragedy they happened every night for a long time. But as a rule they could not stand the daylight. They faded out and shredded away and disappeared in the glad splendor of the sun. They were the creatures of fear and darkness, and they could not live out of their own place. The day gave me cheer and peace, and at night I repented again. In all my boyhood life I am not sure that I ever tried to lead a better life in the daytime—or wanted to. In my age I should never think of wishing to do such a thing. But in my age, as in my youth, night brings me many a deep remorse. I realize that from the cradle up I have been like the rest of the race—never quite sane in the night. When " Injun Joe " died.*. . . But never mind: in another chapter I have already described what a raging hell of repentance I passed through then. I believe that for months I was as pure as the driven snow. After dark.

It was back in those far-distant days—1848 or '9—that Jim Wolf came to us. He was from Shelbyville, a hamlet thirty or forty miles back in the country, and he brought all his native sweetnesses and gentlenesses and simplicities with him. He was approaching seventeen, a grave and slender lad, trustful, honest, a creature to love and cling to. And he was incredibly bashful.

It is to this kind that untoward things happen. My sister gave a " candy-pull " on a winter's night. I was too young to be of the company, and Jim was too diffident. I was sent up to bed early, and Jim followed of his own motion. His room was in the new part of the house, and his window looked out on the roof of the L annex. That roof was six inches deep in snow, and the snow had an ice-crust upon it which was as slick as glass. Out of the comb of the roof projected a short chimney, a common resort for sentimental cats on moonlight nights—and this was a moonlight night. Down at the eaves, below the chimney, a canopy

* Used in " Tom Sawyer."

of dead vines spread away to some posts, making a cozy shelter, and after an hour or two the rollicking crowd of young ladies and gentlemen grouped themselves in its shade, with their saucers of liquid and piping-hot candy disposed about them on the frozen ground to cool. There was joyous chaffing and joking and laughter—peal upon peal of it.

About this time a couple of old disreputable tom-cats got up on the chimney and started a heated argument about something; also about this time I gave up trying to get to sleep, and went visiting to Jim's room. He was awake and fuming about the cats and their intolerable yowling. I asked him, mockingly, why he didn't climb out and drive them away. He was nettled, and said over-boldly that for two cents he *would*.

It was a rash remark, and was probably repented of before it was fairly out of his mouth. But it was too late—he was committed. I knew him; and I knew he would rather break his neck than back down, if I egged him on judiciously.

"Oh, of course you would! Who's doubting it?"

It galled him, and he burst out, with sharp irritation—

"Maybe *you* doubt it!"

"I? Oh no, I shouldn't think of such a thing. You are always doing wonderful things. With your mouth."

He was in a passion, now. He snatched on his yarn socks and began to raise the window, saying in a voice unsteady with anger—

"*You* think I dasn't—*you* do! Think what you blame please —*I* don't care what you think. I'll show you!"

The window made him rage; it wouldn't stay up. I said—

"Never mind, I'll hold it."

Indeed, I would have done anything to help. I was only a boy, and was already in a radiant heaven of anticipation. He climbed carefully out, clung to the window-sill until his feet were safely placed, then began to pick his perilous way on all fours along the glassy comb, a foot and a hand on each side of it. I believe I enjoy it now as much as I did then: yet it is a good deal over fifty years ago. The frosty breeze flapped his short shirt about his lean legs; the crystal roof shone like polished marble in the intense glory of the moon; the unconscious cats sat erect upon the chimney, alertly watching each other, lashing their tails and pouring out their hollow grievances; and slowly and cautiously Jim crept on, flapping as he went, the gay and frolicsome young creatures under the vine-canopy unaware, and outraging these solemnities with their misplaced laughter. Every time Jim slipped I had a hope; but always on he crept and disappointed it. At last he was within reaching distance. He paused, raised himself carefully up, measured his distance deliberately, then made a frantic grab at the nearest cat—and missed. Of course he lost his balance. His heels flew up, he struck on his back, and like a rocket he darted down the roof feet first, crashed through the dead vines and landed in a sitting posture in fourteen saucers of red-hot candy, in the midst of all that party—and dressed as *he* was: this lad who could not look a girl in the face with his clothes on. There was a wild scramble and a storm of shrieks, and Jim fled up the stairs, dripping broken crockery all the way.

The incident was ended. But I was not done with it yet, though I supposed I was. Eighteen or twenty years later I arrived in New York from California, and by that time I had failed in all my other undertakings and had stumbled into literature without intending it. This was early in 1867. I (1867.) was offered a large sum to write something for the " Sunday Mercury," and I answered with the tale of " Jim Wolf and the Cats." I also collected the money for it—twenty-five dollars. It seemed over-pay, but I did not say anything about that, for I was not so scrupulous then as I am now.

A year or two later " Jim Wolf and the Cats " appeared in a Tennessee paper in a new dress—as to spelling; spelling borrowed from Artemus Ward. The appropriator of the tale had a wide reputation in the West, and was exceedingly popular. Deservedly so, I think. He wrote some of the breeziest and funniest things I have ever read, and did his work with distinguished ease and fluency. His name has passed out of my memory.

A couple of years went by; then the original story—my own version — cropped up again and went floating around in the original spelling, and with my name to it. Soon first one paper and then another fell upon me vigorously for " stealing " Jim Wolf and the Cats from the Tennessee man. I got a merciless basting, but I did not mind it. It's all in the game. Besides, I had learned, a good while before that, that it is not wise to keep the fire going under a slander unless you can get some large advantage out of keeping it alive.  Few slanders can stand the wear of silence.

But I was not done with Jim and the Cats yet.  In 1873 I was lecturing in London, in the Queen's Concert Rooms, Han-
**(1873.)** over Square, and was living at the Langham Hotel, Portland Place.  I had no domestic household, and no official household except George Dolby, lecture-agent, and Charles Warren Stoddard, the California poet, now (1900) Professor of
**(1900.)** English Literature in the Roman Catholic University, Washington.  Ostensibly Stoddard was my private secretary; in reality he was merely my comrade—I hired him in order to have his company.  As secretary there was nothing for him to do except to scrap-book the daily reports of the great trial of the Tichborne Claimant for perjury.  But he made a sufficient job out of that, for the reports filled six columns a day and he usually postponed the scrap-booking until Sunday; then he had 36 columns to cut out and paste in—a proper labor for Hercules.  He did his work well, but if he had been older and feebler it would have killed him once a week.  Without doubt he does his literary lectures well, but also without doubt he prepares them fifteen minutes before he is due on his platform and thus gets into them a freshness and sparkle which they might lack if they underwent the staling process of overstudy.

He was good company when he was awake.  He was refined, sensitive, charming, gentle, generous, honest himself and unsuspicious of other people's honesty, and I think he was the purest male I have known, in mind and speech.  George Dolby was something of a contrast to him, but the two were very friendly and sociable together, nevertheless.  Dolby was large and ruddy, full of life and strength and spirits, a tireless and energetic talker, and always overflowing with good-nature and bursting with jollity.  It was a choice and satisfactory menagerie, this pensive poet and this gladsome gorilla.  An indelicate story was a sharp distress to Stoddard; Dolby told him twenty-five a day.  Dolby always came home with us after the lecture, and entertained Stoddard till midnight.  Me too.  After he left, I walked the floor and talked, and Stoddard went to sleep on the sofa.  I hired him for company.

Dolby had been agent for concerts, and theatres, and Charles Dickens and all sorts of shows and " attractions " for many years;

he had known the human being in many aspects, and he didn't much believe in him. But the poet did. The waifs and estrays found a friend in Stoddard: Dolby tried to persuade him that he was dispensing his charities unworthily, but he was never able to succeed.

One night a young American got access to Stoddard at the Concert Rooms and told him a moving tale. He said he was living on the Surrey side, and for some strange reason his remittances had failed to arrive from home; he had no money, he was out of employment, and friendless; his girl-wife and his new baby were actually suffering for food; for the love of heaven could he lend him a sovereign until his remittances should resume? Stoddard was deeply touched, and gave him a sovereign on my account. Dolby scoffed, but Stoddard stood his ground. Each told me his story later in the evening, and I backed Stoddard's judgment. Dolby said we were women in disguise, and not a sane kind of women, either.

The next week the young man came again. His wife was ill with the pleurisy, the baby had the bots, or something, I am not sure of the name of the disease; the doctor and the drugs had eaten up the money, the poor little family was starving. If Stoddard "in the kindness of his heart could only spare him another sovereign," etc., etc. Stoddard was much moved, and spared him a sovereign for me. Dolby was outraged. He spoke up and said to the customer—

"Now, young man, you are going to the hotel with us and state your case to the other member of the family. If you don't make him believe in you I sha'n't honor this poet's drafts in your interest any longer, for I don't believe in you myself."

The young man was quite willing. I found no fault in him. On the contrary, I believed in him at once, and was solicitous to heal the wounds inflicted by Dolby's too frank incredulity; therefore I did everything I could think of to cheer him up and entertain him and make him feel at home and comfortable. I spun many yarns; among others the tale of Jim Wolf and the Cats. Learning that he had done something in a small way in literature, I offered to try to find a market for him in that line. His face lighted joyfully at that, and he said that if I could only sell a small manuscript to Tom Hood's Annual for him it would be the happiest event of his sad life and he would hold me

in grateful remembrance always.  That was a most pleasant night
for three of us, but Dolby was disgusted and sarcastic.

Next week the baby died.  Meantime I had spoken to Tom
Hood and gained his sympathy.  The young man had sent his
manuscript to him, and the very day the child died the money
for the MS. came—three guineas.  The young man came with a
poor little strip of crape around his arm and thanked me, and
said that nothing could have been more timely than that money,
and that his poor little wife was grateful beyond words for the
service I had rendered.  He wept, and in fact Stoddard and I
wept with him, which was but natural.  Also Dolby wept.  At
least he wiped his eyes and wrung out his handkerchief, and
sobbed stertorously and made other exaggerated shows of grief.
Stoddard and I were ashamed of Dolby, and tried to make the
young man understand that he meant no harm, it was only his
way.  The young man said sadly that he was not minding it, his
grief was too deep for other hurts; that he was only thinking of
the funeral, and the heavy expenses which—

We cut that short and told him not to trouble about it, leave it
all to us; send the bills to Mr. Dolby and—

" Yes," said Dolby, with a mock tremor in his voice, " send
them to me, and I will pay them.  What, are you going?  You
must not go alone in your worn and broken condition; Mr. Stoddard and I will go with you.  Come, Stoddard.  We will comfort
the bereaved mamma and get a lock of the baby's hair."

It was shocking.  We were ashamed of him again, and said so.
But he was not disturbed.  He said—

" Oh, I know this kind, the woods are full of them.  I'll make
this offer: if he will show me his family I will give him twenty
pounds.  Come!"  The young man said he would not remain to be
insulted; and he said good-night and took his hat.  But Dolby said
he would go with him, and stay by him until he found the family.
Stoddard went along to soothe the young man and modify Dolby.
They drove across the river and all over Southwark, but did not find
the family.  At last the young man confessed there wasn't any.

The thing he sold to Tom Hood's Annual was " Jim and the
Cats."  And he did not put my name to it.

So that small tale was sold three times.  I am selling it again,
now.  It is one of the best properties I have come across.

*(To be Continued.)*     MARK TWAIN.

# Chapter XVIII

## May 17, 1907. Pages 113–22.

PREFATORY NOTE.—Mr. Clemens began to write his autobiography many years ago, and he continues to add to it day by day. It was his original intention to permit no publication of his memoirs until after his death; but, after leaving "Pier No. 70," he concluded that a considerable portion might now suitably be given to the public. It is that portion, garnered from the quarter-million of words already written, which will appear in this REVIEW during the coming year. No part of the autobiography will be published in book form during the lifetime of the author.—EDITOR N. A. R.

[*Dictated December 21, 1906.*] I wish to insert here some pages of Susy's Biography of me in which the biographer does not scatter, according to her custom, but sticks pretty steadily to a single subject until she has fought it to a finish:

*Feb. 27, '86.*—Last summer while we were in Elmira an article came out in the "Christian Union" by name "What ought he to have done" treating of the government of children, or rather giving an account of a fathers battle with his little baby boy, by the mother of the child and put in the form of a question as to whether the father disciplined the child corectly or not, different people wrote their opinions of the fathers behavior, and told what they thought he should have done. Mamma had long known how to disciplin children, for in fact the bringing up of children had been one of her specialties for many years.

She had a great many theories, but one of them was, that if a child was big enough to be nauty, it was big enough to be whipped and here we all agreed with her. I remember one morning when Dr.—— came up to the farm he had a long discussion with mamma, upon the following topic. Mamma gave *this* as illustrative of one important rule for punishing a child. She said we will suppose the boy has thrown a handkerchief onto the floor, I tell him to pick it up, he refuses. I tell him again, he refuses. Then I say you must either pick up the handkerchief or have a whipping. My theory is never to make a child have a whipping and pick up the handkerchief too. I say "If you do not pick it up, I must punish you," if he doesn't he gets the whipping, but *I* pick up the handkerchief, if he does he gets no punishment. I tell him to do a thing if he disobeys me he is punished for so doing, but not forced to obey me afterwards.

When Clara and I had been very nauty or were being very nauty, the nurse would go and call Mamma and she would appear suddenly and look at us (she had a way of looking at us when she was displeased as if she could see right through us) till we were ready to sink through the floor from embarasment, and total absence of knowing what to say. This look was usually followed with "Clara" or "Susy what do you mean by this? do you want to come to the bathroom with me?" Then followed the climax for Clara and I both new only too well what going to the bath-room meant.

But mamma's first and foremost object was to make the child understand that he is being punished for *his* sake, and because the mother so loves him that she cannot allow him to do wrong; also that it is as hard for her to punish him as for him to be punished and even harder. Mamma never allowed herself to punish us when she was angry with us she never struck us because she was enoyed at us and felt like striking us if we had been nauty and had enoyed her, so that she thought she felt or would show the least bit of temper toward us while punnishing us, she always postponed the punishment until *she* was no more chafed by our behavior. She never humored herself by striking or punishing us because or while she was the least bit enoyed with us.

Our very worst nautinesses were punished by being taken to the bath-room and being whipped by the paper cutter. But after the whipping was over, mamma did not allow us to leave her until we were perfectly happy, and perfectly understood why we had been whipped. I never remember having felt the least bit bitterly toward mamma for punishing me. I always felt I had deserved my punishment, and was much happier for having received it. For after mamma had punished us and shown her displeasure, she showed no signs of further displeasure, but acted as if we had not displeased her in any way.

Ordinary punishments answered very well for Susy. She was a thinker, and would reason out the purpose of them, apply the lesson, and achieve the reform required. But it was much less easy to devise punishments that would reform Clara. This was because she was a philosopher who was always turning her attention to finding something good and satisfactory and entertaining in everything that came her way; consequently it was sometimes pretty discouraging to the troubled mother to find that after all her pains and thought in inventing what she meant to be a severe and reform-compelling punishment, the child had entirely missed the severities through her native disposition to get interest and pleasure out of them as novelties. The mother, in her anxiety to find a penalty that would take sharp hold and do its work effectively, at last resorted, with a sore heart, and with a reproachful conscience, to that punishment which the incorrigible criminal in the penitentiary dreads above all the other punitive miseries which the warden inflicts upon him for his good—solitary confinement in the dark chamber. The grieved and worried mother shut Clara up in a very small clothes-closet and went away and left her there—for fifteen minutes—it was all that the mother-heart could endure. Then she came softly back and listened—listened for the sobs, but there weren't any; there were muffled and inarticulate sounds, but they could not be construed into sobs. The mother waited half an hour longer; by that time she was suffering so intensely with sorrow and compassion for the little prisoner that she was not able to wait any longer for the distressed sounds which she had counted upon to inform her when there had been punishment enough and the reform accomplished. She opened the closet to set the prisoner free and take her back into her loving favor and forgiveness, but the result was not the one expected. The captive had manufactured a fairy cavern out of the closet, and friendly fairies out of the clothes hanging from the hooks, and was having a most sinful and unrepentant good time, and requested permission to spend the rest of the day there!

*From Susy's Biography of Me.*

But Mamma's oppinions and ideas upon the subject of bringing up children has always been more or less of a joke in our family, perticularly since Papa's article in the " Christian Union," and I am sure Clara and I have related the history of our old family paper-cutter, our punishments and privations with rather more pride and triumph than any other sentiment, because of Mamma's way of rearing us.

When the article " What ought he to have done ?" came out Mamma read it, and was very much interested in it. And when papa heard that she had read it he went to work and secretly wrote his opinion of what the father ought to have done.  He told Aunt Susy, Clara and I, about it but mamma was not to see it or hear any thing about it till it came out.  He gave it to Aunt Susy to read, and after Clara and I had gone up to get ready for bed he brought it up for us to read.  He told what he thought the father ought to have done by telling what mamma would have done.  The article was a beautiful tribute to mamma and every word in it true.  But still in writing about mamma he partly forgot that the article was going to be published, I think, and expressed himself more fully than he would do the second time he wrote it; I think the article has done and will do a great deal of good, and I think it would have been perfect for the family and friend's enjoyment, but a little bit too private to have been published as it was.  And Papa felt so too, because the very next day or a few days after, he went down to New York to see if he couldn't get it back before it was published but it was too late, and he had to return without it.  When the Christian Union reached the farm and papa's article in it all ready and waiting to be read to mamma papa hadn't the courage to show it to her (for he knew she wouldn't like it at all) at first, and he didn't but he might have let it go and never let her see it, but finally he gave his consent to her seeing it, and told Clara and I we could take it to her, which we did, with tardiness, and we all stood around mamma while she read it, all wondering what she would say and think about it.

She was too much surprised, (and pleased privately, too) to say much at first, but as we all expected publicly, (or rather when she remembered that this article was to be read by every one that took the Christian Union) she was rather shocked and a little displeased.

Clara and I had great fun the night papa gave it to us to read and then hide, so mamma couldn't see it, for just as we were in the midst of reading it mamma appeared papa following anxiously and asked why we were not in bed? then a scuffle ensued for we told her it was a secret and tried to hide it; but she chased us wherever we went, till she thought it was time for us to go to bed, then she surendered and left us to tuck it under Clara's matress.

A little while after the article was published letters began to come in to papa crittisizing it, there were some very pleasant ones but a few very disagreable.  One of these, the very worst, mamma got hold of and read, to papa's great regret, it was full of the most disagreble things, and so very enoying to papa that he for a time felt he must do something to show the author of it his great displeasure at being so insulted.  But he finally decided not to, because he felt the man had some cause for feeling enoyed at, for papa had spoken of him, (he was the baby's father) rather slightingly in his Christian Union Article.

After all this, papa and mamma both wished I think they might never hear or be spoken to on the subject of the Christian Union article, and whenever any has spoken to me and told me " How much they did enjoy my father's article in the Christian Union " I almost laughed in their faces when I remembered what a great variety of oppinions had been expressed upon the subject of the Christian Union article of papa's.

The article was written in July or August and just the other day papa received quite a bright letter from a gentleman who has read the C. U. article and gave his opinion of it in these words.

It is missing. She probably put the letter between the leaves of the Biography and it got lost out. She threw away the hostile letters, but tried to keep the pleasantest one for her book; surely there has been no kindlier biographer than this one. Yet to a quite creditable degree she is loyal to the responsibilities of her position as historian—not eulogist—and honorably gives me a quiet prod now and then. But how many, many, many she has withheld that I deserved! I could prize them now; there would be no acid in her words, and it is loss to me that she did not set them all down. Oh, Susy, you sweet little biographer, you break my old heart with your gentle charities!

I think a great deal of her work. Her canvases are on their easels, and her brush flies about in a care-free and random way, delivering a dash here, a dash there and another yonder, and one might suppose that there would be no definite result; on the contrary I think that an intelligent reader of her little book must find that by the time he has finished it he has somehow accumulated a pretty clear and nicely shaded idea of the several members of this family—including Susy herself—and that the random dashes on the canvases have developed into portraits. I feel that my own portrait, with some of the defects fined down and others left out, is here; and I am sure that any who knew the mother will recognize her without difficulty, and will say that the lines are drawn with a just judgment and a sure hand. Little creature though Susy was, the penetration which was born in her finds its way to the surface more than once in these pages.

Before Susy began the Biography she let fall a remark now and then concerning my character which showed that she had it under observation. In the Record which we kept of the children's sayings there is an instance of this. She was twelve years old at the time. We had established a rule that each member of the family must bring a fact to breakfast—a fact drawn from a book or from any other source; any fact would answer. Susy's first contribution was in substance as follows. Two great exiles and former opponents in war met in Ephesus—Scipio and Hannibal. Scipio asked Hannibal to name the greatest general the world had produced.

" Alexander "—and he explained why.

" And the next greatest?"

" Pyrrhus "—-and he explained why.

" But where do you place yourself, then?"

" If I had conquered you I would place myself before the others."

Susy's grave comment was—

" That *attracted* me, it was just like papa—he is so frank about his books."

So frank in admiring them, she meant.

[*Thursday, March 28, 1907.*] Some months ago I commented upon a chapter of Susy's Biography wherein she very elaborately discussed an article about the training and disciplining of children, which I had published in the " Christian Union " (this was twenty-one years ago), an article which was full of worshipful praises of Mrs. Clemens as a mother, and which little Clara, and Susy, and I had been hiding from this lovely and admirable mother because we knew she would disapprove of public and printed praises of herself. At the time that I was dictating these comments, several months ago, I was trying to call back to my memory some of the details of that article, but I was not able to do it, and I wished I had a copy of the article so that I could see what there was about it which gave it such large interest for Susy.

Yesterday afternoon I elected to walk home from the luncheon at the St. Regis, which is in 55th Street and Fifth Avenue, for it was a fine spring day and I hadn't had a walk for a year or two, and felt the need of exercise. As I walked along down Fifth Avenue the desire to see that " Christian Union " article came into my head again. I had just reached the corner of 42nd Street then, and there was the usual jam of wagons, carriages, and automobiles there. I stopped to let it thin out before trying to cross the street, but a stranger, who didn't require as much room as I do, came racing by and darted into a crack among the vehicles and made the crossing. But on his way past me he thrust a couple of ancient newspaper clippings into my hand, and said,

" There, you don't know me, but I have saved them in my scrap-book for twenty years, and it occurred to me this morning that perhaps you would like to see them, so I was carrying them down-town to mail them, I not expecting to run across you in this accidental way, of course; but I will give them into your own hands now. Good-by !"—and he disappeared among the wagons.

Those scraps which he had put into my hand were ancient newspaper copies of that " Christian Union " article! It is a handsome instance of mental telegraphy—or if it isn't that, it is a handsome case of coincidence.

*From the Biography.*

*March 14th, '86.*—Mr. Laurence Barrette and Mr. and Mrs. Hutton were here a little while ago, and we had a very interesting visit from them. Papa said Mr. Barette never had acted so well before when he had seen him, as he did the first night he was staying with us. And Mrs.—— said she never had seen an actor on the stage, whom she more wanted to speak with.

Papa has been very much interested of late, in the " Mind Cure " theory. And in fact so have we all. A young lady in town has worked wonders, by using the " Mind Cure " upon people; she is constantly busy now curing peoples deseases in this way—and curing her own even, which to me seems the most remarkable of all.

A little while past, papa was delighted with the knowledge of what he thought the best way of curing a cold, which was by starving it. This starving did work beautifully, and freed him from a great many severe colds. Now he says it wasn't the starving that helped his colds, but the trust in the starving, the mind cure connected with the starving.

I shouldn't wonder if we finally became firm believers in Mind Cure. The next time papa has a cold, I haven't a doubt, he will send for Miss H—— the young lady who is doctoring in the " Mind Cure " theory, to cure him of it.

Mamma was over at Mrs. George Warners to lunch the other day, and Miss H—— was there too. Mamma asked if anything as natural as near sightedness could be cured she said oh yes just as well as other deseases.

When mamma came home, she took me into her room, and told me that perhaps my near-sightedness could be cured by the " Mind Cure " and that she was going to have me try the treatment any way, there could be no harm in it, and there might be great good. If her plan succeeds there certainly will be a great deal in " Mind Cure " to my oppinion, for I am *very* near sighted and so is mamma, and I never expected there could be any more cure for it than for blindness, but now I dont know but what theres a cure for *that*.

It was a disappointment; her near-sightedness remained with

her to the end.   She was born with it, no doubt; yet, strangely
enough, she must have been four years old, and possibly five,
before we knew of its existence.   It is not easy to understand
how that could have happened.   I discovered the defect by accident.   I was half-way up the hall stairs one day at home, and
was leading her by the hand, when I glanced back through the
open door of the dining-room and saw what I thought she would
recognize as a pretty picture.   It was " Stray Kit," the slender,
the graceful, the sociable, the beautiful, the incomparable, the
cat of cats, the tortoise-shell, curled up as round as a wheel and
sound asleep on the fire-red cover of the dining-table, with a
brilliant stream of sunlight falling across her.   I exclaimed about
it, but Susy said she could see nothing there, neither cat nor
table-cloth.   The distance was so slight—not more than twenty
feet, perhaps—that if it had been any other child I should not
have credited the statement.

### From the Biography.

*March 14th, '86.*—Clara sprained her ankle, a little while ago, by
running into a tree, when coasting, and while she was unable to walk
with it she played solotaire with cards a great deal.   While Clara was
sick and papa saw her play solotaire so much, he got very much interested in the game, and finally began to play it himself a little, then
Jean took it up, and at last *mamma*, even played it ocasionally; Jean's
and papa's love for it rapidly increased, and now Jean brings the
cards every night to the table and papa and mamma help her play,
and before dinner is at an end, papa has gotten a separate pack of
cards, and is playing alone, with great interest.   Mamma and Clara
next are made subject to the contagious solatair, and there are four
solotaireans at the table; while you hear nothing but " Fill up the
place " etc.   It is dreadful! after supper Clara goes into the library,
and gets a little red mahogany table, and placing it under the gas
fixture seats herself and begins to play again, then papa follows with
another table of the same discription, and they play solatair till bedtime.

We have just had our Prince and Pauper pictures taken; two groups
and some little single ones.   The groups (the Interview and Lady Jane
Grey scene) were pretty good, the lady Jane scene was perfect, just
as pretty as it could be, the Interview was not so good; and two of
the little single pictures were very good indeed, but one was very bad.
Yet on the whole we think they were a success.

Papa has done a great deal in his life I think, that is good, and very
remarkable, but I think if he had had the advantages with which he
could have developed the gifts which he has made no use of in writing
his books, or in any other way for other peoples pleasure and benefit

outside of his own family and intimate friends, he could have done *more* than he has and a great deal more even. He is known to the public as a humorist, but he has much more in him that is earnest than that is humorous. He has a keen sense of the ludicrous, notices funny stories and incidents knows how to tell them, to improve upon them, and does not forget them. He has been through a great many of the funny adventures related in " Tom Sayer " and in " Huckleberry Finn," *himself* and he lived among just such boys, and in just such villages all the days of his early life. His " Prince and Pauper is his most orriginal, and best production; it shows the most of any of his books what kind of pictures are in his mind, usually. Not that the pictures of England in the 16th Century and the adventures of a little prince and pauper are the kind of things he mainly thinks about; but that *that* book, and those pictures represent the train of thought and imagination he would be likely to be thinking of to-day, to-morrow, or next day, more nearly than those given in " Tom Sawyer or " Huckleberry Finn."*

Papa can make exceedingly bright jokes, and he enjoys funny things, and when he is with people he jokes and laughs a great deal, but still he is more interested in earnest books and earnest subjects to talk upon, than in humorous ones.†

When we are all alone at home, nine times out of ten, he talks about some very earnest subjects, (with an ocasional joke thrown in) and he a good deal more often talks upon such subjects than upon the other kind.

He is as much of a Pholosopher as anything I think. I think he could have done a great deal in this direction if he had studied while young, for he seems to enjoy reasoning out things, no matter what; in a great many such directions he has greater ability than in the gifts which have made him famous.

Thus at fourteen she had made up her mind about me, and in no timorous or uncertain terms had set down her reasons for her opinion. Fifteen years were to pass before any other critic— except Mr. Howells, I think—was to reutter that daring opinion and print it. Right or wrong, it was a brave position for that little analyzer to take. She never withdrew it afterward, nor modified it. She has spoken of herself as lacking physical courage, and has evinced her admiration of Clara's; but she had moral courage, which is the rarest of human qualities, and she kept it functionable by exercising it. I think that in questions of morals

* It is so yet.—M. T.
† She has said it well and correctly. Humor is a subject which has never had much interest for me. This is why I have never examined it, nor written about it nor used it as a topic for a speech. A hundred times it has been offered me as a topic in these past forty years, but in no case has it attracted me.—M. T.

and politics she was usually on my side; but when she was not she had her reasons and maintained her ground. Two years after she passed out of my life I wrote a Philosophy. Of the three persons who have seen the manuscript only one understood it, and all three condemned it. If she could have read it, she also would have condemned it, possibly,—probably, in fact—but she would have understood it. It would have had no difficulties for her on that score; also she would have found a tireless pleasure in analyzing and discussing its problems.

MARK TWAIN.

*(To be Continued.)*

# Chapter XIX

## June 7, 1907. Pages 241–51.

PREFATORY NOTE.—Mr. Clemens began to write his autobiography many years ago, and he continues to add to it day by day. It was his original intention to permit no publication of his memoirs until after his death; but, after leaving "Pier No. 70," he concluded that a considerable portion might now suitably be given to the public. It is that portion, garnered from the quarter-million of words already written, which will appear in this REVIEW during the present year. No part of the autobiography will be published in book form during the lifetime of the author.—EDITOR N. A. R.

### From Susy's Biography of Me.

*March 23, '86.*—The other day was my birthday, and I had a little birthday party in the evening and papa acted some very funny charades with Mr. Gherhardt, Mr. Jesse Grant (who had come up from New York and was spending the evening with us) and Mr. Frank Warner. One of them was "on his knees" honys-sneeze. There were a good many other funny ones, all of which I dont remember. Mr. Grant was very pleasant, and began playing the charades in the most delightful way.

Susy's spelling has defeated me, this time. I cannot make out what "honys-sneeze" stands for. Impromptu charades were almost a nightly pastime of ours, from the children's earliest days —they played in them with me when they were only five or six years old. As they increased in years and practice their love for the sport almost amounted to a passion, and they acted their parts with a steadily increasing ability.  At first they required much drilling; but later they were generally ready as soon as the parts were assigned, and they acted them according to their own devices.  Their stage facility and absence of constraint and self-consciousness in the " Prince and Pauper " was a result of their charading practice.

At ten and twelve Susy wrote plays, and she and Daisy Warner and Clara played them in the library or up-stairs in the school-room, with only themselves and the servants for audience.  They were of a tragic and tremendous sort, and were performed with great energy and earnestness.  They were dramatized (freely) from English history, and in them Mary Queen of Scots and Elizabeth had few holidays.  The clothes were borrowed from the mother's wardrobe and the gowns were longer than necessary, but that was not regarded as a defect.  In one of these plays Jean (three years old, perhaps) was Sir Francis Bacon. She was not dressed for the part, and did not have to say anything, but sat silent and decorous at a tiny table and was kept busy signing death-warrants.  It was a really important office, for few entered those plays and got out of them alive.

*March 26.*—Mamma and Papa have been in New York for two or three days, and Miss Corey has been staying with us.  They are coming home to-day at two o'clock.

Papa has just begun to play chess, and he is very fond of it, so he has engaged to play with Mrs. Charles Warner every morning from 10 to 12, he came down to supper last night, full of this pleasant prospect, but evidently with something on his mind.  Finally he said to mamma in an appologetical tone, Susy Warner and I have a plan.

" Well " mamma said " what now, I wonder?"

Papa said that Susy Warner and he were going to name the chess men after some of the old bible heroes, and then play chess on Sunday.

*April 18, '86.*—Mamma and papa Clara and Daisy have gone to New York to see the " Mikado."  They are coming home to-night at half past seven.

Last winter when Mr. Cable was lecturing with papa, he wrote this letter to him just before he came to visit us.

DEAR UNCLE,—That's one nice thing about me, I never bother any one, to offer me a good thing twice.  You dont ask me to stay over Sunday, but then you dont ask me to leave Saturday night, and knowing the nobility of your nature as I do—thank you, I'll stay till Monday morning.*

Your's and the dear familie's

GEORGE W. CABLE.

[*December 22, 1906.*] It seems a prodigious while ago! Two or three nights ago I dined at a friend's house with a score of other men, and at my side was Cable—actually almost an old man, really almost an old man, that once so young chap! 62 years old, frost on his head, seven grandchildren in stock, and a brand-new wife to re-begin life with!

[*Dictated Nov. 19, 1906.*]

Ever since papa and mamma were married, papa has written his books and then taken them to mamma in manuscript and she has expergated them. Papa read "Huckleberry Finn" to us in manuscript just before it came out, and then he would leave parts of it with mamma to expergate, while he went off up to the study to work, and sometimes Clara and I would be sitting with mamma while she was looking the manuscript over, and I remember so well, with what pangs of regret we used to see her turn down the leaves of the pages, which meant that some delightfully dreadful part must be scratched out. And I remember one part pertickularly which was perfectly fascinating it was dreadful, that Clara and I used to delight in, and oh with what dispair we saw mamma turn down the leaf on which it was written, we thought the book would be almost ruined without it. But we gradually came to feel as mamma did.

It would be a pity to replace the vivacity and quaintness and felicity of Susy's innocent free spelling with the dull and petrified uniformities of the spelling-book. Nearly all the grimness is taken out of the " expergating " of my books by the subtle mollification accidentally infused into the word by Susy's modification of the spelling of it.

I remember the special case mentioned by Susy, and can see the group yet—two-thirds of it pleading for the life of the culprit sentence that was so fascinatingly dreadful and the other third of it patiently explaining why the court could not grant the prayer of the pleaders; but I do not remember what the condemned phrase was. It had much company, and they all went to the gallows; but it is possible that that specially dreadful one which gave those little people so much delight was cunningly devised and put into the book for just that function, and not

* Cable never travelled Sundays.

with any hope or expectation that it would get by the "exper-gator" alive. It is possible, for I had that custom.

Susy's quaint and effective spelling falls quite opportunely into to-day's atmosphere, which is heavy with the rumblings and grumblings and mutterings of the Simplified Spelling Reform. Andrew Carnegie started this storm, a couple of years ago, by moving a simplifying of English orthography, and establishing a fund for the prosecution and maintenance of the crusade. He began gently. He addressed a circular to some hundreds of his friends, asking them to simplify the spelling of a dozen of our badly spelt words—I think they were only words which end with the superfluous *ugh*. He asked that these friends use the suggested spellings in their private correspondence.

By this, one perceives that the beginning was sufficiently quiet and unaggressive.

Next stage: a small committee was appointed, with Brander Matthews for managing director and spokesman. It issued a list of three hundred words, of average silliness as to spelling, and proposed new and sane spellings for these words. The President of the United States, unsolicited, adopted these simplified three hundred officially, and ordered that they be used in the official documents of the Government. It was now remarked, by all the educated and the thoughtful except the clergy that Sheol was to pay. This was most justly and comprehensively descriptive. The indignant British lion rose, with a roar that was heard across the Atlantic, and stood there on his little isle, gazing, red-eyed, out over the glooming seas, snow-flecked with driving spindrift, and lashing his tail—a most scary spectacle to see.

The lion was outraged because we, a nation of children, without any grown-up people among us, with no property in the language, but using it merely by courtesy of its owner the English nation, were trying to defile the sacredness of it by removing from it peculiarities which had been its ornament and which had made it holy and beautiful for ages.

In truth there is a certain sardonic propriety in preserving our orthography, since ours is a mongrel language which started with a child's vocabulary of three hundred words, and now consists of two hundred and twenty-five thousand; the whole lot, with the exception of the original and legitimate three hundred, borrowed, stolen, smouched from every unwatched language under the sun, the spelling of each individual word of the lot locating the source of the theft and preserving the memory of the revered crime.

Why is it that I have intruded into this turmoil and manifested a desire to get our orthography purged of its asininities? Indeed I do not know why I should manifest any interest in the matter, for at bottom I disrespect our orthography most heartily, and as heartily disrespect everything that has been said by anybody in defence of it. Nothing professing to be a defence of our ludicrous spellings has had any basis, so far as my observation goes, except sentimentality. In these " arguments " the term venerable is used instead of mouldy, and hallowed instead of devilish; whereas there is nothing properly venerable or antique about a language which is not yet four hundred years old, and about a jumble of imbecile spellings which were grotesque in the beginning, and which grow more and more grotesque with the flight of the years.

*[Dictated Monday, November 30, 1906.]*

Jean and Papa were walking out past the barn the other day when Jean saw some little newly born baby ducks, she exclaimed as she perceived them " I dont see why God gives us so much ducks when Patrick kills them so."

Susy is mistaken as to the origin of the ducks. They were not a gift, I bought them. I am not finding fault with her, for that would be most unfair. She is remarkably accurate in her statements as a historian, as a rule, and it would not be just to make much of this small slip of hers; besides I think it was a quite natural slip, for by heredity and habit ours was a religious household, and it was a common thing with us whenever anybody did a handsome thing, to give the credit of it to Providence, without examining into the matter. This may be called automatic religion—in fact that is what it is; it is so used to its work that it can do it without your help or even your privity; out of all the facts and statistics that may be placed before it, it will always get the one result, since it has never been taught to seek any other. It is thus the unreflecting cause of much injustice. As we have seen, it betrayed Susy into an injustice toward me. It had to be automatic, for she would have been far from doing me an injustice when in her right mind.  It was a dear little biographer, and she meant me no harm, and I am not censuring her now, but am only desirous of correcting in advance an erroneous impression which her words would be sure to convey to a reader's mind.  No elaboration of this matter is necessary; it is sufficient to say *I* provided the ducks.

It was in Hartford.  The greensward sloped down-hill from the house to the sluggish little river that flowed through the grounds, and Patrick, who was fertile in good ideas, had early conceived the idea of having home-made ducks for our table. Every morning he drove them from the stable down to the river, and the children were always there to see and admire the waddling white procession; they were there again at sunset to see Patrick conduct the procession back to its lodgings in the stable. But this was not always a gay and happy holiday show, with joy in it for the witnesses; no, too frequently there was a tragedy connected with it, and then there were tears and pain for the children.  There was a stranded log or two in the river, and on these certain families of snapping-turtles used to congregate and drowse in the sun and give thanks, in their dumb way, to Providence for benevolence extended to them.  It was but another instance of misplaced credit; it was the young ducks that those pious reptiles were so thankful for — whereas they were *my* ducks.  I bought the ducks.

When a crop of young ducks, not yet quite old enough for the table but approaching that age, began to join the procession, and paddle around in the sluggish water, and give thanks—not to me—for that privilege, the snapping-turtles would suspend their songs of praise and slide off the logs and paddle along under the water and chew the feet of the young ducks.  Presently Patrick would notice that two or three of those little creatures were not moving about, but were apparently at anchor, and were not looking as thankful as they had been looking a short time before. He early found out what that sign meant—a submerged snapping-turtle was taking his breakfast, and silently singing his gratitude. Every day or two Patrick would rescue and fetch up a little duck with incomplete legs to stand upon—nothing left of their extremities but gnawed and bleeding stumps.  Then the children said pitying things and wept — and at dinner we finished the tragedy which the turtles had begun.  Thus, as will be seen—

out of season, at least—it was really the turtles that gave us so much ducks. At my expense.

Papa has written a new version of " There is a happy land " it is—

> " There is a boarding-house
>     Far, far away,
> Where they have ham and eggs,
>     Three times a day,
> Oh dont those boarders yell
> When they hear the dinner-bell,
> They give that land-lord rats
>     Three times a day."

Again Susy has made a small error. It was not I that wrote the song. I heard Billy Rice sing it in the negro minstrel show, and I brought it home and sang it—with great spirit—for the elevation of the household. The children admired it to the limit, and made me sing it with burdensome frequency. To their minds it was superior to the Battle Hymn of the Republic.

How many years ago that was! Where now is Billy Rice? He was a joy to me, and so were the other stars of the nigger-show—Billy Birch, David Wambold, Backus, and a delightful dozen of their brethren, who made life a pleasure to me forty years ago, and later. Birch, Wambold, and Backus are gone years ago; and with them departed to return no more forever, I suppose, the real nigger-show—the genuine nigger-show, the extravagant nigger-show,—the show which to me had no peer and whose peer has not yet arrived, in my experience. We have the grand opera; and I have witnessed, and greatly enjoyed, the first act of every-thing which Wagner created, but the effect on me has always been so powerful that one act was quite sufficient; whenever I have witnessed two acts I have gone away physically exhausted; and whenever I have ventured an entire opera the result has been the next thing to suicide. But if I could have the nigger-show back again, in its pristine purity and perfection, I should have but little further use for opera. It seems to me that to the elevated mind and the sensitive spirit the hand-organ and the nigger-show are a standard and a summit to whose rarefied alti-tude the other forms of musical art may not hope to reach.

[*Dictated September 5, 1906.*] It is years since I have exam-ined " The Children's Record." I have turned over a few of its pages this morning. This book is a record in which Mrs. Clemens and I registered some of the sayings and doings of the children, in the long ago, when they were little chaps. Of course, we wrote these things down at the time because they were of momentary interest—things of the passing hour, and of no permanent value —but at this distant day I find that they still possess an interest for me and also a value, because it turns out that they were *registrations of character.* The qualities then revealed by fitful glimpses, in childish acts and speeches, remained as a permanency in the children's characters in the drift of the years, and were always afterwards clearly and definitely recognizable.

There is a masterful streak in Jean that now and then moves her to set my authority aside for a moment and end a losing argument in that prompt and effective fashion. And here in this old book I find evidence that she was just like that before she was quite four years old.

*From The Children's Record. Quarry Farm, July 7, 1884.*—Yesterday evening our cows (after being inspected and worshipped by Jean from the shed for an hour,) wandered off down into the pasture, and left her bereft. I thought I was going to get back home, now, but that was an error. Jean knew of some more cows, in a field somewhere, and took my hand and led me thitherward. When we turned the corner and took the right-hand road, I saw that we should presently be out of range of call and sight; so I began to argue against continuing the expedition, and Jean began to argue in favor of it—she using English for light skirmishing, and German for "business." I kept up my end with vigor, and demolished her arguments in detail, one after the other, till I judged I had her about cornered. She hesitated a moment, then answered up sharply:

"*Wir werden nichts mehr darüber sprechen!*" (We won't talk any more about it!)

It nearly took my breath away; though I thought I might possibly have misunderstood. I said:

"Why, you little rascal! *Was hast du gesagt?*"

But she said the same words over again, and in the same decided way. I suppose I ought to have been outraged; but I wasn't, I was charmed. And I suppose I ought to have spanked her; but I didn't, I fraternized with the enemy, and we went on and spent half an hour with the cows.

That incident is followed in the "Record" by the following paragraph, which is another instance of a juvenile characteristic maintaining itself into mature age. Susy was persistently and conscientiously truthful throughout her life with the exception of one interruption covering several months, and perhaps a year.

This was while she was still a little child. Suddenly—not gradually—she began to lie; not furtively, but frankly, openly, and on a scale quite disproportioned to her size. Her mother was so stunned, so nearly paralyzed for a day or two, that she did not know what to do with the emergency. Reasonings, persuasions, beseechings, all went for nothing; they produced no effect; the lying went tranquilly on. Other remedies were tried, but they failed. There is a tradition that success was finally accomplished by whipping. I think the Record says so, but if it does it is because the Record is incomplete. Whipping was indeed tried, and was faithfully kept up during two or three weeks, but the results were merely temporary; the reforms achieved were discouragingly brief.

Fortunately for Susy, an incident presently occurred which put a complete stop to all the mother's efforts in the direction of reform. This incident was the chance discovery in Darwin of a passage which said that when a child exhibits a sudden and unaccountable disposition to forsake the truth and restrict itself to lying, the explanation must be sought away back in the past; that an ancestor of the child had had the same disease, at the same tender age; that it was irremovable by persuasion or punishment, and that it had ceased as suddenly and as mysteriously as it had come, when it had run its appointed course. I think Mr. Darwin said that nothing was necessary but to leave the matter alone and let the malady have its way and perish by the statute of limitations.

We had confidence in Darwin, and after that day Susy was relieved of our reformatory persecutions. She went on lying without let or hindrance during several months, or a year; then the lying suddenly ceased, and she became as conscientiously and exactingly truthful as she had been before the attack, and she remained so to the end of her life.

The paragraph in the Record to which I have been leading up is in my handwriting, and is of a date so long posterior to the time of the lying malady that she had evidently forgotten that truth-speaking had ever had any difficulties for her.

Mama was speaking of a servant who had been pretty unveracious, but was now "trying to tell the truth." Susy was a good deal surprised, and said she shouldn't think anybody would have to *try* to tell the truth.

In the Record the children's acts and speeches quite definitely
define their characters. Susy's indicated the presence of mentality — thought — and they were generally marked by gravity.
She was timid, on her physical side, but had an abundance of
moral courage. Clara was sturdy, independent, orderly, practical, persistent, plucky—just a little animal, and very satisfactory.
Charles Dudley Warner said Susy was made of mind, and Clara
of matter.

When Motley, the kitten, died, some one said that the thoughts
of the two children need not be inquired into, they could be
divined: that Susy was wondering if this was the *end* of Motley,
and had his life been worth while; whereas Clara was merely interested in seeing to it that there should be a creditable funeral.

In those days Susy was a dreamer, a thinker, a poet and philosopher, and Clara—well, Clara wasn't. In after-years a passion for music developed the latent spirituality and intellectuality
in Clara, and her practicality took second and, in fact, even third
place. Jean was from the beginning orderly, steady, diligent,
persistent; and remains so. She picked up languages easily, and
kept them.

*Susy aged eleven, Jean three.*—Susy said the other day when she saw
Jean bringing a cat to me of her own motion, " Jean has found out
already that mamma loves morals and papa loves cats."

It is another of Susy's remorselessly sound verdicts.

As a child, Jean neglected my books. When she was nine years
old Will Gillette invited her and the rest of us to a dinner at the
Murray Hill Hotel in New York, in order that we might get
acquainted with Mrs. Leslie and her daughters. Elsie Leslie was
nine years old, and was a great celebrity on the stage. Jean was
astonished and awed to see that little slip of a thing sit up at
table and take part in the conversation of the grown people,
capably and with ease and tranquillity. Poor Jean was obliged
to keep still, for the subjects discussed never happened to hit her
level, but at last the talk fell within her limit and she had her
chance to contribute to it. " Tom Sawyer " was mentioned.
Jean spoke gratefully up and said,

" I know who wrote that book—Harriet Beecher Stowe!"

One evening Susy had prayed, Clara was curled up for sleep; she
was reminded that it was her turn to pray now. She said " Oh! one's
enough," and dropped off to slumber.

*Clara five years old.*—We were in Germany. The nurse, Rosa, was not allowed to speak to the children otherwise than in German. Clara grew very tired of it; by and by the little creature's patience was exhausted, and she said " Aunt Clara, I wish God had made Rosa in English."

*Clara four years old, Susy six.*—This morning when Clara discovered that this is my birthday, she was greatly troubled because she had provided no gift for me, and repeated her sorrow several times. Finally she went musing to the nursery and presently returned with her newest and dearest treasure, a large toy horse, and said, " You shall have this horse for your birthday, papa."

I accepted it with many thanks. After an hour she was racing up and down the room with the horse, when Susy said,

" Why Clara, you gave that horse to papa, and now you've tooken it again."

*Clara.*—" I never give it to him for always; I give it to him for his birthday."

In Geneva, in September, I lay abed late one morning, and as Clara was passing through the room I took her on my bed a moment. Then the child went to Clara Spaulding and said,

" Aunt Clara, papa is a good deal of trouble to me."

" Is he? Why?"

" Well, he wants me to get in bed with him, and I can't do that with jelmuls [gentlemen]--I don't like jelmuls anyway."

" What, you don't like gentlemen! Don't you like Uncle Theodore Crane?"

" Oh yes, but he's not a jelmul, he's a friend."

MARK TWAIN.

*(To be Continued.)*

# Chapter XX

July 5, 1907. Pages 465–74.

PREFATORY NOTE.—Mr. Clemens began to write his autobiography many years ago, and he continues to add to it day by day. It was his original intention to permit no publication of his memoirs until after his death; but, after leaving "Pier No. 70," he concluded that a considerable portion might now suitably be given to the public. It is that portion, garnered from the quarter-million of words already written, which will appear in this REVIEW during the coming year. No part of the autobiography will be published in book form during the lifetime of the author.—EDITOR N. A. R.

[*Notes on "Innocents Abroad." Dictated in Florence, Italy, April, 1904.*]—I will begin with a note upon the dedication. I wrote the book in the months of March and
**(1868.)** April, 1868, in San Francisco. It was published in August, 1869. Three years afterward Mr. Goodman, of Virginia City, Nevada, on whose newspaper I had served ten years before, came East, and we were walking down Broadway one day when he said: " How did you come to steal Oliver Wendell Holmes's dedication and put it in your book?"

I made a careless and inconsequential answer, for I supposed he was joking. But he assured me that he was in earnest. He said: " I'm not discussing the question of whether you stole it or didn't—for that is a question that can be settled in the first bookstore we come to—I am only asking you *how* you came to steal it, for that is where my curiosity is focalized."

I couldn't accommodate him with this information, as I hadn't it in stock. I could have made oath that I had not stolen anything, therefore my vanity was not hurt nor my spirit troubled. At bottom I supposed that he had mistaken another book for mine, and was now getting himself into an untenable place and preparing sorrow for himself and triumph for me. We entered a bookstore and he asked for " The Innocents Abroad " and for the dainty little blue and gold edition of Dr. Oliver Wendell Holmes's poems. He opened the books, exposed their dedications and said: " Read them. It is plain that the author of the second one stole the first one, isn't it ?"

I was very much ashamed, and unspeakably astonished. We continued our walk, but I was not able to throw any gleam of light upon that original question of his. I could not remember ever having seen Dr. Holmes's dedication. I knew the poems, but the dedication was new to me.

I did not get hold of the key to that secret until months afterward, then it came in a curious way, and yet it was a natural way; for the natural way provided by nature and the construction of the human mind for the discovery of a forgotten event is to employ another forgotten event for its resurrection.

I received a letter from the Rev. Dr. Rising, who had been rector of the Episcopal church in Virginia City in my time, in **(1866.)** which letter Dr. Rising made reference to certain things which had happened to us in the Sandwich Islands six years before; among things he made casual mention of the Honolulu Hotel's poverty in the matter of literature. At first I did not see the bearing of the remark, it called nothing to my mind. But presently it did—with a flash ! There was but one book in Mr. Kirchhof's hotel, and that was the first volume of Dr. Holmes's blue and gold series. I had had a fortnight's chance to get well acquainted with its contents, for I had ridden around the big island (Hawaii) on horseback and had brought back so many saddle boils that if there had been a duty on them it would have bankrupted me to pay it. They kept me in my room, unclothed, and in persistent pain for two weeks, with no company but cigars and the little volume of poems. Of course I read them almost constantly; I read them from beginning to end, then read them backwards, then began in the middle and read them both ways, then read them wrong end first and upside down. In a word, I read the book to rags, and was infinitely grateful to the hand that wrote it.

Here we have an exhibition of what repetition can do, when persisted in daily and hourly over a considerable stretch of time, where one is merely reading for entertainment, without thought or intention of preserving in the memory that which is read. It is a process which in the course of years dries all the juice out of a familiar verse of Scripture, leaving nothing but a sapless husk behind. In that case you at least know the origin of the husk, but in the case in point I apparently preserved the husk but presently forgot whence it came. It lay lost in some dim corner of my memory a year or two, then came forward when I needed a dedication, and was promptly mistaken by me as a child of my own happy fancy.

I was new, I was ignorant, the mysteries of the human mind were a sealed book to me as yet, and I stupidly looked upon myself as a tough and unforgivable criminal. I wrote to Dr. Holmes and told him the whole disgraceful affair, implored him in impassioned language to believe that I had never intended to commit this crime, and was unaware that I had committed it until I was confronted with the awful evidence. I have lost his answer, I could better have afforded to lose an uncle. Of these I had a surplus, many of them of no real value to me, but that letter was beyond price, beyond uncledom, and unsparable. In it Dr. Holmes laughed the kindest and healingest laugh over the whole matter, and at considerable length and in happy phrase assured me that there was no crime in unconscious plagiarism; that I committed it every day, that he committed it every day, that every man alive on the earth who writes or speaks commits it every day and not merely once or twice but every time he opens his mouth; that all our phrasings are spiritualized shadows cast multitudinously from our readings; that no happy phrase of ours is ever quite original with us, there is nothing of our own in it except some slight change born of our temperament, character, environment, teachings and associations; that this slight change differentiates it from another man's manner of saying it, stamps it with our special style, and makes it our own for the time being; all the rest of it being old, moldy, antique, and smelling of the breath of a thousand generations of them that have passed it over their teeth before!

In the thirty-odd years which have come and gone since then, I have satisfied myself that what Dr. Holmes said was true.

I wish to make a note upon the preface of the "Innocents." In the last paragraph of that brief preface, I speak of the proprietors of the "Daily Alta California" having "waived their rights" in certain letters which I wrote for that journal while absent on the "Quaker City" trip. I was young then, I am white-headed now, but the insult of that word rankles yet, now that I am reading that paragraph for the first time in many years, reading it for the first time since it was written, perhaps. There were rights, it is true—such rights as the strong are able to acquire over the weak and the absent. Early in '66 George Barnes invited me to resign my reportership on his paper, the San Francisco "Morning Call," and for some months thereafter I was without money or work; then I had a pleasant turn of fortune. The proprietors of the "Sacramento Union," a great and influential daily journal, sent me to the Sandwich Islands to write four letters a month at twenty dollars apiece. I was there four or five months, and returned to find myself about the best known honest man on the Pacific Coast. Thomas McGuire, proprietor of several theatres, said that now was the time to make my fortune—strike while the iron was hot! —break into the lecture field! I did it. I announced a lecture on the Sandwich Islands, closing the advertisement with the remark, "Admission one dollar; doors open at half-past 7, the trouble begins at 8." A true prophecy. The trouble certainly did begin at 8, when I found myself in front of the only audience I had ever faced, for the fright which pervaded me from head to foot was paralyzing. It lasted two minutes and was as bitter as death, the memory of it is indestructible, but it had its compensations, for it made me immune from timidity before audiences for all time to come. I lectured in all the principal Californian towns and in Nevada, then lectured once or twice more in San Francisco, then retired from the field rich—for me— and laid out a plan to sail Westward from San Francisco, and go around the world. The proprietors of the "Alta" engaged me to write an account of the trip for that paper—fifty letters of a column and a half each, which would be about two thousand words per letter, and the pay to be twenty dollars per letter.

I went East to St. Louis to say good-bye to my mother, and then I was bitten by the prospectus of Captain Duncan of the " Quaker City " excursion, and I ended by joining it. During the trip I wrote and sent the fifty letters; six of them miscarried, and I wrote six new ones to complete my contract. Then I put together a lecture on the trip and delivered it in San Francisco at great and satisfactory pecuniary profit, then I branched out into the country and was aghast at the result: I had been entirely forgotten, I never had people enough in my houses to sit as a jury of inquest on my lost reputation! I inquired into this curious condition of things and found that the thrifty owners of that prodigiously rich " Alta " newspaper had *copyrighted* all those poor little twenty-dollar letters, and had threatened with prosecution any journal which should venture to copy a paragraph from them!

And there I was! I had contracted to furnish a large book, concerning the excursion, to the American Publishing Co. of Hartford, and I supposed I should need all those letters to fill it out with. I was in an uncomfortable situation—that is, if the proprietors of this stealthily acquired copyright should refuse to let me use the letters. That is just what they did; Mr. Mac—something—I have forgotten the rest of his name—said his firm were going to make a book out of the letters in order to get back the thousand dollars which they had paid for them. I said that if they had acted fairly and honorably, and had allowed the country press to use the letters or portions of them, my lecture-skirmish on the coast would have paid me ten thousand dollars, whereas the " Alta " had lost me that amount. Then he offered a compromise: he would publish the book and allow me ten per cent. royalty on it. The compromise did not appeal to me, and I said so. I was now quite unknown outside of San Francisco, the book's sale would be confined to that city, and my royalty would not pay me enough to board me three months; whereas my Eastern contract, if carried out, could be profitable to me, for I had a sort of reputation on the Atlantic seaboard acquired through the publication of six excursion-letters in the New York " Tribune " and one or two in the " Herald."

In the end Mr. Mac agreed to suppress his book, on certain conditions: in my preface I must thank the " Alta " for waiving its " rights " and granting me permission. I objected to the thanks. I could not with any large degree of sincerity thank the " Alta " for bankrupting my lecture-raid. After considerable debate my point was conceded and the thanks left out.

Noah Brooks was the editor of the " Alta " at the time, a man of sterling character and equipped with a right heart, also a good historian where facts were not essential. In biographical sketches of me written many years afterward (1902), he was quite eloquent in praises of the generosity of the " Alta " people **(1902.)** in giving to me without compensation a book which, as history had afterward shown, was worth a fortune. After all the fuss, I did not levy heavily upon the " Alta " letters. I found that they were newspaper matter, not book matter. They had been written here and there and yonder, as opportunity had given me a chance working-moment or two during our feverish flight around about Europe or in the furnace-heat of my state-room on board the " Quaker City," therefore they were loosely constructed, and needed to have some of the wind and water squeezed out of them. I used several of them—ten or twelve, perhaps. I wrote the rest of " The Innocents Abroad " in sixty days, and I could have added a fortnight's labor with the pen and gotten along without the letters altogether. I was very young in those days, exceedingly young, marvellously young, younger than I am now, younger than I shall ever be again, by hundreds of years. I worked every night from eleven or twelve until broad day in the morning, and as I did two hundred thousand words in the sixty days, the average was more than three thousand words a day—nothing for Sir Walter Scott, nothing for Louis Stevenson, nothing for plenty of other people, but quite handsome for me. In 1897, when we were living in **(1897.)** Tedworth Square, London, and I was writing the book called " Following the Equator " my average was eighteen hundred words a day; here in Florence (1904), my average **(1904.)** seems to be fourteen hundred words per sitting of four or five hours.*

I was deducing from the above that I have been slowing down steadily in these thirty-six years, but I perceive that my

* With the pen, I mean. This Autobiography is dictated, not written.

statistics have a defect: three thousand words in the spring of
1868 when I was working seven or eight or nine hours at a
sitting has little or no advantage over the sitting of to-
day, covering half the time and producing half the output. Figures often beguile me, particularly when I have the arranging
of them myself; in which case the remark attributed to Disraeli
would often apply with justice and force:

" There are three kinds of lies: lies, damned lies, and statistics."

[*Dictated, January 23, 1907.*]—The proverb says that Providence protects children and idiots. This is really true. I know
it because I have tested it. It did not protect George through
the most of his campaign, but it saved him in his last inning,
and the veracity of the proverb stood confirmed.

I have several times been saved by this mysterious interposition, when I was manifestly in extreme peril. It has been common, all my life, for smart people to perceive in me an easy
prey for selfish designs, and I have walked without suspicion
into the trap set for me, yet have often come out unscathed,
against all the likelihoods. More than forty years ago, in San
(1865.) Francisco, the office staff adjourned, upon conclusion
of its work at two o'clock in the morning, to a great
bowling establishment where there were twelve alleys. I was
invited, rather perfunctorily, and as a matter of etiquette—by
which I mean that I was invited politely, but not urgently.
But when I diffidently declined, with thanks, and explained
that I knew nothing about the game, those lively young fellows
became at once eager and anxious and urgent to have my society.
This flattered me, for I perceived no trap, and I innocently and
gratefully accepted their invitation. I was given an alley all
to myself. The boys explained the game to me, and they also
explained to me that there would be an hour's play, and that the
player who scored the fewest ten-strikes in the hour would have
to provide oysters and beer for the combination. This disturbed
me very seriously, since it promised me bankruptcy, and I was
sorry that this detail had been overlooked in the beginning.
But my pride would not allow me to back out now, so I stayed
in, and did what I could to look satisfied and glad I had come.
It is not likely that I looked as contented as I wanted to, but the
others looked glad enough to make up for it, for they were quite
unable to hide their evil joy. They showed me how to stand,

and how to stoop, and how to aim the ball, and how to let fly; and then the game began. The results were astonishing. In my ignorance I delivered the balls in apparently every way except the right one; but no matter—during half an hour I never started a ball down the alley that didn't score a ten-strike, every time, at the other end. The others lost their grip early, and their joy along with it. Now and then one of them got a ten-strike, but the occurrence was so rare that it made no show alongside of my giant score. The boys surrendered at the end of the half-hour, and put on their coats and gathered around me and in courteous, but sufficiently definite, language expressed their opinion of an experience-worn and seasoned expert who would stoop to lying and deception in order to rob kind and well-meaning friends who had put their trust in him under the delusion that he was an honest and honorable person. I was not able to convince them that I had not lied, for now my character was gone, and they refused to attach any value to anything I said. The proprietor of the place stood by for a while saying nothing, then he came to my defence. He said: " It looks like a mystery, gentlemen, but it isn't a mystery after it's explained. That is a *grooved* alley; you've only to start a ball down it any way you please and the groove will do the rest; it will slam the ball against the northeast curve of the head pin every time, and nothing can save the ten from going down."

It was true. The boys made the experiment and they found that there was no art that could send a ball down that alley and fail to score a ten-strike with it. When I had told those boys that I knew nothing about that game I was speaking only the truth; but it was ever thus, all through my life: whenever I have diverged from custom and principle and uttered a truth, the rule has been that the hearer hadn't strength of mind enough to believe it.

A quarter of a century ago I arrived in London to lecture a few weeks under the management of George Dolby, who had **(1873.)** conducted the Dickens readings in America five or six years before. He took me to the Albemarle and fed me, and in the course of the dinner he enlarged a good deal, and with great satisfaction, upon his reputation as a player of fifteen-ball pool, and when he learned by my testimony that I had never seen the game played, and knew nothing of the art of pocketing

balls, he enlarged more and more, and still more, and kept on
enlarging, until I recognized that I was either in the presence
of the very father of fifteen-ball pool or in the presence of his
most immediate descendant. At the end of the dinner Dolby
was eager to introduce me to the game and show me what he
could do. We adjourned to the billiard-room and he framed the
balls in a flat pyramid and told me to fire at the apex ball and
then go on and do what I could toward pocketing the fifteen,
after which he would take the cue and show me what a past-
master of the game could do with those balls. I did as required.
I began with the diffidence proper to my ignorant estate, and
when I had finished my inning all the balls were in the pockets
and Dolby was burying me under a volcanic irruption of acid
sarcasms.

So I was a liar in Dolby's belief. He thought he had been sold,
and at a cheap rate; but he divided his sarcasms quite fairly
and quite equally between the two of us. He was full of ironical
admiration of his childishness and innocence in letting a wandering and characterless and scandalous American load him up
with deceptions of so transparent a character that they ought
not to have deceived the house cat. On the other hand, he was
remorselessly severe upon me for beguiling him, by studied and
discreditable artifice, into bragging and boasting about his poor
game in the presence of a professional expert disguised in lies
and frauds, who could empty more balls in billiard pockets in
an hour than he could empty into a basket in a day.

In the matter of fifteen-ball pool I never got Dolby's confidence wholly back, though I got it in other ways, and kept it
until his death. I have played that game a number of times
since, but that first time was the only time in my life that I have
ever pocketed all the fifteen in a single inning.

My unsuspicious nature has made it necessary for Providence
to save me from traps a number of times. Thirty years ago, a
**(1876.)** couple of Elmira bankers invited me to play the game of
"Quaker" with them. I had never heard of the game
before, and said that if it required intellect, I should not be
able to entertain them. But they said it was merely a game of
chance, and required no mentality—so I agreed to make a trial
of it. They appointed four in the afternoon for the sacrifice.
As the place, they chose a ground-floor room with a large win-

dow in it. Then they went treacherously around and advertised the " sell " which they were going to play upon me.

I arrived on time, and we began the game—with a large and eager free-list to superintend it. These superintendents were outside, with their noses pressed against the window-pane. The bankers described the game to me. So far as I recollect, the pattern of it was this: they had a pile of Mexican dollars on the table; twelve of them were of even date, fifty of them were of odd dates. The bankers were to separate a coin from the pile and hide it under a hand, and I must guess " odd " or " even." If I guessed correctly, the coin would be mine; if incorrectly, I lost a dollar. The first guess I made was " even," and was right. I guessed again, " even," and took the money. They fed me another one and I guessed " even " again, and took the money. I guessed " even " the fourth time, and took the money. It seemed to me that " even " was a good guess, and I might as well stay by it, which I did. I guessed " even " twelve times, and took the twelve dollars. I was doing as they secretly desired. Their experience of human nature had convinced them that any human being as innocent as my face proclaimed me to be, would repeat his first guess if it won, and would go on repeating it if it should continue to win. It was their belief that an innocent would be almost sure at the beginning to guess " even," and not " odd," and that if an innocent should guess " even " twelve times in succession and win every time, he would go on guessing " even " to the end—so it was their purpose to let me win those twelve even dates and then advance the odd dates, one by one, until I should lose fifty dollars, and furnish those superintendents something to laugh about for a week to come.

But it did not come out in that way; for by the time I had won the twelfth dollar and last even date, I withdrew from the game because it was so one-sided that it was monotonous, and did not entertain me. There was a burst of laughter from the superintendents at the window when I came out of the place, but I did not know what they were laughing at nor whom they were laughing at, and it was a matter of no interest to me anyway. Through that incident I acquired an enviable reputation for smartness and penetration, but it was not my due, for I had not penetrated anything that the cow could not have penetrated.

*(To be Continued.)*     MARK TWAIN.

# Chapter XXI

## August 2, 1907. Pages 689–98.

Prefatory Note.—Mr. Clemens began to write his autobiography many years ago, and he continues to add to it day by day. It was his original intention to permit no publication of his memoirs until after his death; but, after leaving "Pier No. 70," he concluded that a considerable portion might now suitably be given to the public. It is that portion, garnered from the quarter-million of words already written, which will appear in this Review during the present year. No part of the autobiography will be published in book form during the lifetime of the author.—Editor N. A. R.

*From Susy's Biography of Me.*

*Feb. 12, '86.*

Mamma and I have both been very much troubled of late because papa since he has been publishing Gen. Grant's book has seemed to forget his own books and work entirely, and the other evening as papa and I were promonading up and down the library he told me that he didn't expect to write but one more book, and then he was ready to give up work altogether, die, or do anything, he said that he had written more than he had ever expected to, and the only book that he had been pertickularly anxious to write was one locked up in the safe down stairs, not yet published.†

But this intended future of course will never do, and although papa usually holds to his own opinions and intents with outsiders, when

---

† It isn't yet. Title of it, " Captain Stormfield's Visit to Heaven."— S. L. C.

mamma realy desires anything and says that it must be, papa allways gives up his plans (at least so far) and does as she says is right (and she is usually right, if she dissagrees with him at all). It was because he knew his great tendency to being convinced by her, that he published without her knowledge that article in the "Christian Union" concerning the government of children. So judging by the proofs of past years, I think that we will be able to persuade papa to go back to work as before, and not leave off writing with the end of his next story. Mamma says that she sometimes feels, and I do too, that she would rather have papa depend on his writing for a living than to have him think of giving it up.

[*Dictated, November 8, 1906.*] I have a defect of a sort which I think is not common; certainly I hope it isn't: it is rare that I can call before my mind's eye the form and face of either friend or enemy. If I should make a list, now, of persons whom I know in America and abroad—say to the number of even an entire thousand—it is quite unlikely that I could reproduce five of them in my mind's eye. Of my dearest and most intimate friends, I could name eight whom I have seen and talked with four days ago, but when I try to call them before me they are formless shadows. Jean has been absent, this past eight or ten days, in the country, and I wish I could reproduce her in the mirror of my mind, but I can't do it.

It may be that this defect is not constitutional, but a result of lifelong absence of mind and indolent and inadequate observation. Once or twice in my life it has been an embarrassment to me. Twenty years ago, in the days of Susy's Biography of Me, there was a dispute one morning at the breakfast-table about the color of a neighbor's eyes. I was asked for a verdict, but had to confess that if that valued neighbor and old friend had eyes I was not sure that I had ever seen them. It was then mockingly suggested that perhaps I didn't even know the color of the eyes of my own family, and I was required to shut my own at once and testify. I was able to name the color of Mrs. Clemens's eyes, but was not able to even suggest a color for Jean's, or Clara's, or Susy's.

All this talk is suggested by Susy's remark: "The other evening as papa and I were promonading up and down the library." Down to the bottom of my heart I am thankful that I can see *that* picture! And it is not dim, but stands out clear in the unfaded light of twenty-one years ago. In those days

Susy and I used to " promonade " daily up and down the library, with our arms about each other's waists, and deal in intimate communion concerning affairs of State, or the deep questions of human life, or our small personal affairs.

It was quite natural that I should think I had written myself out when I was only fifty years old, for everybody who has ever written has been smitten with that superstition at about that age. Not even yet have I really written myself out. I have merely stopped writing because dictating is pleasanter work, and because dictating has given me a strong aversion to the pen, and because two hours of talking per day is enough, and because— But I am only damaging my mind with this digging around in it for pretexts where no pretext is needed, and where the simple truth is for this one time better than any invention, in this small emergency. I shall never finish my five or six unfinished books, for the reason that by forty years of slavery to the pen I have earned my freedom. I detest the pen and I wouldn't use it again to sign the death warrant of my dearest enemy.

[*Dictated, March 8, 1906.*] For thirty years, I have received an average of a dozen letters a year from strangers who remember me, or whose fathers remember me as boy and young man. But these letters are almost always disappointing. I have not known these strangers nor their fathers. I have not heard of the names they mention; the reminiscences to which they call attention have had no part in my experience; all of which means that these strangers have been mistaking me for somebody else. But at last I have the refreshment, this morning, of a letter from a man who deals in names that were familiar to me in my boyhood. The writer encloses a newspaper clipping which has been wandering through the press for four or five weeks, and he wants to know if Capt. Tonkray, lately deceased, was (as stated in the clipping) the original of " Huckleberry Finn."

I have replied that " Huckleberry Finn " was Frank F. As this inquirer evidently knew the Hannibal of the forties, he will easily recall Frank. Frank's father was at one time Town Drunkard, an exceedingly well-defined and unofficial office of those days. He succeeded " General " Gaines, and for a time he was sole and only incumbent of the office; but afterward Jimmy Finn proved competency and disputed the place with him, so we had two town drunkards at one time—and it made as much trouble in that village as Christendom experienced in the fourteenth century when there were two Popes at the same time.

In " Huckleberry Finn " I have drawn Frank exactly as he was. He was ignorant, unwashed, insufficiently fed; but he had as good a heart as ever any boy had. His liberties were totally unrestricted. He was the only really independent person—boy or man—in the community, and by consequence he was tranquilly and continuously happy, and was envied by all the rest of us. We liked him; we enjoyed his society. And as his society was forbidden us by our parents, the prohibition trebled and quadrupled its value, and therefore we sought and got more of his society than of any other boy's. I heard, four years ago, that he was Justice of the Peace in a remote village in the State of ——, and was a good citizen and was greatly respected.

During Jimmy Finn's term he (Jimmy) was not exclusive; he was not finical; he was not hypercritical; he was largely and handsomely democratic—and slept in the deserted tan-yard with the hogs. My father tried to reform him once, but did not succeed. My father was not a professional reformer. In him the spirit of reform was spasmodic. It only broke out now and then, with considerable intervals between. Once he tried to reform Injun Joe. That also was a failure. It was a failure, and we boys were glad. For Injun Joe, drunk, was interesting and a benefaction to us, but Injun Joe, sober, was a dreary spectacle. We watched my father's experiments upon him with a good deal of anxiety, but it came out all right and we were satisfied. Injun Joe got drunk oftener than before, and became intolerably interesting.

I think that in " Tom Sawyer " I starved Injun Joe to death in the cave. But that may have been to meet the exigencies of romantic literature. I can't remember now whether the real Injun Joe died in the cave or out of it, but I do remember that the news of his death reached me at a most unhappy time— that is to say, just at bedtime on a summer night when a prodigious storm of thunder and lightning accompanied by a deluging rain that turned the streets and lanes into rivers, caused me to repent and resolve to lead a better life. I can remember those awful thunder-bursts and the white glare of the lightning yet, and the wild lashing of the rain against the window-panes. By my teachings I perfectly well knew what all that wild riot was for—Satan had come to get Injun Joe. I had no shadow of doubt about it. It was the proper thing when a person like Injun Joe was required in the under world, and I should have thought it strange and unaccountable if Satan had come for him in a less impressive way. With every glare of lightning I shrivelled and shrunk together in mortal terror, and in the interval of black darkness that followed I poured out my lamentings over my lost condition, and my supplications for just one more chance, with an energy and feeling and sincerity quite foreign to my nature.

But in the morning I saw that it was a false alarm and concluded to resume business at the old stand and wait for another reminder.

The axiom says " History repeats itself." A week or two ago Mr. Blank-Blank dined with us. At dinner he mentioned a circumstance which flashed me back over about sixty years and landed me in that little bedroom on that tempestuous night, and brought to my mind how creditable to me was my conduct through the whole night, and how barren it was of moral spot or fleck during that entire period: he said Mr. X was sexton, or something, of the Episcopal church in his town, and had been for many years the competent superintendent of all the church's worldly affairs, and was regarded by the whole congregation as a stay, a blessing, a priceless treasure. But he had a couple of defects—not large defects, but they seemed large when flung against the background of his profoundly religious character: he drank a good deal, and he could outswear a brakeman. A movement arose to persuade him to lay aside these vices, and after consulting with his pal, who occupied the same position as himself in the other Episcopal church, and whose defects were duplicates of his own and had inspired regret in the congregation he was serving, they concluded to try for reform—not wholesale, but half at a time. They took the liquor pledge and waited for results. During nine days the results were entirely satisfactory, and they were recipients of many compliments and much congratulation. Then on New-year's eve they had business a mile and a half out of town, just beyond the State line. Everything went well with them that evening in the barroom of the inn—but at last the celebration of the occasion by those villagers came to be of a burdensome nature. It was a bitter cold night and the multitudinous hot toddies that were circulating began by and by to exert a powerful influence upon the new prohibitionists. At last X's friend remarked,

" X, does it occur to you that we are *outside the diocese?*"

That ended reform No. 1. Then they took a chance in reform No. 2. For a while that one prospered, and they got much applause. I now reach the incident which sent me back a matter of sixty years, as I have remarked a while ago.

One morning Mr. Blank-Blank met X on the street and said,

" You have made a gallant struggle against those defects of yours. I am aware that you failed on No. 1, but I am also aware that you are having better luck with No. 2."

" Yes," X said; " No. 2 is all right and sound up to date, and we are full of hope."

Blank-Blank said, " X, of course you have your troubles like other people, but they never show on the outside. I have never seen you when you were not cheerful. Are you always cheerful? Really always cheerful?"

" Well, no," he said, " no, I can't say that I am always cheerful, but—well, you know that kind of a night that comes: *say*— you wake up 'way in the night and the whole world is sunk in gloom and there are storms and earthquakes and all sorts of disasters in the air threatening, and you get cold and clammy; and when that happens to me I recognize how sinful I am and it all goes clear to my heart and wrings it and I have such terrors and terrors!—oh, they are indescribable, those terrors that assail me, and I slip out of bed and get on my knees and pray and pray and promise that I *will* be good, if I can only have another chance. And then, you know, in the morning the sun shines out *so* lovely, and the birds sing and the whole world is so beautiful, and—*b' God, I rally!*"

Now I will quote a brief paragraph from this letter which I have a minute ago spoken of. The writer says:

You no doubt are at a loss to know who I am. I will tell you. In my younger days I was a resident of Hannibal, Mo., and you and I were schoolmates attending Mr. Dawson's school along with Sam and Will Bowen and Andy Fuqua and others whose names I have forgotten. I was then about the smallest boy in school, for my age, and they called me little Aleck for short.

I only dimly remember him, but I knew those other people as well as I knew the town drunkards. I remember Dawson's schoolhouse perfectly. If I wanted to describe it I could save myself the trouble by conveying the description of it to these pages from "Tom Sawyer." I can remember the drowsy and inviting summer sounds that used to float in through the open windows from that distant boy-Paradise, Cardiff Hill (Holliday's Hill), and mingle with the murmurs of the studying pupils and make them the more dreary by the contrast. I remember Andy Fuqua, the oldest pupil—a man of twenty-five. I remember the youngest pupil, Nannie Owsley, a child of seven. I remember George Robards, eighteen or twenty years old, the only pupil who studied Latin. I remember—in some cases vividly, in others vaguely—the rest of the twenty-five boys and girls. I remember Mr. Dawson very well. I remember his boy, Theodore, who was as good as he could be. In fact, he was inordinately good, extravagantly good, offensively good, detestably good—and he had pop-eyes—and I would have drowned him if I had had a chance. In that school we were all about on an equality, and, so far as I remember, the passion of envy had no place in our hearts, except in the case of Arch Fuqua—the other one's brother. Of course we all went barefoot in the summer-time. Arch Fuqua was about my own age—ten or eleven. In the winter we could stand him, because he wore shoes then, and his great gift was hidden from our sight and we were enabled to forget it. But in the summer-time he was a bitterness to us. He was our envy, for he could double back his big toe and let it fly and you could hear it snap thirty yards. There was not another boy in the school that could approach this feat. He had not a rival as regards a physical distinction—except in Theodore Eddy, who could work his ears like a horse. But he was no real rival, because you couldn't hear him work his ears; so all the advantage lay with Arch Fuqua.

I am not done with Dawson's school; I will return to it in a later chapter.

[*Dictated at Hamilton, Bermuda, January 6, 1907.*] "That reminds me." In conversation we are always using that phrase, and seldom or never noticing how large a significance it bears. It stands for a curious and interesting fact, to wit: that sleeping or waking, dreaming or talking, the thoughts which swarm through our heads are almost constantly, almost continuously, accompanied by a like swarm of reminders of incidents and episodes of our past. A man can never know what a large traffic this commerce of association carries on in our minds until he sets out to write his autobiography; he then finds that a thought is seldom born to him that does not immediately remind him of some event, large or small, in his past experience. Quite naturally these remarks remind me of various things, among others this: that sometimes a thought, by the power of association, will bring back to your mind a lost word or a lost name which you have not been able to recover by any other process known to your mental equipment. Yesterday we had an instance of this. Rev. Joseph H. Twichell is with me on this flying trip to Bermuda. He was with me on my last visit to Bermuda, and to-day we were trying to remember when it was. We thought it was somewhere in the neighborhood of thirty years ago, but that was as near as we could get at the date. Twichell said that the landlady in whose boarding-house we sojourned in that ancient time could doubtless furnish us the date, and we must look her up. We wanted to see her, anyway, because she and her blooming daughter of eighteen were the only persons whose acquaintance we had made at that time, for we were travelling under fictitious names, and people who wear aliases are not given to seeking society and bringing themselves under suspicion. But at this point in our talk we encountered an obstruction: we could not recall the landlady's name. We hunted all around through our minds for that name, using all the customary methods of research, but without success; the name was gone from us, apparently permanently. We finally gave the matter up, and fell to talking about something else. The talk wandered from one subject to another, and finally arrived at Twichell's school-days in Hartford—the Hartford of something more than half a century ago—and he mentioned several of his schoolmasters, dwelling with special interest upon the peculiarities of an aged one named Olney. He remarked that Olney, humble village schoolmaster as he was, was yet a man of superior parts, and had published text-books which had enjoyed a wide currency in America in their day. I said I remembered those books, and had studied Olney's Geography in school when I was a boy. Then Twichell said,

"That reminds me—our landlady's name was a name that was associated with school-books of some kind or other fifty or sixty years ago. I wonder what it was. I believe it began with K."

Association did the rest, and did it instantly. I said,

"Kirkham's Grammar!"

That settled it. Kirkham was the name; and we went out to seek for the owner of it. There was no trouble about that, for Bermuda is not large, and is like the earlier Garden of Eden, in that everybody in it knows everybody else, just as it was in the serpent's headquarters in Adam's time. We easily found Miss Kirkham—she that had been the blooming girl of a generation before—and she was still keeping boarders; but her mother had passed from this life. She settled the date for us, and did it with certainty, by help of a couple of uncommon circumstances, events of that ancient time. She said we had sailed from Bermuda on the 24th of May, 1877, which was the day on which her only nephew was born—and he is now thirty years of age. The other unusual circumstance—she called it an unusual circumstance, and I didn't say anything—was that on that day the Rev. Mr. Twichell (bearing the assumed name of Peters) had made a statement to her which she regarded as a fiction. I remembered the circumstance very well. We had bidden the young girl good-by and had gone fifty yards, perhaps, when Twichell said he had forgotten something (I doubted it) and must go back. When he rejoined me he was silent, and this alarmed me, because I had not seen an example of it before. He seemed quite uncomfortable, and I asked him what the trouble was. He said he had been inspired to give the girl a pleasant surprise, and so had gone back and said to her—

"That young fellow's name is not Wilkinson—that's Mark Twain."

She did not lose her mind; she did not exhibit any excitement at all, but said quite simply, quite tranquilly,

"Tell it to the marines, Mr. Peters—if that should happen to be *your* name."

It was very pleasant to meet her again. We were white-headed, but she was not; in the sweet and unvexed spiritual atmosphere of the Bermudas one does not achieve gray hairs at forty-eight.

I had a dream last night, and of course it was born of association, like nearly everything else that drifts into a person's head, asleep or awake. On board ship, on the passage down, Twichell was talking about the swiftly developing possibilities of aerial navigation, and he quoted those striking verses of Tennyson's which forecast a future when air-borne vessels of war shall meet and fight above the clouds and redden the earth below with a rain of blood. This picture of carnage and blood and death reminded me of something which I had read a fortnight ago— statistics of railway accidents compiled by the United States Government, wherein the appalling fact was set forth that on our 200,000 miles of railway we annually kill 10,000 persons outright and injure 80,000. The war-ships in the air suggested the railway horrors, and three nights afterward the railway horrors suggested my dream. The work of association was going on in my head, unconsciously, all that time. It was an admirable dream, what there was of it.

In it I saw a funeral procession; I saw it from a mountain peak; I saw it crawling along and curving here and there, serpentlike, through a level vast plain. I seemed to see a hundred miles of the procession, but neither the beginning of it nor the end of it was within the limits of my vision. The procession was in ten divisions, each division marked by a sombre flag, and the whole represented ten years of our railway activities in the accident line; each division was composed of 80,000 cripples, and was bearing its own year's 10,000 mutilated corpses to the grave: in the aggregate 800,000 cripples and 100,000 dead, drenched in blood!

MARK TWAIN.

*(To be Continued.)*

# Chapter XXII

August 16, 1907. Pages 8–21.

PREFATORY NOTE.—Mr. Clemens began to write his autobiography many years ago, and he continues to add to it day by day. It was his original intention to permit no publication of his memoirs until after his death; but, after leaving " Pier No. 70," he concluded that a considerable portion might now suitably be given to the public. It is that portion, garnered from the quarter-million of words already written, which will appear in this REVIEW during the present year. No part of the autobiography will be published in book form during the lifetime of the author.—EDITOR N. A. R.

[*Dictated, October 10, 1906.*] Susy has named a number of the friends who were assembled at Onteora at the time of our **(1890.)** visit, but there were others—among them Laurence Hutton, Charles Dudley Warner, and Carroll Beckwith, and their wives. It was a bright and jolly company. Some of those choice spirits are still with us; the others have passed from this life: Mrs. Clemens, Susy, Mr. Warner, Mary Mapes Dodge, Laurence Hutton, Dean Sage—peace to their ashes! Susy is in error in thinking Mrs. Dodge was not there at that time; we were her guests.

We arrived at nightfall, dreary from a tiresome journey; but the dreariness did not last. Mrs. Dodge had provided a home-made banquet, and the happy company sat down to it, twenty strong, or more. Then the thing happened which always happens at large dinners, and is always exasperating: everybody talked to his elbow-mates and all talked at once, and gradually raised their voices higher, and higher, and higher, in the desperate effort to be heard. It was like a riot, an insurrection; it was an intolerable volume of noise. Presently I said to the lady next me—

" I will subdue this riot, I will silence this racket. There is only one way to do it, but I know the art.  You must tilt your head toward mine and seem to be deeply interested in what I am saying; I will talk in a low voice; then, just because our neighbors won't be able to hear me, they will *want* to hear me.  If I mumble long enough—say two minutes—you will see that the dialogues will one after another come to a standstill, and there will be silence, not a sound anywhere but my mumbling."

Then in a very low voice I began:

" When I went out to Chicago, eleven years ago, to witness the Grant festivities, there was a great banquet on the first night, with six hundred ex-soldiers present.  The gentleman who sat next me was Mr. X. X.  He was very hard of hearing, and he had a habit common to deaf people of shouting his remarks instead of delivering them in an ordinary voice.  He would handle his knife and fork in reflective silence for five or six minutes at a time and then suddenly fetch out a shout that would make you jump out of the United States."

By this time the insurrection at Mrs. Dodge's table—at least that part of it in my immediate neighborhood—had died down, and the silence was spreading, couple by couple, down the long table.  I went on in a lower and still lower mumble, and most impressively—

" During one of Mr. X. X.'s mute intervals, a man opposite us approached the end of a story which he had been telling his elbow-neighbor.  He was speaking in a low voice—there was much noise—I was deeply interested, and straining my ears to catch his words, stretching my neck, holding my breath, to hear, unconscious of everything but the fascinating tale.  I heard him say, ' At this point he seized her by her long hair—she shrieking and begging—bent her neck across his knee, and with one awful sweep of the razor—'

" HOW DO YOU LIKE CHICA-A-AGO?!!!"

That was X. X.'s interruption, hearable at thirty miles.  By the time I had reached that place in my mumblings Mrs. Dodge's dining-room was so silent, so breathlessly still, that if you had dropped a thought anywhere in it you could have heard it smack the floor.*  When I delivered that yell the entire dinner company jumped as one person, and punched their heads through the ceiling, damaging it, for it was only lath and plaster, and it all

* This was tried.  I well remember it.—M. T., *October, '06.*

came down on us, and much of it went into the victuals and made them gritty, but no one was hurt. Then I explained why it was that I had played that game, and begged them to take the moral of it home to their hearts and be rational and merciful thenceforth, and cease from screaming in mass, and agree to let one person talk at a time and the rest listen in grateful and unvexed peace. They granted my prayer, and we had a happy time all the rest of the evening; I do not think I have ever had a better time in my life. This was largely because the new terms enabled me to keep the floor—now that I had it—and do all the talking myself. I do like to hear myself talk. Susy has exposed this in her Biography of me.

Dean Sage was a delightful man, yet in one way a terror to his friends, for he loved them so well that he could not refrain from playing practical jokes on them. We have to be pretty deeply in love with a person before we can do him the honor of joking familiarly with him. Dean Sage was the best citizen I have known in America. It takes courage to be a good citizen, and he had plenty of it. He allowed no individual and no corporation to infringe his smallest right and escape unpunished. He was very rich, and very generous, and benevolent, and he gave away his money with a prodigal hand; but if an individual or corporation infringed a right of his, to the value of ten cents, he would spend thousands of dollars' worth of time and labor and money and persistence on the matter, and would not lower his flag until he had won his battle or lost it.

He and Rev. Mr. Harris had been classmates in college, and to the day of Sage's death they were as fond of each other as an engaged pair. It follows, without saying, that whenever Sage found an opportunity to play a joke upon Harris, Harris was sure to suffer.

Along about 1873 Sage fell a victim to an illness which reduced him to a skeleton, and defied all the efforts of the physicians to cure it. He went to the Adirondacks and took Harris with him. Sage had always been an active man, and he couldn't idle any day wholly away in inanition, but walked every day to the limit of his strength. One day, toward nightfall, the pair came upon a humble log cabin which bore these words painted upon a shingle: "Entertainment for Man and Beast." They were obliged to stop there for the night, Sage's strength being exhausted. They entered the cabin and found its owner and sole occupant there, a rugged and sturdy and simple-hearted man of middle age. He cooked supper and placed it before the travellers —salt junk, boiled beans, corn bread and black coffee. Sage's stomach could abide nothing but the most delicate food, therefore this banquet revolted him, and he sat at the table unemployed, while Harris fed ravenously, limitlessly, gratefully; for he had been chaplain in a fighting regiment all through the war, and had kept in perfection the grand and uncritical appetite and splendid physical vigor which those four years of tough fare and activity had furnished him. Sage went supperless to bed, and tossed and writhed all night upon a shuck mattress that was full of attentive and interested corn-cobs. In the morning Harris was ravenous again, and devoured the odious breakfast as contentedly and as delightedly as he had devoured its twin the night before. Sage sat upon the porch, empty, and contemplated the performance and meditated revenge. Presently he beckoned to the landlord and took him aside and had a confidential talk with him. He said,

"I am the paymaster. What is the bill?"

"Two suppers, fifty cents; two beds, thirty cents; two breakfasts, fifty cents—total, a dollar and thirty cents."

Sage said, "Go back and make out the bill and fetch it to me here on the porch. Make it thirteen dollars."

"Thirteen dollars! Why, it's impossible! I am no robber. I am charging you what I charge everybody. It's a dollar and thirty cents, and that's all it is."

"My man, I've got something to say about this as well as you. It's thirteen dollars. You'll make out your bill for that, and you'll *take* it, too, or you'll not get a cent."

The man was troubled, and said, "I don't understand this. I can't make it out."

"Well, I understand it. I know what I am about. It's thirteen dollars, and I want the bill made out for that. There's no other terms. Get it ready and bring it out here. I will examine it and be outraged. You understand? I will dispute the bill. You must stand to it. You must refuse to take less. I will begin to lose my temper; you must begin to lose yours. I will call you hard names; you must answer with harder ones. I will raise my voice; you must raise yours. You must go into a rage—

foam at the mouth, if you can; insert some soap to help it along. Now go along and follow your instructions."

The man played his assigned part, and played it well. He brought the bill and stood waiting for results. Sage's face began to cloud up, his eyes to snap, and his nostrils to inflate like a horse's; then he broke out with—

"*Thirteen dollars!* You mean to say that you charge thirteen dollars for these damned inhuman hospitalities of yours? Are you a professional buccaneer? Is it your custom to—"

The man burst in with spirit: "Now, I don't want any more out of you—that's a plenty. The bill is thirteen dollars and you'll *pay* it—that's all; a couple of characterless adventurers bilking their way through this country and attempting to dictate terms to a gentleman! a gentleman who received you supposing you were gentlemen yourselves, whereas in my opinion hell's full of—"

Sage broke in—

"Not another word of that!—I won't have it. I regard you as the lowest-down thief that ever—"

"Don't you use that word again! By ——, I'll take you by the neck and—"

Harris came rushing out, and just as the two were about to grapple he pushed himself between them and began to implore—

"Oh, Dean, don't, *don't*—now, Mr. Smith, control yourself! Oh, think of your family, Dean!—think what a scandal—"

But they burst out with maledictions, imprecations and all the hard names they could dig out of the rich accumulations of their educated memories, and in the midst of it the man shouted—

"When *gentlemen* come to this house, I treat them *as* gentlemen. When people come to this house with the ordinary appetites of gentlemen, I charge them a dollar and thirty cents for what I furnished you; but when a man brings a hell-fired Famine here that gorges a barrel of pork and four barrels of beans at two sittings—"

Sage broke in, in a voice that was eloquent with remorse and self-reproach, "I never thought of that, and I ask your pardon; I am ashamed of myself and of my friend. Here's your thirteen dollars, and my apologies along with it."

[*Dictated March 12, 1906.*] I have always taken a great in-

terest in other people's duels. One always feels an abiding interest in any heroic thing which has entered into his own experience.

In 1878, fourteen years after my unmaterialized duel, Mes-
sieurs Fortu and Gambetta fought a duel which made heroes of
**(1878.)** both of them in France, but made them rather ridicu-
lous throughout the rest of the world. I was living in
Munich that fall and winter, and I was so interested in that
funny tragedy that I wrote a long account of it, and it is in one
of my books, somewhere—an account which had some inaccu-
racies in it, but as an exhibition of the *spirit* of that duel, I think
it was correct and trustworthy. And when I was living in
Vienna, thirty-four years after my ineffectual duel, my interest
in that kind of incident was still strong; and I find here among
my Autobiographical manuscripts of that day a chapter which I
began concerning it, but did not finish. I wanted to finish it,
but held it open in the hope that the Italian ambassador, M.
Nigra, would find time to furnish me the *full* history of Señor
Cavalotti's adventures in that line. But he was a busy man;
there was always an interruption before he could get well started;
so my hope was never fulfilled. The following is the unfinished
chapter:

As concerns duelling. This pastime is as common in Austria to-day
as it is in France. But with this difference, that here in the Austrian
**(1898.)** States the duel is dangerous, while in France it is not. Here
it is tragedy, in France it is comedy; here it is a solemnity,
there it is monkey-shines; here the duellist risks his life, there he does
not even risk his shirt. Here he fights with pistol or sabre, in France
with a hairpin—a blunt one. Here the desperately wounded man tries
to walk to the hospital; there they paint the scratch so that they can
find it again, lay the sufferer on a stretcher, and conduct him off the
field with a band of music.

At the end of a French duel the pair hug and kiss and cry, and praise
each other's valor; then the surgeons make an examination and pick
out the scratched one, and the other one helps him on to the litter and
pays his fare; and in return the scratched one treats to champagne and
oysters in the evening, and then "the incident is closed," as the French
say. It is all polite, and gracious, and pretty, and impressive. At the
end of an Austrian duel the antagonist that is alive gravely offers his
hand to the other man, utters some phrases of courteous regret, then
bids him good-by and goes his way, and that incident also is closed.
The French duellist is painstakingly protected from danger, by the rules
of the game. His antagonist's weapon cannot reach so far as his body;
if he get a scratch it will not be above his elbow. But in Austria the

rules of the game do not provide against danger, they carefully provide *for* it, usually. Commonly the combat must be kept up until one of the men is disabled; a non-disabling slash or stab does not retire him.

For a matter of three months I watched the Viennese journals, and whenever a duel was reported in their telegraphic columns I scrap-booked it. By this record I find that duelling in Austria is not confined to journalists and old maids, as in France, but is indulged in by military men, journalists, students, physicians, lawyers, members of the legis-lature, and even the Cabinet, the Bench and the police. Duelling is for-bidden by law; and so it seems odd to see the makers and administrators of the laws dancing on their work in this way. Some months ago Count Bodeni, at that time Chief of the Government, fought a pistol-duel here in the capital city of the Empire with representative Wolf, and both of those distinguished Christians came near getting turned out of the Church—for the Church as well as the State forbids duelling.

In one case, lately, in Hungary, the police interfered and stopped a duel after the first innings. This was a sabre-duel between the chief of police and the city attorney. Unkind things were said about it by the newspapers. They said the police remembered their duty uncom-monly well when their own officials were the parties concerned in duels. But I think the underlings showed good bread-and-butter judgment. If their superiors had carved each other well, the public would have asked, Where were the police? and their places would have been endangered; but custom does not require them to be around where mere unofficial citizens are explaining a thing with sabres.

There was another duel—a double duel—going on in the immediate neighborhood at the time, and in this case the police obeyed custom and did not disturb it. Their bread and butter was not at stake there. In this duel a physician fought a couple of surgeons, and wounded both—one of them lightly, the other seriously. An undertaker wanted to keep people from interfering, but that was quite natural again.

Selecting at random from my record, I next find a duel at Tarnopol between military men. An officer of the Tenth Dragoons charged an officer of the Ninth Dragoons with an offence against the laws of the card-table. There was a defect or a doubt somewhere in the matter, and this had to be examined and passed upon by a Court of Honor. So the case was sent up to Lemberg for this purpose. One would like to know what the defect was, but the newspaper does not say. A man here who has fought many duels and has a graveyard, says that probably the matter in question was as to whether the accusation was true or not; that if the charge was a very grave one—cheating, for instance—proof of its truth would rule the guilty officer out of the field of honor; the Court would not allow a gentleman to fight with such a person. You see what a solemn thing it is; you see how particular they are; any lit-tle careless act can lose you your privilege of getting yourself shot, here. The Court seems to have gone into the matter in a searching and careful fashion, for several months elapsed before it reached a decision. It then sanctioned a duel and the accused killed his accuser.

Next I find a duel between a prince and a major; first with pistols —no result satisfactory to either party; then with sabres, and the major badly hurt.

Next, a sabre-duel between journalists—the one a strong man, the other feeble and in poor health. It was brief; the strong one drove his sword through the weak one, and death was immediate.

Next, a duel between a lieutenant and a student of medicine. According to the newspaper report these are the details. The student was in a restaurant one evening: passing along, he halted at a table to speak with some friends; near by sat a dozen military men; the student conceived that one of these was "staring" at him; he asked the officer to step outside and explain. This officer and another one gathered up their caps and sabres and went out with the student. Outside—this is the student's account—the student introduced himself to the offending officer and said, "You seemed to stare at me"; for answer, the officer struck at the student with his fist; the student parried the blow; both officers drew their sabres and attacked the young fellow, and one of them gave him a wound on the left arm; then they withdrew. This was Saturday night. The duel followed on Monday, in the military riding-school — the customary duelling-ground all over Austria, apparently. The weapons were pistols. The duelling terms were somewhat beyond custom in the matter of severity, if I may gather that from the statement that the combat was fought "*unter sehr schweren Bedingungen*"—to wit, "Distance, 15 steps—with 3 steps advance." There was but one exchange of shots. The student was hit. "He put his hand on his breast, his body began to bend slowly forward, then collapsed in death and sank to the ground."

It is pathetic. There are other duels in my list, but I find in each and all of them one and the same ever-recurring defect—the *principals* are never present, but only their sham representatives. The *real* principals in any duel are not the duellists themselves, but their families. They do the mourning, the suffering, theirs is the loss and theirs the misery. They stake all that, the duellist stakes nothing but his life, and that is a trivial thing compared with what his death must cost those whom he leaves behind him. Challenges should not mention the duellist; he has nothing much at stake, and the real vengeance cannot reach him. The challenge should summon the offender's old gray mother, and his young wife and his little children,—these, or any to whom he is a dear and worshipped possession—and should say, "You have done me no harm, but I am the meek slave of a custom which requires me to crush the happiness out of your hearts and condemn you to years of pain and grief, in order that I may wash clean with your tears a stain which has been put upon me by another person."

The logic of it is admirable: a person has robbed me of a penny; I must beggar ten innocent persons to make good my loss. Surely nobody's "honor" is worth all that.

Since the duellist's family are the real principals in a duel, the State ought to compel them to be present at it. Custom, also, ought to be so amended as to require it; and without it no duel ought to be allowed to go on. If that student's unoffending mother had been present and watching the officer through her tears as he raised his pistol, he—why, he would have fired in the air. We know that. For we know how we are all made. Laws ought to be based upon the ascertained facts of our nature. It would be a simple thing to make a duelling law which would stop duelling.

As things are now, the mother is never invited. She submits to this; and without outward complaint, for she, too, is the vassal of custom, and custom requires her to conceal her pain when she learns the disastrous news that her son must go to the duelling-field, and by the powerful force that is lodged in habit and custom she is enabled to obey this trying requirement—a requirement which exacts a miracle of her, and gets it. Last January a neighbor of ours who has a young son in the army was wakened by this youth at three o'clock one morning, and she sat up in bed and listened to his message:

" I have come to tell you something, mother, which will distress you, but you must be good and brave, and bear it. I have been affronted by a fellow officer, and we fight at three this afternoon. Lie down and sleep, now, and think no more about it."

She kissed him good night and lay down paralyzed with grief and fear, but said nothing. But she did not sleep; she prayed and mourned till the first streak of dawn, then fled to the nearest church and implored the Virgin for help; and from that church she went to another and another and another; church after church, and still church after church, and so spent all the day until three o'clock on her knees in agony and tears; then dragged herself home and sat down comfortless and desolate, to count the minutes, and wait, with an outward show of calm, for what had been ordained for her—happiness, or endless misery. Presently she heard the clank of a sabre—she had not known before what music was in that sound!—and her son put his head in and said:

" X was in the wrong, and he apologized."

So that incident was closed; and for the rest of her life the mother will always find something pleasant about the clank of a sabre, no doubt.

In one of my listed duels—however, let it go, there is nothing particularly striking about . it except that the seconds interfered. And prematurely, too, for neither man was dead. This was certainly irregular. Neither of the men liked it. It was a duel with cavalry sabres, between an editor and a lieutenant. The editor walked to the hospital, the lieutenant was carried. In this country an editor who can write well is valuable, but he is not likely to remain so unless he can handle a sabre with charm.

The following very recent telegram shows that also in France duels are humanely stopped as soon as they approach the (French) danger-point:

" *Reuter's Telegram.*—PARIS, *March 5.*—The duel between Colonels Henry and Picquart took place this morning in the Riding School of the Ecole Militaire, the doors of which were strictly guarded in order to prevent intrusion. The combatants, who fought with swords, were in position at ten o'clock.

"At the first reengagement Lieutenant-Colonel Henry was slightly scratched in the fore arm, and just at the same moment his own blade appeared to touch his adversary's neck. Senator Ranc, who was Colonel Picquart's second, stopped the fight, but as it was found that his principal had not been touched, the combat continued. A very sharp encounter ensued, in which Colonel Henry was wounded in the elbow, and the duel terminated."

After which, the stretcher and the band. In lurid contrast with this delicate flirtation, we have this fatal duel of day before yesterday in Italy, where the earnest Austrian duel is in vogue. I knew Cavalotti slightly, and this gives me a sort of personal interest in his duel. I first saw him in Rome several years ago. He was sitting on a block of stone in the Forum, and was writing something in his note-book—a poem or a challenge, or something like that—and the friend who pointed him out to me said, "That is Cavalotti—he has fought thirty duels; do not disturb him." I did not disturb him.

[*May 13, 1907.*] It is a long time ago. Cavalotti—poet, orator, satirist, statesman, patriot—was a great man, and his death was deeply lamented by his countrymen: many monuments to his memory testify to this. In his duels he killed several of his antagonists and disabled the rest. By nature he was a little irascible. Once when the officials of the library of Bologna threw out his books the gentle poet went up there and challenged the whole fifteen! His parliamentary duties were exacting, but he proposed to keep coming up and fighting duels between trains until all those officials had been retired from the activities of life. Although he always chose the sword to fight with, he had never had a lesson with that weapon. When game was called he waited for nothing, but always plunged at his opponent and rained such a storm of wild and original thrusts and whacks upon him that the man was dead or crippled before he could bring his science to bear. But his latest antagonist discarded science, and won. He held his sword straight forward like a lance when Cavalotti made his plunge—with the result that he impaled himself upon it. It entered his mouth and passed out at the back of his neck. Death was instantaneous.

[*Dictated December 20, 1906.*] Six months ago, when I was recalling early days in San Francisco, I broke off at a place where

I was about to tell about Captain Osborn's odd adventure at the
" What Cheer," or perhaps it was at another cheap feeding-place
—the " Miners' Restaurant." It was a place where one could get
good food on the cheapest possible terms, and its popularity was
great among the multitudes whose purses were light. It was a
good place to go to, to observe mixed humanity. Captain Osborn
and Bret Harte went there one day and took a meal, and in the
course of it Osborn fished up an interesting reminiscence of a
dozen years before and told about it. It was to this effect:

He was a midshipman in the navy when the Californian gold
craze burst upon the world and set it wild with excitement. His
ship made the long journey around the Horn and was approaching her goal, the Golden Gate, when an accident happened.

" It happened to me," said Osborn. " I fell overboard. There
was a heavy sea running, but no one was much alarmed about
me, because we had on board a newly patented life-saving device
which was believed to be competent to rescue anything that could
fall overboard, from a midshipman to an anchor. Ours was the
only ship that had this device; we were very proud of it, and had
been anxious to give its powers a practical test. This thing was
lashed to the garboard-strake of the main-to'gallant mizzen-yard
amidships,* and there was nothing to do but cut the lashings
and heave it over; it would do the rest. One day the cry of
' Man overboard!' brought all hands on deck. Instantly
the lashings were cut and the machine flung joyously over.
Damnation, it went to the bottom like an anvil! By the time
that the ship was brought to and a boat manned, I was become
but a bobbing speck on the waves half a mile astern and losing
my strength very fast; but by good luck there was a common
seaman on board who had practical ideas in his head and hadn't
waited to see what the patent machine was going to do, but had
run aft and sprung over after me the moment the alarm was
cried through the ship. I had a good deal of a start of him, and
the seas made his progress slow and difficult, but he stuck to his
work and fought his way to me, and just in the nick of time he
put his saving arms about me when I was about to go down. He
held me up until the boat reached us and rescued us. By that
time I was unconscious, and I was still unconscious when we
arrived at the ship. A dangerous fever followed, and I was de-

* Can this be correct? I think there must be some mistake—M. T.

lirious for three days; then I came to myself and at once inquired for my benefactor, of course. He was gone. We were lying at anchor in the Bay and every man had deserted to the gold-mines except the commissioned officers. I found out nothing about my benefactor but his name—Burton Sanders—a name which I have held in grateful memory ever since. Every time I have been on the Coast, these twelve or thirteen years, I have tried to get track of him, but have never succeeded. I wish I could find him and make him understand that his brave act has never been forgotten by me. Harte, I would rather see him and take him by the hand than any other man on the planet."

At this stage or a little later there was an interruption. A waiter near by said to another waiter, pointing,

" Take a look at that tramp that's coming in. Ain't that the one that bilked the house, last week, out of ten cents?"

" I believe it is. Let him alone—don't pay any attention to him; wait till we can get a good look at him."

The tramp approached timidly and hesitatingly, with the air of one unsure and apprehensive. The waiters watched him furtively. When he was passing behind Harte's chair one of them said,

" He's the one!"—and they pounced upon him and proposed to turn him over to the police as a bilk. He begged piteously. He confessed his guilt, but said he had been driven to his crime by necessity—that when he had eaten the plate of beans and slipped out without paying for it, it was because he was starving, and hadn't the ten cents to pay for it with. But the waiters would listen to no explanations, no palliations; he must be placed in custody. He brushed his hand across his eyes and said meekly that he would submit, being friendless. Each waiter took him by an arm and faced him about to conduct him away. Then his melancholy eyes fell upon Captain Osborn, and a light of glad and eager recognition flashed from them. He said,

" Weren't you a midshipman once, sir, in the old ' Lancaster ' ?"

" Yes," said Osborn. " Why ?"

" Didn't you fall overboard?"

" Yes, I did. How do you come to know about it?"

" Wasn't there a new patent machine aboard, and didn't they throw it over to save you?"

" Why, yes," said Osborn, laughing gently, " but it didn't do it."

" No, sir, it was a sailor that done it."

" It certainly was. Look here, my man, you are getting distinctly interesting. Were you of our crew?"

" Yes, sir, I was."

" I reckon you may be right. You do certainly know a good deal about that incident. What is your name?"

" Burton Sanders."

The Captain sprang up, excited, and said,

" Give me your hand! Give me both your hands! I'd rather shake them than inherit a fortune!"—and then he cried to the waiters, " Let him go!—take your hands off! He is my guest, and can have anything and everything this house is able to furnish. I am responsible."

There was a love-feast, then. Captain Osborn ordered it regardless of expense, and he and Harte sat there and listened while the man told stirring adventures of his life and fed himself up to the eyebrows. Then Osborn wanted to be benefactor in his turn, and pay back some of his debt. The man said it could all be paid with ten dollars—that it had been so long since he had owned that amount of money that it would seem a fortune to him, and he should be grateful beyond words if the Captain could spare him that amount. The Captain spared him ten broad twenty-dollar gold pieces, and made him take them in spite of his modest protestations, and gave him his address and said he must never fail to give him notice when he needed grateful service.

Several months later Harte stumbled upon the man in the street. He was most comfortably drunk, and pleasant and chatty. Harte remarked upon the splendidly and movingly dramatic incident of the restaurant, and said,

" How curious and fortunate and happy and interesting it was that you two should come together, after that long separation, and at exactly the right moment to save you from disaster and turn your defeat by the waiters into a victory. A preacher could make a great sermon out of that, for it does look as if the hand of Providence was in it."

The hero's face assumed a sweetly genial expression, and he said,

" Well now, it wasn't Providence this time. I was running the arrangements myself."

" How do you mean?"

" Oh, I hadn't ever seen the gentleman before. I was at the next table, with my back to you the whole time he was telling about it. I saw my chance, and slipped out and fetched the two waiters with me and offered to give them a commission out of what I could get out of the Captain if they would do a quarrel act with me and give me an opening. So, then, after a minute or two I straggled back, and you know the rest of it as well as I do."

MARK TWAIN.

*(To be Continued.)*

# Chapter XXIII

October, 1907. Pages 161–73.

PREFATORY NOTE.—Mr. Clemens began to write his autobiography many years ago, and he continues to add to it day by day. It was his original intention to permit no publication of his memoirs until after his death; but, after leaving "Pier No. 70," he concluded that a considerable portion might now suitably be given to the public. It is that portion, garnered from the quarter-million of words already written, which will appear in this REVIEW during the present year. No part of the autobiography will be published in book form during the lifetime of the author.—EDITOR N. A. R.

[*Dictated March 9, 1906.*] . . . I am talking of a time sixty years ago, and upwards. I remember the names of some of those **(1845.)** schoolmates, and, by fitful glimpses, even their faces rise dimly before me for a moment—only just long enough to be recognized; then they vanish. I catch glimpses of George Robards, the Latin pupil—slender, pale, studious, bending over his book and absorbed in it, his long straight black hair hanging down below his jaws like a pair of curtains on the sides of his face. I can see him give his head a toss and flirt one of the curtains back around his head—to get it out of his way, apparently; really to show off. In that day it was a great thing among the boys to have hair of so flexible a sort that it could be flung back in that way, with a flirt of the head. George Robards was the envy of us all. For there was no hair among

236

us that was so competent for this exhibition as his—except, perhaps, the yellow locks of Will Bowen and John Robards. My hair was a dense ruck of short curls, and so was my brother Henry's. We tried all kinds of devices to get these crooks straightened out so that they would flirt, but we never succeeded. Sometimes, by soaking our heads and then combing and brushing our hair down tight and flat to our skulls, we could get it straight, temporarily, and this gave us a comforting moment of joy; but the first time we gave it a flirt it all shrivelled into curls again and our happiness was gone.

John Robards was the little brother of George; he was a wee chap with silky golden curtains to his face which dangled to his shoulders and below, and could be flung back ravishingly. When he was twelve years old he crossed the plains with his father amidst the rush of the gold-seekers of '49; and I remember the departure of the cavalcade when it spurred westward. We were all there to see and to envy. And I can still see that proud little chap sailing by on a great horse, with his long locks streaming out behind. We were all on hand to gaze and envy when he returned, two years later, in unimaginable glory—*for he had travelled!* None of us had ever been forty miles from home. But he had crossed the Continent. He had been in the gold-mines, that fairyland of our imagination. And he had done a still more wonderful thing. He had been in ships—in ships on the actual ocean; in ships on three actual oceans. For he had sailed down the Pacific and around the Horn among icebergs and through snow-storms and wild wintry gales, and had sailed on and turned the corner and flown northward in the trades and up through the blistering equatorial waters—and there in his brown face were the proofs of what he had been through. We would have sold our souls to Satan for the privilege of trading places with him.

I saw him when I was out on that Missouri trip four years ago. He was old then—though not quite so old as I—and the burden of life was upon him. He said his granddaughter, twelve years old, had read my books and would like to see me. It was a pathetic time, for she was a prisoner in her room and marked for death. And John knew that she was passing swiftly away. Twelve years old—just her grandfather's age when he rode away on that great journey with his yellow hair flapping behind him.

In her I seemed to see that boy again. It was as if he had come back out of that remote past and was present before me in his golden youth. Her malady was heart disease, and her brief life came to a close a few days later.

Another of those schoolboys was John Garth. He became a prosperous banker and a prominent and valued citizen; and a few years ago he died, rich and honored. *He died.* It is what I have to say about so many of those boys and girls. The widow still lives, and there are grandchildren. In her pantalette days and my barefoot days she was a schoolmate of mine. I saw John's tomb when I made that Missouri visit.

Her father, Mr. Kercheval, had an apprentice in the early days when I was nine years old, and he had also a slave woman who had many merits. But I can't feel very kindly or forgivingly toward either that good apprentice boy or that good slave woman, for they saved my life. One day when I was playing on a loose log which I supposed was attached to a raft—but it wasn't—it tilted me into Bear Creek. And when I had been under water twice and was coming up to make the third and fatal descent my fingers appeared above the water and that slave woman seized them and pulled me out. Within a week I was in again, and that apprentice had to come along just at the wrong time, and he plunged in and dived, pawed around on the bottom and found me, and dragged me out and emptied the water out of me, and I was saved again. I was drowned seven times after that before I learned to swim—once in Bear Creek and six times in the Mississippi. I do not now know who the people were who interfered with the intentions of a Providence wiser than themselves, but I hold a grudge against them yet. When I told the tale of these remarkable happenings to Rev. Dr. Burton of Hartford, he said he did not believe it. *He slipped on the ice the very next year and sprained his ankle.*

Will Bowen was another schoolmate, and so was his brother, Sam, who was his junior by a couple of years. Before the Civil War broke out, both became St. Louis and New Orleans pilots. Both are dead, long ago.

[*Dictated March 16, 1906.*] We will return to those school-children of sixty years ago. I recall Mary Miller. She was not **(1845.)** my first sweetheart, but I think she was the first one that furnished me a broken heart. I fell in love with her when she was eighteen and I was nine, but she scorned me, and I recognized that this was a cold world. I had not noticed that temperature before. I believe I was as miserable as even a grown man could be. But I think that this sorrow did not remain with me long. As I remember it, I soon transferred my worship to Artimisia Briggs, who was a year older than Mary Miller. When I revealed my passion to her she did not scoff at it. She did not make fun of it. She was very kind and gentle about it. But she was also firm, and said she did not want to be pestered by children.

And there was Mary Lacy. She was a schoolmate. But she also was out of my class because of her advanced age. She was pretty wild and determined and independent. But she married, and at once settled down and became in all ways a model matron and was as highly respected as any matron in the town. Four years ago she was still living, and had been married fifty years.

Jimmie McDaniel was another schoolmate. His age and mine about tallied. His father kept the candy-shop and he was the most envied little chap in the town—after Tom Blankenship (" Huck Finn ")—for although we never saw him eating candy, we supposed that it was, nevertheless, his ordinary diet. He pretended that he never ate it, and didn't care for it because there was nothing forbidden about it—there was plenty of it and he could have as much of it as he wanted. He was the first human being to whom I ever told a humorous story, so far as I can remember. This was about Jim Wolfe and the cats; and I gave him that tale the morning after that memorable episode. I thought he would laugh his teeth out. I had never been so proud and happy before, and have seldom been so proud and happy since. I saw him four years ago when I was out there. He wore a beard, gray and venerable, that came half-way down to his knees, and yet it was not difficult for me to recognize him. He had been married fifty-four years. He had many children and grandchildren and great-grandchildren, and also even posterity, they all said—thousands—yet the boy to whom I had told the cat story when we were callow juveniles was still present in that cheerful little old man.

Artimisia Briggs got married not long after refusing me. She married Richmond, the stone mason, who was my Methodist Sunday-school teacher in the earliest days, and he had one dis-

tinction which I envied him: at some time or other he had hit
his thumb with his hammer and the result was a thumb nail
which remained permanently twisted and distorted and curved
and pointed, like a parrot's beak.  I should not consider it an
ornament now, I suppose, but it had a fascination for me then,
and a vast value, because it was the only one in the town.  He
was a very kindly and considerate Sunday-school teacher, and
patient and compassionate, so he was the favorite teacher with us
little chaps.  In that school they had slender oblong pasteboard
blue tickets, each with a verse from the Testament printed on it,
and you could get a blue ticket by reciting two verses.  By reciting five verses you could get three blue tickets, and you could
trade these at the bookcase and borrow a book for a week.  I
was under Mr. Richmond's spiritual care every now and then
for two or three years, and he was never hard upon me.  I always recited the same five verses every Sunday.  He was always
satisfied with the performance.  He never seemed to notice that
these were the same five foolish virgins that he had been hearing
about every Sunday for months.  I always got my tickets and ex-
changed them for a book.  They were pretty dreary books, for
there was not a bad boy in the entire bookcase.  They were *all*
good boys and good girls and drearily uninteresting, but they
were better society than none, and I was glad to have their
company and disapprove of it.

Twenty years ago Mr. Richmond had become possessed of Tom
Sawyer's cave in the hills three miles from town, and had made
a tourist-resort of it.  In 1849 when the gold-seekers were
streaming through our little town of Hannibal, many of our
grown men got the gold fever, and I think that all the boys had
it.  On the Saturday holidays in summer-time we used to borrow
**(1849.)** skiffs whose owners were not present and go down the
river three miles to the cave hollow (Missourian for " valley "), and there we staked out claims and pretended to dig gold,
panning out half a dollar a day at first; two or three times as much,
later, and by and by whole fortunes, as our imaginations became
inured to the work. Stupid and unprophetic lads!  We were
doing this in play and never suspecting.  Why, that cave hollow
and all the adjacent hills were made of gold!  But we did not
know it.  We took it for dirt.  We left its rich secret in its own
peaceful possession and grew up in poverty and went wandering

about the world struggling for bread—and this because we had not the gift of prophecy. That region was all dirt and rocks to us, yet all it needed was to be ground up and scientifically handled and it was gold. That is to say, the whole region was a cement-mine—and they make the finest kind of Portland cement there now, five thousand barrels a day, with a plant that cost $2,000,000.

For a little while Reuel Gridley attended that school of ours. He was an elderly pupil; he was perhaps twenty-two or twenty-three years old. Then came the Mexican War and he volunteered. A company of infantry was raised in our town and Mr. Hickman, a tall, straight, handsome athlete of twenty-five, was made captain of it and had a sword by his side and a broad yellow stripe down the leg of his gray pants. And when that company marched back and forth through the streets in its smart uniform —which it did several times a day for drill—its evolutions were attended by all the boys whenever the school hours permitted. I can see that marching company yet, and I can almost feel again the consuming desire that I had to join it. But they had no use for boys of twelve and thirteen, and before I had a chance in another war the desire to kill people to whom I had not been introduced had passed away.

I saw the splendid Hickman in his old age. He seemed about the oldest man I had ever seen—an amazing and melancholy contrast with the showy young captain I had seen preparing his warriors for carnage so many, many years before. Hickman is dead—it is the old story. As Susy said, " What is it all for?"

Reuel Gridley went away to the wars and we heard of him no more for fifteen or sixteen years. Then one day in Carson City while I was having a difficulty with an editor on the sidewalk —an editor better built for war than I was—I heard a voice say, " Give him the best you've got, Sam, I'm at your back." It was Reuel Gridley. He said he had not recognized me by my face but by my drawling style of speech.

He went down to the Reese River mines about that time and presently he lost an election bet in his mining camp, and by the terms of it he was obliged to buy a fifty-pound sack of self-raising flour and carry it through the town, preceded by music, and deliver it to the winner of the bet. Of course the whole camp was present and full of fluid and enthusiasm. The winner of the bet put up the sack at auction for the benefit of the United States Sanitary Fund, and sold it. The excitement grew and grew. The sack was sold over and over again for the benefit of the Fund. The news of it came to Virginia City by telegraph. It produced great enthusiasm, and Reuel Gridley was begged by telegraph to bring the sack and have an auction in Virginia City. He brought it. An open barouche was provided, also a brass band. The sack was sold over and over again at Gold Hill, then was brought up to Virginia City toward night and sold—and sold again, and again, and still again, netting twenty or thirty thousand dollars for the Sanitary Fund. Gridley carried it across California and sold it at various towns. He sold it for large sums in Sacramento and in San Francisco. He brought it East, sold it in New York and in various other cities, then carried it out to a great Fair at St. Louis, and went on selling it; and finally made it up into small cakes and sold those at a dollar apiece. First and last, the sack of flour which had originally cost ten dollars, perhaps, netted more than two hundred thousand dollars for the Sanitary Fund. Reuel Gridley has been dead these many, many years—it is the old story.

In that school were the first Jews I had ever seen. It took me a good while to get over the awe of it. To my fancy they were clothed invisibly in the damp and cobwebby mould of antiquity. They carried me back to Egypt, and in imagination I moved among the Pharaohs and all the shadowy celebrities of that remote age. The name of the boys was Levin. We had a collective name for them which was the only really large and handsome witticism that was ever born in that Congressional district. We called them " Twenty-two "—and even when the joke was old and had been worn threadbare we always followed it with the explanation, to make sure that it would be understood, " Twice Levin—twenty-two."

There were other boys whose names remain with me. Irving Ayres—but no matter, he is dead. Then there was George Butler, whom I remember as a child of seven wearing a blue leather belt with a brass buckle, and hated and envied by all the boys on account of it. He was a nephew of General Ben Butler and fought gallantly at Ball's Bluff and in several other actions of the Civil War. He is dead, long and long ago.

Will Bowen (dead long ago), Ed Stevens (dead long ago)

and John Briggs were special mates of mine. John is still
living.

In 1845, when I was ten years old, there was an epidemic of
measles in the town and it made a most alarming slaughter
**(1845.)** among the little people. There was a funeral almost
daily, and the mothers of the town were nearly demented
with fright. My mother was greatly troubled. She worried
over Pamela and Henry and me, and took constant and extraordinary pains to keep us from coming into contact with the
contagion. But upon reflection I believed that her judgment
was at fault. It seemed to me that I could improve upon it
if left to my own devices. I cannot remember now whether I
was frightened about the measles or not, but I clearly remember
that I grew very tired of the suspense I suffered on account of
being continually under the threat of death. I remember that
I got so weary of it and so anxious to have the matter settled one
way or the other, and promptly, that this anxiety spoiled my
days and my nights. I had no pleasure in them. I made up
my mind to end this suspense and be done with it. Will Bowen
was dangerously ill with the measles and I thought I would go
down there and catch them. I entered the house by the front
way and slipped along through rooms and halls, keeping sharp
watch against discovery, and at last I reached Will's bed-chamber
in the rear of the house on the second floor and got into it un-
captured. But that was as far as my victory reached. His
mother caught me there a moment later and snatched me out
of the house and gave me a most competent scolding and drove
me away. She was so scared that she could hardly get her words
out, and her face was white. I saw that I must manage better
next time, and I did. I hung about the lane at the rear of the
house and watched through cracks in the fence until I was convinced that the conditions were favorable; then I slipped through
the back yard and up the back way and got into the room and
into the bed with Will Bowen without being observed. I don't
know how long I was in the bed. I only remember that Will
Bowen, as society, had no value for me, for he was too sick to
even notice that I was there. When I heard his mother coming
I covered up my head, but that device was a failure. It was
dead summer-time—the cover was nothing more than a limp
blanket or sheet, and anybody could see that there were two of us

under it. It didn't remain two very long. Mrs. Bowen snatched
me out of the bed and conducted me home herself, with a grip
on my collar which she never loosened until she delivered me
into my mother's hands along with her opinion of that kind of
a boy.

It was a good case of measles that resulted. It brought me
within a shade of death's door. It brought me to where I no
longer took any interest in anything, but, on the contrary, felt a
total absence of interest—which was most placid and enchanting.
I have never enjoyed anything in my life any more than I enjoyed dying that time. I *was,* in effect, dying. The word had
been passed and the family notified to assemble around the bed
and see me off. I knew them all. There was no doubtfulness
in my vision. They were all crying, but that did not affect me.
I took but the vaguest interest in it, and that merely because I
was the centre of all this emotional attention and was gratified
by it and vain of it.

When Dr. Cunningham had made up his mind that nothing
more could be done for me he put bags of hot ashes all over
me. He put them on my breast, on my wrists, on my ankles;
and so, very much to his astonishment—and doubtless to my regret—he dragged me back into this world and set me going
again.

[*Dictated July 26, 1907.*] In an article entitled "England's
Ovation to Mark Twain," Sydney Brooks—but never mind that,
now.

I was in Oxford by seven o'clock that evening (June 25, 1907),
and trying on the scarlet gown which the tailor had been constructing, and found it right—right and surpassingly becoming.
At half past ten the next morning we assembled at All Souls
College and marched thence, gowned, mortar-boarded and in
double file, down a long street to the Sheldonian Theatre, between
solid walls of the populace, very much hurrah'd and limitlessly
kodak'd. We made a procession of considerable length and
distinction and picturesqueness, with the Chancellor, Lord Curzon,
late Viceroy of India, in his rich robe of black and gold, in the
lead, followed by a pair of trim little boy train-bearers, and the
train-bearers followed by the young Prince Arthur of Connaught,
who was to be made a D.C.L. The detachment of D.C.L.'s were
followed by the Doctors of Science, and these by the Doctors of

Literature, and these in turn by the Doctors of Music. Sidney Colvin marched in front of me; I was coupled with Sidney Lee, and Kipling followed us; General Booth, of the Salvation Army, was in the squadron of D.C.L.'s.

Our journey ended, we were halted in a fine old hall whence we could see, through a corridor of some length, the massed audience in the theatre. Here for a little time we moved about and chatted and made acquaintanceships; then the D.C.L.'s were summoned, and they marched through that corridor and the shouting began in the theatre. It would be some time before the Doctors of Literature and of Science would be called for, because each of those D.C.L.'s had to have a couple of Latin speeches made over him before his promotion would be complete —one by the Regius Professor of Civil Law, the other by the Chancellor. After a while I asked Sir William Ramsay if a person might smoke here and not get shot. He said, " Yes," but that whoever did it and got caught would be fined a guinea, and perhaps hanged later. He said he knew of a place where we could accomplish at least as much as half of a smoke before any informers would be likely to chance upon us, and he was ready to show the way to any who might be willing to risk the guinea and the hanging. By request he led the way, and Kipling, Sir Norman Lockyer and I followed. We crossed an unpopulated quadrangle and stood under one of its exits—an archway of massive masonry—and there we lit up and began to take comfort. The photographers soon arrived, but they were courteous and friendly and gave us no trouble, and we gave them none. They grouped us in all sorts of ways and photographed us at their diligent leisure, while we smoked and talked. We were there more than an hour; then we returned to headquarters, happy, content, and greatly refreshed. Presently we filed into the theatre, under a very satisfactory hurrah, and waited in a crimson column, dividing the crowded pit through the middle, until each of us in his turn should be called to stand before the Chancellor and hear our merits set forth in sonorous Latin. Meantime, Kipling and I wrote autographs until some good kind soul interfered in our behalf and procured for us a rest.

I will now save what is left of my modesty by quoting a paragraph from Sydney Brooks's " Ovation."

     *      *      *      *      *      *

Let those stars take the place of it for the present.  Sydney
Brooks has done it well.  It makes me proud to read it; as proud
as I was in that old day, sixty-two years ago, when I lay dying,
the centre of attraction, with one eye piously closed upon the
fleeting vanities of this life—an excellent effect—and the other
open a crack to observe the tears, the sorrow, the admiration—all
for me—all for me!

Ah, that was the proudest moment of my long life—until
Oxford!

&ast;          &ast;          &ast;          *          *          *

Most Americans have been to Oxford and will remember what a
dream of the Middle Ages it is, with its crooked lanes, its gray
and stately piles of ancient architecture and its meditation-breed-
ing air of repose and dignity and unkinship with the noise and
fret and hurry and bustle of these modern days.  As a dream of the
Middle Ages Oxford was not perfect until Pageant day arrived and
furnished certain details which had been for generations lacking.
These details began to appear at mid-afternoon on the 27th.  At
that time singles, couples, groups and squadrons of the three thousand five hundred costumed characters who were to take part in
the Pageant began to ooze and drip and stream through house
doors, all over the old town, and wend toward the meadows outside
the walls.  Soon the lanes were thronged with costumes which Oxford had from time to time seen and been familiar with in bygone
centuries—fashions of dress which marked off centuries as by
dates, and mile-stoned them back, and back, and back, until history faded into legend and tradition, when Arthur was a fact
and the Round Table a reality.  In this rich commingling of
quaint and strange and brilliantly colored fashions in dress the
dress-changes of Oxford for twelve centuries stood livid and
realized to the eye; Oxford as a dream of the Middle Ages was
complete now as it had never, in our day, before been complete;
at last there was no discord; the mouldering old buildings, and the
picturesque throngs drifting past them, were in harmony; soon—
astonishingly soon!—the only persons that seemed out of place,
and grotesquely and offensively and criminally out of place were
such persons as came intruding along clothed in the ugly and
odious fashions of the twentieth century; they were a bitterness to
the feelings, an insult to the eye.

The make-ups of illustrious historic personages seemed perfect,

both as to portraiture and costume; one had no trouble in recog
nizing them.   Also, I was apparently quite easily recognizable
myself.   The first corner I turned brought me suddenly face to
face with Henry VIII, a person whom I had been implacably dis-
liking for sixty years; but when he put out his hand with royal
courtliness and grace and said, " Welcome, well-beloved stranger,
to my century and to the hospitalities of my realm," my old prejudices vanished away and I forgave him.   I think now that Henry
the Eighth has been over-abused, and that most of us, if we had
been situated as he was, domestically, would not have been able to
get along with as limited a graveyard as he forced himself to put
up with.   I feel now that he was one of the nicest men in history.
Personal contact with a king is more effective in removing baleful
prejudices than is any amount of argument drawn from tales and
histories.   If I had a child I would name it Henry the Eighth,
regardless of sex.

Do you remember Charles the First?—and his broad slouch
with the plume in it? and his slender, tall figure? and his body
clothed in velvet doublet with lace sleeves, and his legs in leather,
with long rapier at his side and his spurs on his heels?   I encountered him at the next corner, and knew him in a moment—knew
him as perfectly and as vividly as I should know the Grand Chain
in the Mississippi if I should see it from the pilot-house after all
these years.   He bent his body and gave his hat a sweep that
fetched its plume within an inch of the ground, and gave me a
welcome that went to my heart.   This king has been much
maligned; I shall understand him better hereafter, and shall regret him more than I have been in the habit of doing these fifty
or sixty years.   He did some things in his time, which might better have been left undone, and which cast a shadow upon his
name—we all know that, we all concede it—but our error has been
in regarding them as crimes and in calling them by that name,
whereas I perceive now that they were only indiscretions.   At
every few steps I met persons of deathless name whom I had never
encountered before outside of pictures and statuary and history,
and these were most thrilling and charming encounters.   I had
hand-shakes with Henry the Second, who had not been seen in the
Oxford streets for nearly eight hundred years; and with the Fair
Rosamond, whom I now believe to have been chaste and blameless, although I had thought differently about it before; and with

Shakespeare, one of the pleasantest foreigners I have ever gotten acquainted with; and with Roger Bacon; and with Queen Elizabeth, who talked five minutes and never swore once—a fact which gave me a new and good opinion of her and moved me to forgive her for beheading the Scottish Mary, if she really did it, which I now doubt; and with the quaintly and anciently clad young King Harold Harefoot, of near nine hundred years ago, who came flying by on a bicycle and smoking a pipe, but at once checked up and got off to shake with me; and also I met a bishop who had lost his way because this was the first time he had been inside the walls of Oxford for as much as twelve hundred years or thereabouts. By this time I had grown so used to the obliterated ages and their best-known people that if I had met Adam I should not have been either surprised or embarrassed; and if he had come in a racing automobile and a cloud of dust, with nothing on but his fig-leaf, it would have seemed to me all right and harmonious.

MARK TWAIN.

*(To be Continued.)*

# Chapter XXIV

## November, 1907. Pages 327–36.

PREFATORY NOTE.—Mr. Clemens began to write his autobiography many years ago, and he continues to add to it day by day. It was his original intention to permit no publication of his memoirs until after his death; but, after leaving " Pier No. 70," he concluded that a considerable portion might now suitably be given to the public. It is that portion, garnered from the quarter-million of words already written, which will appear in this REVIEW during the present year. No part of the autobiography will be published in book form during the lifetime of the author.—EDITOR N. A. R.

*From Susy's Biography of Me* [1885–6].

Mamma and papa have returned from Onteora and they have had a delightful visit. Mr. Frank Stockton was down in Virginia and could not reach Onteora in time, so they did not see him, and Mrs. Mary Mapes Dodge was ill and couldn't go to Onteora, but Mrs. General Custer was there, and mamma said that she was a very attractive, sweet appearing woman.

[*Dictated October 9, 1906.*] Onteora was situated high up in the Catskill Mountains, in the centre of a far-reaching solitude. I do not mean that the region was wholly uninhabited; there were farmhouses here and there, at generous distances apart. Their occupants were descendants of ancestors who had built the houses in Rip Van Winkle's time, or earlier; and those ancestors were not more primitive than were this posterity of theirs. The city people were as foreign and unfamiliar and strange to them as monkeys would have been, and they would have respected the monkeys as much as they respected these elegant summer-resorters. The resorters were a puzzle to them, their ways were so strange and their interests so trivial. They drove the resorters over the mountain roads and listened in shamed surprise at their bursts of enthusiasm over the scenery. The farmers had had that scenery on exhibition from their mountain roosts all their lives, and had never noticed anything remarkable about it. By way of an incident: a pair of these primitives were overheard chatting about the resorters, one day, and in the course of their talk this remark was dropped:

" I was a-drivin' a passel of 'em round about yisterday evenin', quiet ones, you know, still and solemn, and all to wunst they busted out to make your hair lift and I judged hell was to pay. Now what do you reckon it was? It wa'n't anything but jest one of them common damned yaller sunsets."

In those days—

[*Tuesday, October 16, 1906.*] . . . Warner is gone. Stockton is gone. I attended both funerals. Warner was a near neighbor, from the autumn of '71 until his death, nineteen years afterward. It is not the privilege of the most of us to have many intimate friends—a dozen is our aggregate—but I think he could count his by the score. It is seldom that a man is so beloved by both sexes and all ages as Warner was. There was a charm about his spirit, and his ways, and his words, that won all that came within the sphere of its influence. Our children adopted him while they were little creatures, and thenceforth, to the end, he was " Cousin Charley " to them. He was " Uncle Charley " to the children of more than one other friend. Mrs. Clemens was very fond of him, and he always called her by her first name—shortened. Warner died, as she died, and as I would die—without premonition, without a moment's warning.

Uncle Remus still lives, and must be over a thousand years old. Indeed, I know that this must be so, because I have seen a new photograph of him in the public prints within the last month or so, and in that picture his aspects are distinctly and strikingly geological, and one can see he is thinking about the mastodons and plesiosaurians that he used to play with when he was young.

It is just a quarter of a century since I have seen Uncle Remus. He visited us in our home in Hartford and was reverently devoured by the big eyes of Susy and Clara, for I made a deep and awful impression upon the little creatures—who knew his book by heart through my nightly declamation of its tales to them—by revealing to them privately that he was the real Uncle Remus whitewashed so that he could come into people's houses the front way.

He was the bashfulest grown person I have ever met. When there were people about he stayed silent, and seemed to suffer until they were gone. But he was lovely, nevertheless; for the sweetness and benignity of the immortal Remus looked out from his eyes, and the graces and sincerities of his character shone in his face.

It may be that Jim Wolf was as bashful as Harris. It hardly seems possible, yet as I look back fifty-six years and consider Jim Wolf, I am almost persuaded that he was. He was our long slim apprentice in my brother's printing-office in Hannibal. He was seventeen, and yet he was as much as four times as bashful as I was, though I was only fourteen. He boarded and slept in the house, but he was always tongue-tied in the presence of my sister, and when even my gentle mother spoke to him he could not answer save in frightened monosyllables. He would not enter a room where a girl was; nothing could persuade him to do such a thing. Once when he was in our small parlor alone, two majestic old maids entered and seated themselves in such a way that Jim could not escape without passing by them. He would as soon have thought of passing by one of Harris's plesiosaurians ninety feet long. I came in presently, was charmed with the situation, and sat down in a corner to watch Jim suffer, and enjoy it. My mother followed a minute later and sat down with the visitors and began to talk. Jim sat upright in his chair, and during a quarter of an hour he did not change his position by a shade—neither General Grant nor a bronze image could have maintained that immovable pose more successfully. I mean as to body and limbs; with the face there was a difference. By fleeting revealments of the face I saw that something was happening—something out of the common. There would be a sudden twitch of the muscles of the face, an instant distortion, which in the next instant had passed and left no trace. These twitches gradually grew in frequency, but no muscle outside of the face lost any of its rigidity, or betrayed any interest in what was happening to Jim. I mean if something *was* happening to him, and I knew perfectly well that that was the case. At last a pair of tears began to swim slowly down his cheeks amongst the twitchings, but Jim sat still and let them run; then I saw his right hand steal along his thigh until half-way to his knee, then take a vigorous grip upon the cloth.

That was a *wasp* that he was grabbing! A colony of them were climbing up his legs and prospecting around, and every time he winced they stabbed him to the hilt—so for a quarter of an hour one group of excursionists after another climbed up Jim's legs and resented even the slightest wince or squirm that he indulged himself with, in his misery. When the entertainment had become nearly unbearable, he conceived the idea of gripping them between his fingers and putting them out of commission. He succeeded with many of them, but at great cost, for, as he couldn't see the wasp, he was as likely to take hold of the wrong end of him as he was the right; then the dying wasp gave him a punch to remember the incident by.

If those ladies had stayed all day, and if all the wasps in Missouri had come and climbed up Jim's legs, nobody there would ever have known it but Jim and the wasps and me. There he would have sat until the ladies left.

When they finally went away we went up-stairs and he took his clothes off, and his legs were a picture to look at. They looked as if they were mailed all over with shirt buttons, each with a single red hole in the centre. The pain was intolerable—no, would have been intolerable, but the pain of the presence of those ladies had been so much harder to bear that the pain of the wasps' stings was quite pleasant and enjoyable by comparison.

Jim never could enjoy wasps. I remember once—

*From Susy's Biography of Me* [1885–6].

Mamma has given me a very pleasant little newspaper scrap about papa, to copy. I will put it in here.

[*Thursday, October 11, 1906.*] It was a rather strong compliment; I think I will leave it out. It was from James Redpath.

The chief ingredients of Redpath's make-up were honesty, sincerity, kindliness, and pluck. He wasn't afraid. He was one of Ossawatomie Brown's right-hand men in the bleeding Kansas days; he was all through that struggle. He carried his life in his hands, and from one day to another it wasn't worth the price of a night's lodging. He had a small body of daring men under him, and they were constantly being hunted by the " jayhawkers," who were proslavery Missourians, guerillas, modern free lances.

[*Friday, October 12, 1906*] . . . I can't think of the name of that daredevil guerilla who led the jayhawkers and chased

Redpath up and down the country, and, in turn, was chased by Redpath. By grace of the chances of war, the two men never met in the field, though they several times came within an ace of it.

Ten or twelve years later, Redpath was earning his living in Boston as chief of the lecture business in the United States. Fifteen or sixteen years after his Kansas adventures I became a public lecturer, and he was my agent. Along there somewhere was a press dinner, one November night, at the Tremont Hotel in Boston, and I attended it. I sat near the head of the table, with Redpath between me and the chairman; a stranger sat on my other side. I tried several times to talk with the stranger, but he seemed to be out of words and I presently ceased from troubling him. He was manifestly a very shy man, and, moreover, he might have been losing sleep the night before.

The first man called up was Redpath. At the mention of the name the stranger started, and showed interest. He fixed a fascinated eye on Redpath, and lost not a word of his speech. Redpath told some stirring incidents of his career in Kansas, and said, among other things:

"Three times I came near capturing the gallant jayhawker chief, and once he actually captured *me,* but didn't know me and let me go, because he said he was hot on Redpath's trail and couldn't afford to waste time and rope on inconsequential small fry."

My stranger was called up next, and when Redpath heard his name he, in turn, showed a startled interest. The stranger said, bending a caressing glance upon Redpath and speaking gently—I may even say sweetly:

"You realize that I was that jayhawker chief. I am glad to know you now and take you to my heart and call you friend"— then he added, in a voice that was pathetic with regret, "but if I had only known you then, what tumultuous happiness I should have had in your society!—while it lasted."

The last quarter of a century of my life has been pretty constantly and faithfully devoted to the study of the human race— that is to say, the study of myself, for, in my individual person, I am the entire human race compacted together. I have found that there is no ingredient of the race which I do not possess in either a small way or a large way. When it is small, as compared with the same ingredient in somebody else, there is still enough of it for all the purposes of examination. In my contacts with the species I find no one who possesses a quality which I do not possess. The shades of difference between other people and me serve to make variety and prevent monotony, but that is all; broadly speaking, we are all alike; and so by studying myself carefully and comparing myself with other people, and noting the divergences, I have been enabled to acquire a knowledge of the human race which I perceive is more accurate and more comprehensive than that which has been acquired and revealed by any other member of our species. As a result, my private and concealed opinion of myself is not of a complimentary sort. It follows that my estimate of the human race is the duplicate of my estimate of myself.

I am not proposing to discuss all of the peculiarities of the human race, at this time; I only wish to touch lightly upon one or two of them. To begin with, I wonder why a man should prefer a good billiard-table to a poor one; and why he should prefer straight cues to crooked ones; and why he should prefer round balls to chipped ones; and why he should prefer a level table to one that slants; and why he should prefer responsive cushions to the dull and unresponsive kind. I wonder at these things, because when we examine the matter we find that the essentials involved in billiards are as competently and exhaustively furnished by a bad billiard outfit as they are by the best one. One of the essentials is amusement. Very well, if there is any more amusement to be gotten out of the one outfit than out of the other, the facts are in favor of the bad outfit. The bad outfit will always furnish thirty per cent. more fun for the players and for the spectators than will the good outfit. Another essential of the game is that the outfit shall give the players full opportunity to exercise their best skill, and display it in a way to compel the admiration of the spectators. Very well, the bad outfit is nothing behind the good one in this regard. It is a difficult matter to estimate correctly the eccentricities of chipped balls and a slanting table, and make the right allowance for them and secure a count; the finest kind of skill is required to accomplish the satisfactory result. Another essential of the game is that it shall add to the interest of the game by furnishing opportunities to bet. Very well, in this regard no good outfit can claim any advantage over a bad one. I know, by experience, that a bad outfit is as valuable as the best one; that an outfit that couldn't be sold at auction for seven dollars is just as valuable for all the essentials of the game as an outfit that is worth a thousand.

I acquired some of this learning in Jackass Gulch, California, more than forty years ago. Jackass Gulch had once been a rich and thriving surface-mining camp. By and by its gold deposits were exhausted; then the people began to go away, and the town began to decay, and rapidly; in my time it had disappeared. Where the bank, and the city hall, and the church, and the gambling-dens, and the newspaper office, and the streets of brick blocks had been, was nothing now but a wide and beautiful expanse of green grass, a peaceful and charming solitude. Half a dozen scattered dwellings were still inhabited, and there was still one saloon of a ruined and rickety character struggling for life, but doomed. In its bar was a billiard outfit that was the counterpart of the one in my father-in-law's garret. The balls were chipped, the cloth was darned and patched, the table's surface was undulating, and the cues were headless and had the curve of a parenthesis—but the forlorn remnant of marooned miners played games there, and those games were more entertaining to look at than a circus and a grand opera combined. Nothing but a quite extraordinary skill could score a carom on that table—a skill that required the nicest estimate of force, distance, and how much to allow for the various slants of the table and the other formidable peculiarities and idiosyncrasies furnished by the contradictions of the outfit. Last winter, here in New York, I saw Hoppe and Schaefer and Sutton and the three or four other billiard champions of world-wide fame contend against each other, and certainly the art and science displayed were a wonder to see; yet I saw nothing there in the way of science and art that was more wonderful than shots which I had seen Texas Tom make on the wavy surface of that poor old wreck in the perishing saloon at Jackass Gulch forty years before. Once I saw Texas Tom make a string of seven points on a single inning!—all calculated shots, and not a fluke or a scratch among them. I often saw him make runs of four, but when he made his great string of seven, the boys went wild with enthusiasm and admiration. The joy and the noise exceeded that which the great gathering at Madison Square produced when Sutton scored five hundred points at the eighteen-inch game, on a world-famous night last winter. With practice, that champion could score nineteen or twenty on the Jackass Gulch table; but to start with, Texas Tom would show him miracles that would astonish him; also it might have another handsome result: it might persuade the great experts to discard their own trifling game and bring the Jackass Gulch outfit here and exhibit their skill in a game worth a hundred of the discarded one, for profound and breathless interest, and for displays of almost superhuman skill.

In my experience, games played with a fiendish outfit furnish ecstasies of delight which games played with the other kind cannot match. Twenty-seven years ago my budding little family spent the summer at Bateman's Point, near Newport, Rhode Island. It was a comfortable boarding-place, well stocked with sweet mothers and little children, but the male sex was scarce; however, there was another young fellow besides myself, and he and I had good times—Higgins was his name, but that was not his fault. He was a very pleasant and companionable person. On the premises there was what had once been a bowling-alley. It was a single alley, and it was estimated that it had been out of repair for sixty years—but not the balls, the balls were in good condition; there were forty-one of them, and they ranged in size from a grapefruit up to a lignum-vitæ sphere that you could hardly lift. Higgins and I played on that alley day after day. At first, one of us located himself at the bottom end to set up the pins in case anything should happen to them, but nothing happened. The surface of that alley consisted of a rolling stretch of elevations and depressions, and neither of us could, by any art known to us, persuade a ball to stay on the alley until it should accomplish something. Little balls and big, the same thing always happened—the ball left the alley before it was half-way home and went thundering down alongside of it the rest of the way and made the gamekeeper climb out and take care of himself. No matter, we persevered, and were rewarded. We examined the alley, noted and located a lot of its peculiarities, and little by little we learned how to deliver a ball in such a way that it would travel home and knock down a pin or two. By and by we succeeded in improving our game to a point where we were able to get all of the pins with thirty-five balls—so we made it a thirty-five-ball game. If the player did not succeed with thirty-five, he had lost the game. I suppose that all the balls, taken together, weighed five hundred pounds, or maybe a ton—or along there somewhere—but anyway it was hot weather, and by the time that a player had sent thirty-five of them home he was in a drench of perspiration, and physically exhausted.

Next, we started cocked hat—that is to say, a triangle of three pins, the other seven being discarded. In this game we used the three smallest balls and kept on delivering them until we got the three pins down. After a day or two of practice we were able to get the chief pin with an output of four balls, but it cost us a great many deliveries to get the other two; but by and by we succeeded in perfecting our art—at least we perfected it to our limit. We reached a scientific excellence where we could get the three pins down with twelve deliveries of the three small balls, making thirty-six shots to conquer the cocked hat.

Having reached our limit for daylight work, we set up a couple of candles and played at night. As the alley was fifty or sixty feet long, we couldn't see the pins, but the candles indicated their locality. We continued this game until we were able to knock down the invisible pins with thirty-six shots. Having now reached the limit of the candle game, we changed and played it left-handed. We continued the left-handed game until we conquered its limit, which was fifty-four shots. Sometimes we sent down a succession of fifteen balls without getting anything at all. We easily got out of that old alley five times the fun that anybody could have gotten out of the best alley in New York.

One blazing hot day, a modest and courteous officer of the regular army appeared in our den and introduced himself. He was about thirty-five years old, well built and militarily erect and straight, and he was hermetically sealed up in the uniform of that ignorant old day—a uniform made of heavy material, and much properer for January than July. When he saw the venerable alley, and glanced from that to the long procession of shining balls in the trough, his eye lit with desire, and we judged that he was our meat. We politely invited him to take a hand, and he could not conceal his gratitude; though his breeding, and the etiquette of his profession, made him try. We explained the game to him, and said that there were forty-one balls, and that the player was privileged to extend his inning and keep on playing until he had used them all up—repeatedly—and that for every ten-strike he got a prize. We didn't name the prize—it wasn't necessary, as no prize would ever be needed or called for. He started a sarcastic smile, but quenched it, according to the etiquette of his profession. He merely remarked that he would like to select a couple of medium balls and one small one, adding that he didn't think he would need the rest.

Then he began, and he was an astonished man. He couldn't get a ball to stay on the alley. When he had fired about fifteen balls and hadn't yet reached the cluster of pins, his annoyance began to show out through his clothes. He wouldn't let it show in his face; but after another fifteen balls he was not able to control his face; he didn't utter a word, but he exuded mute blasphemy from every pore. He asked permission to take off his coat, which was granted; then he turned himself loose, with bitter determination, and although he was only an infantry officer he could have been mistaken for a battery, he got up such a volleying thunder with those balls. Presently he removed his cravat; after a little he took off his vest; and still he went bravely on. Higgins was suffocating. My condition was the same, but it would not be courteous to laugh; it would be better to burst, and we came near it. That officer was good pluck. He stood to his work without uttering a word, and kept the balls going until he had expended the outfit four times, making four times forty-one shots; then he had to give it up, and he did; for he was no longer able to stand without wobbling. He put on his clothes, bade us a courteous good-by, invited us to call at the Fort, and started away. Then he came back, and said,

" What is the prize for the ten-strike?"

We had to confess that we had not selected it yet.

He said, gravely, that he thought there was no occasion for hurry about it.

I believe Bateman's alley was a better one than any other in America, in the matter of the essentials of the game. It compelled skill; it provided opportunity for bets; and if you could get a stranger to do the bowling for you, there was more and wholesomer and delightfuler entertainment to be gotten out of his industries than out of the finest game by the best expert, and played upon the best alley elsewhere in existence.

MARK TWAIN.

*(To be Continued.)*

# Chapter XXV

## December, 1907. Pages 481–94

PREFATORY NOTE.—Mr. Clemens began to write his autobiography many years ago, and he continues to add to it day by day. It was his original intention to permit no publication of his memoirs until after his death; but, after leaving "Pier No. 70," he concluded that a considerable portion might now suitably be given to the public. It is that portion, garnered from the quarter-million of words already written, which will appear in this REVIEW during the present year. No part of the autobiography will be published in book form during the lifetime of the author.—EDITOR N. A. R.

*January 11, 1906.* Answer to a letter received this morning:

DEAR MRS. H.,—I am forever your debtor for reminding me of that curious passage in my life. During the first year or two after it happened, I could not bear to think of it. My pain and shame were so intense, and my sense of having been an imbecile so settled, established and confirmed, that I drove the episode entirely from my mind—and so all these twenty-eight or twenty-nine years I have lived in the conviction that my performance of that time was coarse, vulgar and destitute of humor. But your suggestion that you and your family found humor in it twenty-eight years ago moved me to look into the matter. So I commissioned a Boston typewriter to delve among the Boston papers of that bygone time and send me a copy of it.

It came this morning, and if there is any vulgarity about it I am not able to discover it. If it isn't innocently and ridiculously funny, I am no judge. I will see to it that you get a copy.

Address of Samuel L. Clemens (" Mark Twain ")
From a report of the dinner given by the Publishers
of the Atlantic Monthly in honor of the
Seventieth Anniversary of the
Birth of John Greenleaf Whittier, at the Hotel Bruns-
wick, Boston, December 17, 1877,
as published in the
BOSTON EVENING TRANSCRIPT,
December 18, 1877

Mr. Chairman—This is an occasion peculiarly meet for the digging up of pleasant reminiscences concerning literary folk; therefore I will drop lightly into history myself. Standing here on the shore of the Atlantic and contemplating certain of its largest literary billows, I am reminded of a thing which happened to me thirteen years ago, when I had just succeeded in stirring up a little Nevadian literary puddle myself, whose spume-flakes were beginning to blow thinly Cali-forniawards. I started an inspection tramp through the southern mines of California. I was callow and conceited, and I resolved to try the virtue of my *nom de guerre*. I very soon had an opportunity. I knocked at a miner's lonely log cabin in the foothills of the Sierras just at nightfall. It was snowing at the time. A jaded, melancholy man of fifty, barefooted, opened the door to me. When he heard my *nom de guerre* he looked more dejected than before. He let me in—pretty re-luctantly, I thought—and after the customary bacon and beans, black coffee and hot whiskey, I took a pipe. This sorrowful man had not said three words up to this time. Now he spoke up and said, in the voice of one who is secretly suffering, " You're the fourth—I'm going to move." " The fourth what?" said I. " The fourth littery man that has been here in twenty-four hours—I'm going to move." " You don't tell me!" said I; " who were the others?" " Mr. Longfellow, Mr. Emerson and Mr. Oliver Wendell Holmes—consound the lot!"

You can easily believe I was interested. I supplicated—three hot whiskeys did the rest—and finally the melancholy miner began. Said he—

" They came here just at dark yesterday evening, and I let them in of course. Said they were going to the Yosemite. They were a rough lot, but that's nothing; everybody looks rough that travels afoot. Mr. Emerson was a seedy little bit of a chap, red-headed. Mr. Holmes was as fat as a balloon; he weighed as much as three hundred, and had double chins all the way down to his stomach. Mr. Longfellow was built like a prize-fighter. His head was cropped and bristly, like as if he had a wig made of hair-brushes. His nose lay straight down his face, like a finger with the end joint tilted up. They had been drink-ing, I could see that. And what queer talk they used! Mr. Holmes inspected this cabin, then he took me by the buttonhole, and says he—

" ' Through the deep caves of thought
I hear a voice that sings,
Build thee more stately mansions,
O my soul!'

" Says I, ' I can't afford it, Mr. Holmes, and moreover I don't want to.' Blamed if I liked it pretty well, either, coming from a stranger, that way. However, I started to get out my bacon and beans, when Mr. Emerson came and looked on awhile, and then *he* takes me aside by the buttonhole and says—

" ' Give me agates for my meat;
Give me cantharids to eat;
From air and ocean bring me foods,
From all zones and altitudes.'

" Says I, ' Mr. Emerson, if you'll excuse me, this ain't no hotel.' You see it sort of riled me—I warn't used to the ways of littery swells. But I went on a-sweating over my work, and next comes Mr. Long-fellow and buttonholes me, and interrupts me. Says he,

" ' Honor be to Mudjekeewis!
You shall hear how Pau-Puk-Keewis—'

" But I broke in, and says I, ' Beg your pardon, Mr. Longfellow, if you'll be so kind as to hold your yawp for about five minutes and let me get this grub ready, you'll do me proud.' Well, sir, after they'd filled up I set out the jug. Mr. Holmes looks at it and then he fires up all of a sudden and yells—

" ' Flash out a stream of blood-red wine!
For I would drink to other days.'

" By George, I was getting kind of worked up. I don't deny it, I was getting kind of worked up. I turns to Mr. Holmes, and says I, ' Looky here, my fat friend, I'm a-running this shanty, and if the court knows herself, you'll take whiskey straight or you'll go dry.' Them's the very words I said to him. Now I don't want to sass such famous littery people, but you see they kind of forced me. There ain't nothing onreasonable 'bout me; I don't mind a passel of guests a-treadin' on my tail three or four times, but when it comes to *standing* on it it's different, ' and if the court knows herself,' I says, ' you'll take whiskey straight or you'll go dry.' Well, between drinks they'd swell around the cabin and strike attitudes and spout; and pretty soon they got out a greasy old deck and went to playing euchre at ten cents a corner—on trust. I began to notice some pretty suspicious things. Mr. Emerson dealt, looked at his hand, shook his head, says—

" ' I am the doubter and the doubt—'

and ca'mly bunched the hands and went to shuffling for a new layout. Says he—

> " ' They reckon ill who leave me out;
>   They know not well the subtle ways I keep.
>   I pass and deal *again!*'

Hang'd if he didn't go ahead and do it, too!  O, he was a cool one!
Well, in about a minute, things were running pretty tight, but all of
a sudden I see by Mr. Emerson's eye he judged he had 'em.  He had
already corralled two tricks and each of the others one.  So now he kind
of lifts a little in his chair and says—

> " ' I tire of globes and aces!—
>   Too long the game is played!'

—and down he fetched a right bower.  Mr. Longfellow smiles as sweet
as pie and says—

> " ' Thanks, thanks to thee, my worthy friend,
>   For the lesson thou hast taught,'

—and blamed if he didn't down with *another* right bower!  Emerson
claps his hand on his bowie, Longfellow claps his on his revolver, and I
went under a bunk.  There was going to be trouble; but that monstrous
Holmes rose up, wobbling his double chins, and says he, ' Order, gentlemen; the first man that draws, I'll lay down on him and smother him!'
All quiet on the Potomac, you bet!

" They were pretty how-come-you-so, by now, and they begun to blow.
Emerson says, ' The nobbiest thing I ever wrote was Barbara Friet-
chie.'  Says Longfellow, ' It don't begin with my Biglow Papers.'
Says Holmes, ' My Thanatopsis lays over 'em both.  They mighty near
ended in a fight.  Then they wished they had some more company
—and Mr. Emerson pointed to me and says—

> " ' Is yonder squalid peasant all
>   That this proud nursery could breed?'

He was a-whetting his bowie on his boot—so I let it pass.  Well, sir,
next they took it into their heads that they would like some music; so
they made me stand up and sing ' When Johnny Comes Marching Home'
till I dropped—at thirteen minutes past four this morning.  That's
what I've been through, my friend.  When I woke at seven, they were
leaving, thank goodness, and Mr. Longfellow had my only boots on, and
his'n under his arm.  Says I, ' Hold on, there, Evangeline, what are you
going to do with *them?*'  He says, ' Going to make tracks with 'em;
because—

> " ' Lives of great men all remind us
>   We can make our lives sublime;
>   And, departing, leave behind us
>   Footprints on the sands of time.'

As I said, Mr. Twain, you are the fourth in twenty-four hours—and
I'm going to move; I ain't suited to a littery atmosphere."

I said to the miner, " Why, my dear sir, *these* were not the gracious singers to whom we and the world pay loving reverence and homage; these were impostors."

The miner investigated me with a calm eye for a while; then said he, "Ah! impostors, were they? Are *you?*"

I did not pursue the subject, and since then I have not travelled on my *nom de guerre* enough to hurt. Such was the reminiscene I was moved to contribute, Mr. Chairman. In my enthusiasm I may have exaggerated the details a little, but you will easily forgive me that fault, since I believe it is the first time I have ever deflected from perpendicular fact on an occasion like this.

What I have said to Mrs. H. is true. I did suffer during a year or two from the deep humiliations of that episode. But at last, in 1888, in Venice, my wife and I came across Mr. and Mrs. A. P. C., of Concord, Massachusetts, and a friendship began then of the sort which nothing but death terminates. The C.'s were very bright people and in every way charming and companionable. We were together a month or two in Venice and several months in Rome, afterwards, and one day that lamented break of mine was mentioned. And when I was on the point of lathering those people for bringing it to my mind when I had gotten the memory of it almost squelched, I perceived with joy that the C.'s were indignant about the way that my performance had been received in Boston. They poured out their opinions most freely and frankly about the frosty attitude of the people who were present at that performance, and about the Boston newspapers for the position they had taken in regard to the matter. That position was that I had been irreverent beyond belief, beyond imagination. Very well, I had accepted that as a fact for a year or two, and had been thoroughly miserable about it whenever I thought of it—which was not frequently, if I could help it. Whenever I thought of it I wondered how I ever could have been inspired to do so unholy a thing. Well, the C.'s comforted me, but they did not persuade me to continue to think about the unhappy episode. I resisted that. I tried to get it out of my mind, and let it die, and I succeeded. Until Mrs. H.'s letter came, it had been a good twenty-five years since I had thought of that matter; and when she said that the thing was funny I wondered if possibly she might be right. At any rate, my curiosity was aroused, and I wrote to Boston and got the whole thing copied, as above set forth.

I vaguely remember some of the details of that gathering—

dimly I can see a hundred people—no, perhaps fifty—shadowy figures sitting at tables feeding, ghosts now to me, and nameless forever more. I don't know who they were, but I can very distinctly see, seated at the grand table and facing the rest of us, Mr. Emerson, supernaturally grave, unsmiling; Mr. Whittier, grave, lovely, his beautiful spirit shining out of his face; Mr. Longfellow, with his silken white hair and his benignant face; Dr. Oliver Wendell Holmes, flashing smiles and affection and all good-fellowship everywhere like a rose-diamond whose facets are being turned toward the light first one way and then another—a charming man, and always fascinating, whether he was talking or whether he was sitting still (what *he* would call still, but what would be more or less motion to other people). I can see those figures with entire distinctness across this abyss of time.

One other feature is clear—Willie Winter (for these past thousand years dramatic editor of the " New York Tribune," and still occupying that high post in his old age) was there. He was much younger then than he is now, and he showed it. It was always a pleasure to me to see Willie Winter at a banquet. During a matter of twenty years I was seldom at a banquet where Willie Winter was not also present, and where he did not read a charming poem written for the occasion. He did it this time, and it was up to standard: dainty, happy, choicely phrased, and as good to listen to as music, and sounding exactly as if it was pouring unprepared out of heart and brain.

Now at that point ends all that was pleasurable about that notable celebration of Mr. Whittier's seventieth birthday—because *I* got up at that point and followed Winter, with what I have no doubt I supposed would be the gem of the evening—the gay oration above quoted from the Boston paper. I had written it all out the day before and had perfectly memorized it, and I stood up there at my genial and happy and self-satisfied ease, and began to deliver it. Those majestic guests, that row of venerable and still active volcanoes, listened, as did everybody else in the house, with attentive interest. Well, I delivered myself of—we'll say the first two hundred words of my speech. I was expecting no returns from that part of the speech, but this was not the case as regarded the rest of it. I arrived now at the dialogue: ' The old miner said, " You are the fourth, I'm going to move." " The fourth what?" said I. He answered, " The fourth littery man that has been here in twenty-four hours. I am going to move." "Why, you don't tell me," said I. "Who were the others?" "Mr. Longfellow, Mr. Emerson, Mr. Oliver Wendell Holmes, consound the lot—"'

Now then the house's *attention* continued, but the expression of interest in the faces turned to a sort of black frost. I wondered what the trouble was. I didn't know. I went on, but with difficulty—I struggled along, and entered upon that miner's fearful description of the bogus Emerson, the bogus Holmes, the bogus Longfellow, always hoping—but with a gradually perishing hope—that somebody would laugh, or that somebody would at least smile, but nobody did. I didn't know enough to give it up and sit down, I was too new to public speaking, and so I went on with this awful performance, and carried it clear through to the end, in front of a body of people who seemed turned to stone with horror. It was the sort of expression their faces would have worn if I had been making these remarks about the Deity and the rest of the Trinity; there is no milder way in which to describe the petrified condition and the ghastly expression of those people.

When I sat down it was with a heart which had long ceased to beat. I shall never be as dead again as I was then. I shall never be as miserable again as I was then. I speak now as one who doesn't know what the condition of things may be in the next world, but in this one I shall never be as wretched again as I was then. Howells, who was near me, tried to say a comforting word, but couldn't get beyond a gasp. There was no use—he understood the whole size of the disaster. He had good intentions, but the words froze before they could get out. It was an atmosphere that would freeze anything. If Benvenuto Cellini's salamander had been in that place he would not have survived to be put into Cellini's autobiography. There was a frightful pause. There was an awful silence, a desolating silence. Then the next man on the list had to get up—there was no help for it. That was Bishop — Bishop had just burst handsomely upon the world with a most acceptable novel, which had appeared in the "Atlantic Monthly," a place which would make any novel respectable and any author noteworthy. In this case the novel itself was recognized as being, without extraneous help, respectable. Bishop was away up in the public favor, and he was an object of high interest, consequently there was a sort of national expectancy in the air; we may say our American millions were standing, from Maine to Texas and from Alaska to Florida, holding their breath, their lips parted, their hands ready to applaud when Bishop should get up on that occasion, and for the first time in his life speak in public. It was under these damaging conditions that he got up to "make good," as the vulgar say. I had spoken several times before, and that is the reason why I was able to go on without dying in my tracks, as I ought to have done—but Bishop had had no experience. He was up facing those awful deities—facing those other people, those strangers—facing human beings for the first time in his life, with a speech to utter. No doubt it was well packed away in his memory, no doubt it was fresh and usable, until I had been heard from. I suppose that after that, and under the smothering pall of that dreary silence, it began to waste away and disappear out of his head like the rags breaking from the edge of a fog, and presently there wasn't any fog left. He didn't go on—he didn't last long. It was not many sentences after his first before he began to hesitate, and break, and lose his grip, and totter, and wobble, and at last he slumped down in a limp and mushy pile.

Well, the programme for the occasion was probably not more than one-third finished, but it ended there. Nobody rose. The next man hadn't strength enough to get up, and everybody looked so dazed, so stupefied, paralyzed, it was impossible for anybody to do anything, or even try. Nothing could go on in that strange atmosphere. Howells mournfully, and without words, hitched himself to Bishop and me and supported us out of the room. It was very kind—he was most generous. He towed us tottering away into some room in that building, and we sat down there. I don't know what my remark was now, but I know the nature of it. It was the kind of remark you make when you know that nothing in the world can help your case. But Howells was honest—he had to say the heart-breaking things he did say: that there was no help for this calamity, this shipwreck, this cataclysm; that this was the most disastrous thing that had ever happened in anybody's history—and then he added, "That is, for *you*—and consider what you have done for Bishop. It is bad enough in your case, you deserve to suffer. You have committed this crime, and you deserve to have all you are going to get. But here is an innocent man. Bishop had never done you any harm, and see what you have done to him. He can never hold his head up again. The world can never look upon Bishop as being a live person. He is a corpse."

That is the history of that episode of twenty-eight years ago, which pretty nearly killed me with shame during that first year or two whenever it forced its way into my mind.

Now, then, I take that speech up and examine it. As I said, it arrived this morning, from Boston. I have read it twice, and unless I am an idiot, it hasn't a single defect in it from the first word to the last. It is just as good as good can be. It is smart; it is saturated with humor. There isn't a suggestion of coarseness or vulgarity in it anywhere. What could have been the matter with that house? It is amazing, it is incredible, that they didn't shout with laughter, and those deities the loudest of them all. Could the fault have been with me? Did I lose courage when I saw those great men up there whom I was going to describe in such a strange fashion? If that happened, if I showed doubt, that can account for it, for you can't be successfully funny if you show that you are afraid of it. Well, I can't account for it, but if I had those beloved and revered old literary immortals back here now on the platform at Carnegie Hall I would take that same old speech, deliver it, word for word, and melt them till they'd run all over that stage. Oh, the fault must have been with *me,* it is not in the speech at all.

[*Dictated October 3, 1907.*] In some ways, I was always honest; even from my earliest years I could never bring myself to use money which I had acquired in questionable ways; many a time I tried, but principle was always stronger than desire. Six or eight months ago, Lieutenant-General Nelson A. Miles was given a great dinner-party in New York, and when he and I were chatting together in the drawing-room before going out to dinner he said,

" I've known you as much as thirty years, isn't it?"

I said, " Yes, that's about it, I think."

He mused a moment or two and then said,

" I wonder we didn't meet in Washington in 1867; you were there at that time, weren't you?"

I said, " Yes, but there was a difference; I was not known then; I had not begun to bud—I was an obscurity; but you had been adding to your fine Civil War record; you had just come back

from your brilliant Indian campaign in the Far West, and had
been rewarded with a brigadier-generalship in the regular army,
and everybody was talking about you and praising you. If you
had met me, you wouldn't be able to remember it now—unless
some unusual circumstance of the meeting had burnt it into your
memory. It is forty years ago, and people don't remember no-
bodies over a stretch of time like that."

I didn't wish to continue the conversation along that line,
so I changed the subject. I could have proven to him, without
any trouble, that we did meet in Washington in 1867, but I
thought it might embarrass one or the other of us, so I didn't do
it. I remember the incident very well. This was the way of it:

I had just come back from the Quaker City Excursion, and
had made a contract with Bliss of Hartford to write " The Innocents Abroad." I was out of money, and I went down to Washington to see if I could earn enough there to keep me in bread and
butter while I should write the book. I came across William
Clinton, brother of the astronomer, and together we invented a
scheme for our mutual sustenance; we became the fathers and
originators of what is a common feature in the newspaper world
now—the syndicate. We became the old original first Newspaper Syndicate on the planet; it was on a small scale, but that
is usual with untried new enterprises. We had twelve journals
on our list; they were all weeklies, all obscure and poor, and all
scattered far away among the back settlements. It was a proud
thing for those little newspapers to have a Washington correspondence, and a fortunate thing for us that they felt in that
way about it. Each of the twelve took two letters a week from
us, at a dollar per letter; each of us wrote one letter per week
and sent off six duplicates of it to these benefactors, thus acquiring twenty-four dollars a week to live on—which was all we
needed, in our cheap and humble quarters.

Clinton was one of the dearest and loveliest human beings I
have ever known, and we led a charmed existence together, in a
contentment which knew no bounds. Clinton was refined by
nature and breeding; he was a gentleman by nature and breeding;
he was highly educated; he was of a beautiful spirit; he was
pure in heart and speech. He was a Scotchman, and a Presbyterian; a Presbyterian of the old and genuine school, being honest and sincere in his religion, and loving it, and finding serenity

and peace in it. He hadn't a vice—unless a large and grateful sympathy with Scotch whiskey may be called by that name. I didn't regard it as a vice, because he was a Scotchman, and Scotch whiskey to a Scotchman is as innocent as milk is to the rest of the human race. In Clinton's case it was a virtue, and not an economical one. Twenty-four dollars a week would really have been riches to us if we hadn't had to support that jug; because of the jug we were always sailing pretty close to the wind, and any tardiness in the arrival of any part of our income was sure to cause us some inconvenience.

I remember a time when a shortage occurred; we had to have three dollars, and we had to have it before the close of the day. I don't know now how we happened to want all that money at one time; I only know we had to have it. Clinton told me to go out and find it—and he said he would also go out and see what he could do. He didn't seem to have any doubt that we would succeed, but I knew that that was his religion working in him; I hadn't the same confidence; I hadn't any idea where to turn to raise all that bullion, and I said so. I think he was ashamed of me, privately, because of my weak faith. He told me to give myself no uneasiness, no concern; and said in a simple, confident, and unquestioning way, " the Lord will provide." I saw that he fully believed the Lord would provide, but it seemed to me that if he had had my experience—

But never mind that; before he was done with me his strong faith had had its influence, and I went forth from the place almost convinced that the Lord really would provide.

I wandered around the streets for an hour, trying to think up some way to get that money, but nothing suggested itself. At last I lounged into the big lobby of the Ebbitt House, which was then a new hotel, and sat down. Presently a dog came loafing along. He paused, glanced up at me and said, with his eyes, " Are you friendly?" I answered, with my eyes, that I was. He gave his tail a grateful little wag and came forward and rested his jaw on my knee and lifted his brown eyes to my face in a winningly affectionate way. He was a lovely creature—as beautiful as a girl, and he was made all of silk and velvet. I stroked his smooth brown head and fondled his drooping ears, and we were a pair of lovers right away. Pretty soon Brigadier-General Miles, the hero of the land, came strolling by in his blue and gold splendors, with everybody's admiring gaze upon him. He saw the dog and stopped, and there was a light in his eye which showed that he had a warm place in his heart for dogs like this gracious creature; then he came forward and patted the dog and said,

" He is very fine—he is a wonder; would you sell him?"

I was greatly moved; it seemed a marvellous thing to me, the way Clinton's prediction had come true. I said,

" Yes."

The General said,

" What do you ask for him?"

" Three dollars."

The General was manifestly surprised. He said,

" Three dollars? Only three dollars? Why, that dog is a most uncommon dog; he can't possibly be worth less than fifty. If he were mine, I wouldn't take a hundred for him. I'm afraid you are not aware of his value. Reconsider your price if you like, I don't wish to wrong you."

But if he had known me he would have known that I was no more capable of wronging him than he was of wronging me. I responded with the same quiet decision as before,

" No—three dollars. That is his price."

" Very well, since you insist upon it," said the General, and he gave me three dollars and led the dog away, and disappeared up-stairs.

In about ten minutes a gentle-faced middle-aged gentleman came along, and began to look around here and there and under tables and everywhere, and I said to him,

" Is it a dog you are looking for?"

His face was sad, before, and troubled; but it lit up gladly now, and he answered,

" Yes—have you seen him?"

" Yes," I said, " he was here a minute ago, and I saw him follow a gentleman away. I think I could find him for you if you would like me to try."

I have seldom seen a person look so grateful—and there was gratitude in his voice, too, when he conceded that he would like me to try. I said I would do it with great pleasure, but that as it might take a little time I hoped he would not mind paying me something for my trouble. He said he would do it most gladly—repeating that phrase "most gladly"—and asked me how much. I said—

" Three dollars."

He looked surprised, and said,

" Dear me, it is nothing! I will pay you ten, quite willingly."

But I said,

" No, three is the price "—and I started for the stairs without waiting for any further argument, for Clinton had said that that was the amount that the Lord would provide, and it seemed to me that it would be sacrilegious to take a penny more than was promised.

I got the number of the General's room from the office-clerk, as I passed by his wicket, and when I reached the room I found the General there caressing his dog, and quite happy. I said,

" I am sorry, but I have to take the dog again."

He seemed very much surprised, and said,

" Take him again? Why, he is my dog; you sold him to me, and at your own price."

" Yes," I said, " it is true—but I have to have him, because the man wants him again."

" What man?"

" The man that owns him; he wasn't my dog."

The General looked even more surprised than before, and for a moment he couldn't seem to find his voice; then he said,

" Do you mean to tell me that you were selling another man's dog—and knew it?"

" Yes, I knew it wasn't my dog."

" Then why did you sell him?"

I said,

" Well, that is a curious question to ask. I sold him because you wanted him. You offered to buy the dog; you can't deny that. I was not anxious to sell him—I had not even thought of selling him, but it seemed to me that if it could be any accommodation to you—"

He broke me off in the middle, and said,

" *Accommodation* to me? It is the most extraordinary spirit of accommodation I have ever heard of—the idea of your selling a dog that didn't belong to you—"

I broke him off there, and said,

" There is no relevancy about this kind of argument; you said yourself that the dog was probably worth a hundred dollars, I only asked you three; was there anything unfair about that? You offered to pay more, you know you did. I only asked you three; you can't deny it."

"Oh, what in the world has that to do with it! The crux of the matter is that you didn't own the dog—can't you see that? You seem to think that there is no impropriety in selling property that isn't yours provided you sell it cheap. Now, then—"

I said,

"Please don't argue about it any more. You can't get around the fact that the price was perfectly fair, perfectly reasonable—considering that I didn't own the dog—and so arguing about it is only a waste of words. I have to have him back again because the man wants him; don't you see that I haven't any choice in the matter? Put yourself in my place. Suppose you had sold a dog that didn't belong to you; suppose you—"

"Oh," he said, "don't muddle my brains any more with your idiotic reasonings! Take him along, and give me a rest."

So I paid back the three dollars and led the dog down-stairs and passed him over to his owner, and collected three for my trouble.

I went away then with a good conscience, because I had acted honorably; I never could have used the three that I sold the dog for, because it was not rightly my own, but the three I got for restoring him to his rightful owner was righteously and properly mine, because I had earned it. That man might never have gotten that dog back at all, if it hadn't been for me. My principles have remained to this day what they were then. I was always honest; I know I can never be otherwise. It is as I said in the beginning—I was never able to persuade myself to use money which I had acquired in questionable ways.

Now, then, that is the tale. Some of it is true.

MARK TWAIN.

# A CATALOG OF SELECTED DOVER
# BOOKS IN ALL FIELDS OF INTEREST

CONCERNING THE SPIRITUAL IN ART, Wassily Kandinsky. Pioneering work by father of abstract art. Thoughts on color theory, nature of art. Analysis of earlier masters. 12 illustrations. 80pp. of text. 5⅜ x 8½. 23411-8 Pa. $4.95

ANIMALS: 1,419 Copyright-Free Illustrations of Mammals, Birds, Fish, Insects, etc., Jim Harter (ed.). Clear wood engravings present, in extremely lifelike poses, over 1,000 species of animals. One of the most extensive pictorial sourcebooks of its kind. Captions. Index. 284pp. 9 x 12. 23766-4 Pa. $14.95

CELTIC ART: The Methods of Construction, George Bain. Simple geometric techniques for making Celtic interlacements, spirals, Kells-type initials, animals, humans, etc. Over 500 illustrations. 160pp. 9 x 12. (USO) 22923-8 Pa. $9.95

AN ATLAS OF ANATOMY FOR ARTISTS, Fritz Schider. Most thorough reference work on art anatomy in the world. Hundreds of illustrations, including selections from works by Vesalius, Leonardo, Goya, Ingres, Michelangelo, others. 593 illustrations. 192pp. 7⅛ x 10¼. 20241-0 Pa. $9.95

CELTIC HAND STROKE-BY-STROKE (Irish Half-Uncial from "The Book of Kells"): An Arthur Baker Calligraphy Manual, Arthur Baker. Complete guide to creating each letter of the alphabet in distinctive Celtic manner. Covers hand position, strokes, pens, inks, paper, more. Illustrated. 48pp. 8¼ x 11. 24336-2 Pa. $3.95

EASY ORIGAMI, John Montroll. Charming collection of 32 projects (hat, cup, pelican, piano, swan, many more) specially designed for the novice origami hobbyist. Clearly illustrated easy-to-follow instructions insure that even beginning papercrafters will achieve successful results. 48pp. 8¼ x 11. 27298-2 Pa. $3.50

THE COMPLETE BOOK OF BIRDHOUSE CONSTRUCTION FOR WOOD-WORKERS, Scott D. Campbell. Detailed instructions, illustrations, tables. Also data on bird habitat and instinct patterns. Bibliography. 3 tables. 63 illustrations in 15 figures. 48pp. 5¼ x 8½. 24407-5 Pa. $2.50

BLOOMINGDALE'S ILLUSTRATED 1886 CATALOG: Fashions, Dry Goods and Housewares, Bloomingdale Brothers. Famed merchants' extremely rare catalog depicting about 1,700 products: clothing, housewares, firearms, dry goods, jewelry, more. Invaluable for dating, identifying vintage items. Also, copyright-free graphics for artists, designers. Co-published with Henry Ford Museum & Greenfield Village. 160pp. 8¼ x 11. 25780-0 Pa. $10.95

HISTORIC COSTUME IN PICTURES, Braun & Schneider. Over 1,450 costumed figures in clearly detailed engravings—from dawn of civilization to end of 19th century. Captions. Many folk costumes. 256pp. 8⅜ x 11¾. 23150-X Pa. $12.95

CATALOG OF DOVER BOOKS

THE INFLUENCE OF SEA POWER UPON HISTORY, 1660–1783, A. T. Mahan. Influential classic of naval history and tactics still used as text in war colleges. First paperback edition. 4 maps. 24 battle plans. 640pp. 5⅜ x 8½. 25509-3 Pa. $14.95

THE STORY OF THE TITANIC AS TOLD BY ITS SURVIVORS, Jack Winocour (ed.). What it was really like. Panic, despair, shocking inefficiency, and a little heroism. More thrilling than any fictional account. 26 illustrations. 320pp. 5⅜ x 8½. 20610-6 Pa. $8.95

FAIRY AND FOLK TALES OF THE IRISH PEASANTRY, William Butler Yeats (ed.). Treasury of 64 tales from the twilight world of Celtic myth and legend: "The Soul Cages," "The Kildare Pooka," "King O'Toole and his Goose," many more. Introduction and Notes by W. B. Yeats. 352pp. 5⅜ x 8½. 26941-8 Pa. $8.95

BUDDHIST MAHAYANA TEXTS, E. B. Cowell and Others (eds.). Superb, accurate translations of basic documents in Mahayana Buddhism, highly important in history of religions. The Buddha-karita of Asvaghosha, Larger Sukhavativyuha, more. 448pp. 5⅜ x 8½. 25552-2 Pa. $12.95

ONE TWO THREE . . . INFINITY: Facts and Speculations of Science, George Gamow. Great physicist's fascinating, readable overview of contemporary science: number theory, relativity, fourth dimension, entropy, genes, atomic structure, much more. 128 illustrations. Index. 352pp. 5⅜ x 8½. 25664-2 Pa. $8.95

ENGINEERING IN HISTORY, Richard Shelton Kirby, et al. Broad, nontechnical survey of history's major technological advances: birth of Greek science, industrial revolution, electricity and applied science, 20th-century automation, much more. 181 illustrations. ". . . excellent . . ."–Isis. Bibliography. vii + 530pp. 5⅜ x 8¼. 26412-2 Pa. $14.95

DALÍ ON MODERN ART: The Cuckolds of Antiquated Modern Art, Salvador Dalí. Influential painter skewers modern art and its practitioners. Outrageous evaluations of Picasso, Cézanne, Turner, more. 15 renderings of paintings discussed. 44 calligraphic decorations by Dalí. 96pp. 5⅜ x 8½. (USO) 29220-7 Pa. $4.95

ANTIQUE PLAYING CARDS: A Pictorial History, Henry René D'Allemagne. Over 900 elaborate, decorative images from rare playing cards (14th–20th centuries): Bacchus, death, dancing dogs, hunting scenes, royal coats of arms, players cheating, much more. 96pp. 9¼ x 12¼. 29265-7 Pa. $12.95

MAKING FURNITURE MASTERPIECES: 30 Projects with Measured Drawings, Franklin H. Gottshall. Step-by-step instructions, illustrations for constructing handsome, useful pieces, among them a Sheraton desk, Chippendale chair, Spanish desk, Queen Anne table and a William and Mary dressing mirror. 224pp. 8⅛ x 11¼. 29338-6 Pa. $13.95

THE FOSSIL BOOK: A Record of Prehistoric Life, Patricia V. Rich et al. Profusely illustrated definitive guide covers everything from single-celled organisms and dinosaurs to birds and mammals and the interplay between climate and man. Over 1,500 illustrations. 760pp. 7½ x 10⅛. 29371-8 Pa. $29.95

*Prices subject to change without notice.*

Available at your book dealer or write for free catalog to Dept. GI, Dover Publications, Inc., 31 East 2nd St., Mineola, N.Y. 11501. Dover publishes more than 500 books each year on science, elementary and advanced mathematics, biology, music, art, literary history, social sciences and other areas.